'The India growth story has attracted considerable attention and interest in development literature. From being a laggard, the country has now emerged as one of the fastest-growing countries in the world. Most commentators tell this story as a unitary one glossing over the fact that India is a federation of an assortment of states whose growth performance has been wildly divergent. Biswa Swarup Misra's Development Drivers of Indian States takes us on an informed empirical excursion on the factors that explain the differential growth performance of Indian states. In this way, it is an essential addition to this small but growing literature on the economic performance of Indian states'.

Sunil Mani, *Director and Professor,*
RBI Chair, Centre for Development Studies,
Trivandrum, Kerala

'An excellent book on Development Drivers of States by the author with a rich knowledge on the topic. The range of issues-growth and its decomposition, regional inequality, the impact of economic and social infrastructure on productivity and inequality, and political accountability in Indian States are outstanding research output of best standards on the subject'.

K.R. Shanmugam, *Director,*
Madras School of Economics

'Inequality of income among Indian states has been a major challenge for policy makers in India. India, to sustain a growth level of about 8 to 10%, requires contribution from majority of the states. Prof. Misra in this well researched book brings out the factors contributing to inequality – lack of investment in education and health, unwillingness of the political leadership in laggard states – which requires immediate attention of the political leadership. This book is highly recommended for policymakers, academicians, and researchers'.

B.A. Prabhakar, *Former Chairman and*
Managing Director, Andhra Bank

Development and Economic Growth in India

Notwithstanding the improved growth performance of India, development disparity across its states has widened in the first two decades of the 21st century. This book examines development drivers of Indian states and what the necessary course corrections could be to achieve balanced regional growth.

The book begins with a discussion on the evolution of growth and inequality across the states and delves into decomposing growth. It looks at three broad themes which are decomposition of growth and determinants of TFP, impact of Infrastructure on growth and inequality, and the institutional dimension of growth and explains why they are pivotal for sustainable growth in Indian states.

This book will be a useful reference to those interested in understanding growth and inequality in India.

Biswa Swarup Misra is the Dean (Academics) and Professor of Economics at the Xavier Institute of Management, XIM University, Bhubaneswar, India. Prior to joining Academics, he was an economist at the Reserve Bank of India. He has also served as the Chief Economist of Bank of India and Bank of Baroda, on sabbatical from XIM. He has publications in Journals such as *Development Policy Review*, *Comparative Economic Studies*, *Journal of Asia Pacific Economy*, *Review of Urban and Regional Development Studies*, *Journal of International Development*, *Journal of Quantitative Economics*, *India Growth and Development Review*, *Indian Economic Journal*, and RBI's Occasional Papers on issues related to development, banking, credit cooperatives, and infrastructure.

Routledge Studies in Development Economics

173 **Digital Financial Inclusion and Regulation**
Ogochukwu Monye

174 **Household Demand for Consumer Goods in Developing Countries**
A Comparative Perspective with Developed Countries
Eliyathamby A. Selvanathan, Saroja Selvanathan and Maneka Jayasinghe

175 **Unlocking Private Investment in Sustainable Infrastructure in Asia**
Edited by Bhajan Grewal, Nella Hendriyetty, Iskandar Abdullaev, Chul Ju Kim, Naoyuki Yoshino and Eisa Khan Ayoob Ayoob

176 **The Political Economy of Bilateral Aid**
Implications for Global Development
Peter Blunt with Cecilia Escobar and Vlassis Missos

177 **Development and Economic Growth in India**
Drivers for Indian States
Biswa Swarup Misra

178 **Towards a Sustainable Economy**
The Case of Bangladesh
Edited by Moazzem Hossain, Qazi Kholiquzzaman Ahmad and Mazharul M Islam

For more information about this series, please visit: www.routledge.com/Routledge-Studies-in-Development-Economics/book-series/SE0266

Development and Economic Growth in India

Drivers for Indian States

Biswa Swarup Misra

Routledge
Taylor & Francis Group
LONDON AND NEW YORK

First published 2023
by Routledge
4 Park Square, Milton Park, Abingdon, Oxon OX14 4RN

and by Routledge
605 Third Avenue, New York, NY 10158

Routledge is an imprint of the Taylor & Francis Group, an informa business

British Library Cataloguing-in-Publication Data
A catalogue record for this book is available from the British Library

Library of Congress Cataloging-in-Publication Data
Names: Misra, Biswa Swarup, 1975– author.
Title: Development and economic growth in India : drivers for Indian states / Biswa Swarup Misra.
Description: Milton Park, Abingdon, Oxon ; New York, NY : Routledge, 2023. |
Series: Routledge studies in development economics |
Includes bibliographical references and index.
Subjects: LCSH: India—Economic conditions—21st century. |
Indic states—Economic conditions—21st century. |
Infrastructure (Economics)—India—History—21st century
Classification: LCC HC435.4 .M57 2022 |
DDC 338.954—dc23/eng/20220809
LC record available at https://lccn.loc.gov/2022035470

ISBN: 978-1-032-24388-7 (hbk)
ISBN: 978-1-032-24389-4 (pbk)
ISBN: 978-1-003-27835-1 (ebk)

DOI: 10.4324/9781003278351

Typeset in Galliard
by codeMantra

For
My Parents – Srinivas Misra and Satyavama Misra
Wife – Jyotirmayee
Son – Gaurav

Contents

Tables

Annexure

Graphs

Foreword

Given the vast diversity in geography, natural resources, and cultural and historical experience, it was expected that development performance of the Indian states would also differ and suitable policy framework would need to be evolved at the state level within the broader national context. Various institutional and economic frameworks have guided the state-level strategies over the last 75 years of development effort. Policy analysis has focused on the questions of what has worked and what should be the future course of policies to accelerate development. It is in this line of research that the present book by Prof. B.S. Misra provides new insights and makes important contributions to the analysis of India's economic performance across states. It revisits some issues that have been addressed in the literature either at the national level or at the state level and also offers new perspectives on political accountability, estimates of productivity growth, and its determinants at the state level.

The objective of an assessment of India's potential to achieve high rates economic growth on a sustained basis provides an overall focus to the diverse topics covered in the book. The book sets the overall context by exploring the potential growth of the Indian economy through the various phases of its recent history. Prof. Misra convincingly argues why a 10% economic growth is feasible but cannot be taken for granted.

The analysis of inequality and growth has been at the core of development policy debate. Dissecting growth in several ways, the book finds that growth has been primarily driven by a few states in the southern and the western regions of India, highlighting the need for broad basing growth and closing the slack in the eastern and northern regions of the country. An interesting finding is that volatility is not due to agricultural performance, but because of the services sector. Using a variety of measures of inequality, Professor Misra concludes there has been an increase in inequality between States.

Growth decomposition for Indian states is also an important contribution of the book to identify the drivers of development. The analysis includes rigorous estimation of labour and capital inputs for the states to quantify productivity growth in the growth-accounting framework. That the administrative reorganisation does not necessarily lead to improved productivity is an important takeaway. The analysis underscores the need for computing productivity growth at the state level. I am sure the book will serve as a motivation for both researchers and policymakers to pay greater attention to estimating productivity growth for the states.

The book also highlights the relative neglect of building both health and education infrastructure in the states and its adverse effects on productivity and intra-state income inequality. The analysis of determinants of productivity taking into account spatial interaction is analytically rich and methodologically innovative. The chapter on political accountability and incentives for good governance rounds off a wide body of work the book presents.

The findings provide both the test of various hypotheses and also offer suggestions for the future course of policies. I am sure researchers and policymakers would find the analysis timely and valuable.

Shashanka Bhide
Former Senior Advisor, National Council of
Applied Economic Research (NCAER)

Preface

India offers limitless opportunities for economic growth in the 21st century, as structural factors are in its favour. However, converting those opportunities for tangible improvement in living standards involves considerable challenges. This book traces the performance of the Indian economy and the states in the first two decades of the 21st century to identify those challenges.

The Indian policymakers intend to create an innovation-based ecosystem to achieve higher rates of growth. Innovation rests on application of knowledge. This book highlights the urgent need to focus on human capital formation in addition to the current priority of the government to build economic infrastructure.

The period following 2014 has been quite eventful in terms of introducing some long-pending and game-changing reforms by a government that enjoys support of the masses. The world has witnessed a major health crisis in the last two years followed by geo political tensions arising from the Russia–Ukraine war. As all good things do not last forever, the not so good things also come to an end. As and when normalcy is restored, India should do much better than the present times.

Writing this book has been an enriching experience for me and I hope going through it will be a rewarding experience for the readers. I hope the research community will pursue the issues studied in the book further to get additional insights which will help in better policymaking in India.

Acknowledgements

Working on a book which requires massive amount of data on diverse set of indicators encompassing a wide range of topics would not have been possible without support from Xavier Institute of Management, XIM University, Bhubaneswar, where I work. I am grateful to Xavier Institute of Management, for its excellent working conditions and research atmosphere.

I owe deep gratitude to Fr. Tony Uvary, Vice Chancellor, XIM University, for encouraging my research pursuits and providing a wonderful working environment and the state-of-the-art infrastructure facilities.

My sincere gratitude to Fr. S. Tony Raj, Registrar, XIM University and Fr. V. Arockia Das, CFO of XIM University, for their understanding, encouragement, and kind appreciation of my work and for extending the moral support and comfort at the workplace.

While working on this project, I have benefited immensely from my interactions with Shri Akshya Kumar Panda, former Senior Economic Advisor to Government of India, and Prof. Nawal Kishore Chaudhary, my research guide. I am grateful for their guidance, support, and encouragement.

I am grateful to my colleagues Prof. Biresh Kumar Sahoo, Prof. Amar KJR Nayak, Prof. W.S.William, Prof. D.V Ramana, Prof. Ajit Kumar, Prof. Shridhar Kuamr Dash, Prof. Krishna Das Gupta, and Prof. Ranjan Kuamr Mohanty for being available for discussion, debate, and arguments despite their hectic schedules.

The library of Xavier Institute of Management has been a great source of support while working on the Book. I am grateful to all the members of the staff and especially Dr. Deepak Khuntia and Dr. Sribatsa Prahdan who head the library in the two campuses of the XIM University for their timely help on many occasions. I am thankful to Shri Dayanidhi Mishra and Ms. Sangeeta Shanti Barla, who provided active cooperation while working on this project. My student Supratik Biswal has been instrumental in processing a large amount of data used in the book. His excellent command over excel helped to make things easier. Thanks are also due to Satrujit, my student for working on the index for the Book.

I am grateful to my friend Dr. Biswa Prakash Pati who has made himself available for discussion on so many occasions despite his hectic schedule. Thanks are also due to my friends Satyabrat Pradhan, Dr. Sameer Behera, Shri Amitabh Khuntia, and Lala Susanta Ray for sharing lighter moments. They have been a constant source of strength.

I owe a great deal to Yong Ling Lam, senior commissioning editor of Routledge, and her entire team, who have been instrumental in the smooth completion of this work.

I am grateful to Suganya Karuppasamy of codemantra for her support in finalising the Manuscript.

I am grateful to Srinivas Misra, my father and role model. He has been a constant source of encouragement and inspiration in all my efforts. He takes more interest than I do in my academic pursuits and keenly follows my academic engagements. He acts as the sounding board for my research ideas. As a voracious reader, himself, he has inculcated in me the habit of reading. His thoughts to a great extent have also influenced my worldview.

I take this opportunity to thank my sisters, Kalyani, Basanti, Pratima, and Prativa, and my brother, Satya Swarup, who have always been affectionate and encouraging. I am equally grateful to Shri Rabindra Kumar Dash, my father-in-law, for encouraging my academic pursuits.

I am grateful to Prof. Suman Mahapatra, Shri Amitabha Sadangi, Shri Ramaknata Mishra, and Shri Sudhansu Sekhar Dash, for their support and advice.

I take this opportunity to express my gratitude to Shri Jitendranath Rath and Smt. Anupama Rath who have been very affectionate and extended unconditional support during my formative days. They have been a great source of inspiration and serve as role models.

Shri Sanjib Bishoyi, a family friend, appreciates my work and has encouraged me to work on this book. His association for more than three decades has been a great strength and I am grateful for his timely help on many occasions.

Above all, I am indebted to my wife, Lipi, for graciously enduring a perpetually distracted husband, his nocturnal working hours, and the sight of books and reading materials scattered all around the house. She has been highly patient in her disposition and has sacrificed her comforts to accommodate my demanding time schedules.

This long list of people who have been instrumental in one way or other would remain incomplete without the mention of Gaurav, whose innocent questions have contributed to my thought process. I adore the calm disposition of Gaurav and his subtle sense of humour which makes the environment at home much more amenable for academic pursuits.

1 The Indian growth story

I Introduction

The policies and initiatives of the central government set the broad framework within which states operate. India has seen a spate of policy initiatives in the post-2015 period which if implemented in the right spirit can create limitless opportunities. In view of the subdued growth performance in the last few years despite several policy initiatives before the global pandemic, COVID-19 has given rise to scepticism about Indian growth prospects (Acharya, 2022). In this backdrop, the present chapter analyses the growth potential of the Indian economy in the medium term. The rest of the chapter is structured as follows. We begin with analysing the feasibility of India becoming a US$5 trillion economy and argue that why a 10% per annum growth may not be infeasible by analysing the resource use efficiency and productivity of the Indian economy in the recent times. Section II discusses pro-growth initiatives in six dimensions viz, governance, inclusion, entrepreneurship, infrastructure, resolution, and sustainability which augur well for attaining higher levels of productivity. Notwithstanding the growth-oriented measures, the challenges for achieving higher sustainable rates of growth are discussed in Section III. There are certain reforms which are work in progress and if implemented properly can boost India's growth potential. We discuss such reform measures in Section V. Section VI provides an overall assessment of the growth potential keeping in view the policy initiatives and challenges. The chapter concludes with a discussion of competitive federalism pursued by the central government in the post-2015 period which has implications for the development prospects of the states in Section VII.

II Feasibility of GDP surpassing US$5 trillion by 2026

The growth of the Indian economy in the recent years portrays a mixed picture. The GDP growth accelerated from 7.4% in 2015[1] to 8% and 8.3%,

DOI: 10.4324/9781003278351-1

respectively, in 2016 and 2017 (Table 1.1). However, beginning with 2018, there has been a successive deceleration of growth till 2020. While the growth slowdown was gradual in 2018 and 2019, it was quite sharp in 2020. Compared to 6.9% in 2018 and 6.6% in 2019, GDP growth decelerated sharply to 4.2% in 2020.

The severity of the growth slowdown can be appreciated from the fact that growth averaged 6.8% during the period 2015–20 and it jumps to 7.4% per annum during 2015–19 if we exclude 2020 from the analysis. The post 2020 period is marked with the adverse effects of COVID-19 when growth registered a negative 7.25% in 2021 due to cliff effects and scarring generated by the pandemic (Reserve Bank of India, 2022). The GDP is estimated[2] to have surpassed its pre-COVID level in 2022 after withstanding three successive waves of the pandemic. The negative externality associated with the Russia–Ukraine war has posed additional challenges. It is common to lose sight of the large picture while grappling with the challenges at hand and managing existential issues. Hence, we traverse the growth path envisioned before the pandemic struck the world.

It is worthwhile to recall that the Prime Minister of India in the year 2019 had set a target of Indian GDP attaining the US$5trillin mark by 2023–24. With almost two years of economic growth lost due to COVID, the target has been shifted to 2026 (Economic Times, 2022). How is India placed to meet this target? Just to put things into perspective, nominal GDP in 2021 was Rs. 197.45 lakh crores and the average Dollar–Rupee exchange rate was 74.26. Thus, nominal GDP in dollar terms was US$2.66 trillion in 2021. Nominal GDP needs to grow at 13.5% for five years beginning with 2022 so as to reach US$5 trillion by the end of 2026. A 13.5% nominal growth would translate into a real growth of around 7.5% if inflation is assumed to average around 6%. India has grown at around 7.25% per annum during 2001–20. Given the growth experience of the last two decades, aiming for 7.5% growth is just business as usual and is not reflective of the several transformational initiatives taken by the government in the last eight years.

Given India's low production base, a large proportion of its population in the working age, political stability, and political intent to improve living standards, a moot question that arises is whether India can attain a 10% per annum growth in the next two decades. When posed with a 10% growth benchmark, the first question one confronts is whether such a growth target realistic? Many readers would be circumspect about India achieving 10% per annum growth rate when the economy's growth had dipped to 4.2% in 2020. Hence, aiming for 10% growth is likely to be viewed as not only ambitious but devoid of reality and unattainable. Before we write off the 10% growth target, it will be useful to understand the

Table 1.1 Key Macro Indicators of the Indian Economy 2001–21

1	*2*	*3*	*4*	*5*	*6*	*7*	*8*	*9*	*10*
Year	*Growth*	*Inflation*	*Exchange Rate (Rs/$)*	*Fiscal deficit of the centre*	*Combined Fiscal Deficit*	*Exports*	*CAD*	*Lending Rate*	*Real GDP*
2000–01	3.84	3.64	45.68	5.46	9.20	9.70	–0.57	11.00–12.00	43.27
2001–02	4.82	3.22	47.69	5.98	9.60	9.21	0.70	11.00–12.00	45.35
2002–03	3.80	3.72	48.40	5.72	9.30	10.44	1.23	10.75–11.50	47.08
2003–04	7.86	3.87	45.95	4.34	8.30	10.91	2.32	10.25–11.00	50.78
2004–05	7.92	5.73	44.93	3.88	7.20	12.02	–0.35	10.25–11.00	54.80
2005–06	7.92	5.62	44.27	3.96	6.50	12.82	-1.21	10.25–12.75	59.15
2006–07	8.06	8.40	45.25	3.32	5.10	13.71	-1.02	12.25–14.75	63.91
2007–08	7.66	6.94	40.26	2.54	4.00	13.66	-1.29	12.25–15.75	68.81
2008–09	3.09	9.19	45.99	5.99	8.30	15.76	-2.33	11.50–16.75	70.93
2009–10	7.86	7.04	47.44	6.46	9.30	13.60	-2.85	11.00–15.75	76.51
2010–11	8.50	10.53	45.56	4.80		15.29	-2.87	8.25–9.50	83.01
2011–12	5.24	8.73	47.92	5.91	7.84	16.99	–4.29	10.00–10.75	87.36
2012–13	5.46	7.93	54.41	4.93	6.88	16.77	–4.82	9.70–10.25	92.13
2013–14	6.39	6.19	60.50	4.48	6.67	17.16	-1.74	10.00–10.25	98.01
2014–15	7.41	3.33	61.14	4.10	6.71	15.52	-1.32	10.00–10.25	105.28
2015–16	8.00	2.28	65.47	3.87	6.92	12.66	-1.05	9.30–9.70	113.69
2016–17	8.26	3.24	67.07	3.48	6.93	12.21	-0.63	7.75–8.20	123.08
2017–18	6.80	3.97	64.45	3.46	5.83	11.65	-1.84	7.80–7.95	131.45
2018–19	6.53	3.74	69.92	3.44	5.80	12.49	-2.12	8.05–8.55	140.03
2019–20	4.04	3.57	70.90	4.59	6.90	11.16	-0.86	7.45–7.90	145.69
2020–21	-7.25	4.61	74.23	9.36	6.30	11.14	0.90	6.65–7.15	135.13

Notes: FDI and FII are in US$Billion.
Exports refers to export of commodities.
Real GDP growth is calculated on GDP at market price at 2011–12 base.
Combined fiscal deficit refers to the deficit for Centre and States taken together.
Inflation refers to GDP deflator-based inflation.
Exchange rate refers to annual average financial year exchange rate between US Dollar and Rupee.
Real GDP refers to absolute values of real GDP at market price at 2011–12 prices and is expressed in Rs. Trillion.
For combined fiscal deficit (Col.6), Data for 2019–20 are Revised Estimates and data for 2020–21 are Budget Estimates.
For central government fiscal deficit (Col.5), Data for 2020–21 are Revised Estimates.

genesis of the successive decline in growth rate during 2018–20. It is also important to take stock of the productivity growth and efficiency of the Indian economy during the last few years to form a view.

The sharp decline in GDP growth for the year 2020 can either be seen as blip or as a reflection of medium-term growth prospects of India hovering around 5%. Part of the reason for around 4% growth in 2020 can be attributed to a series of shock that the Indian economy experienced during 2015–19. The first shock to the system came from an attempt by the central bank to clean the balance sheet of the commercial banks by undertaking a special asset quality review in Nov 2015. The need for asset quality review (AQR) was felt because the public sector banks had adopted a 'pretend and extend' approach to the non-performing assets in their infrastructure portfolio (Mundra, 2016). The reason behind such a lackadaisical approach of the government-owned banks dates to their massive lending to infrastructure projects for stimulating the economy post the global financial crisis(GFC). Though the government had encouraged the public sector banks to lend to infrastructure projects, it could not grant necessary land and environmental clearances for many projects. Thus, the infrastructure projects faced both time and cost overruns leading to their loss of viability (Rajan, 2016a). The banks on their part were more comfortable to lend for working capital and lacked the underwriting capabilities needed for infrastructure projects.

Without a time-bound resolution framework, the Reserve Bank of India (RBI) as the banking regulator came up with a number of debt restructuring schemes to revive stalled projects. The banks made use of the debt restructuring schemes to delay recognising the non performing assets(NPAs) in their books. As the central bank suspected that banks may be hiding the true NPA on their books, it went for an asset quality review. Following the AQR, there was a sharp jump in the non-performing asset of the public sector banks which accounted for the largest share in bank credit in India (Rajan, 2016b). The high NPA levels identified from the AQR made banks shy of lending. The non-banking finance companies (NBFCs) had filled the void in lending created by the commercial banks. However, the bankruptcy of one of the large NBFCs in 2019 created a near systemic crisis and led to a squeeze in credit to small and medium enterprises.

The stress observed in the NBFC space beginning with the debt default by IL&FS in Sep 2018 followed by a squeeze in liquidity for the entire sector must have contributed its share to the severe growth slowdown in 2020. The overall credit growth following the IL&FS crisis slowed down from 13.4% in 2019 to 6.1% in 2020. Following AQR, the Indian economy was subject to two more dislocations caused by demonetisation in Nov 2016 and a hasty implementation of GST on July 2017. Thus, the very low growth rate in 2020 is the cumulative effect the three shocks and may not be indicative of the medium-term growth potential of the Indian economy. While a 5% medium-term growth may not be a true reflection of the potential of the Indian economy, are there good reasons to believe in achieving a 10% per annum growth. Tracing the resource use efficiency and productivity of the Indian economy in the recent times can give an idea about the potential growth of the Indian economy.

Seen from a different perspective, there has been a substantial improvement in resource use efficiency during 2015–18 which had declined post the global financial crisis (GFC) during the period 2010–14. Indian policymakers responded to the GFC by pursuing expansionary monetary and fiscal policy. The policy stimulus stoked inflationary pressures towards the later part of 2010 and the entire 2011. The central bank, in response to the high inflation, increased policy rate successively for 13 times between March 2010 and October 2011. High inflation for a prolonged period 2011–14 created uncertainty for business (Table 1.1). The central bank's hands off approach to capital inflows after the GFC also contributed its bit to macroeconomic mismanagement. The central bank's reluctance to absorb capital inflows after the GFC in building the forex reserves led to an appreciation of the rupee during 2010–11 hurting India's export competitiveness. Several scams involving the government were also reported in the post GFC period. The vulnerability of the Indian economy was clear when it faced a near balance of payment crisis in 2013 after the US Fed announced to wind up its quantitative easing. Growth of Indian economy slowed to 5.2% and 5.5% in 2012 and 2013 compared to 8.5% in 2011. The inability of the Indian economy to use resources efficiently in the post GFC period is reflected through an increase in incremental capital output ratio (ICOR) from 6.4 during 2005–09 to 7.2 during 2010–14. However, various reforms implemented between 2015 and 2020 resulted in a dramatic drop in the ICOR to 4.1, indicating increased resource use efficiency. From a comparative perspective, the overall ICOR during 2001–20 was 4.6. Seen from the perspective of productivity growth, the post-2000 period experienced total factor productivity (TFP) growth of 4.3% for the period 2001–18. The TFP growth at 3.1% per annum was much higher during 2005–09 compared to 2.7% during the period 2001–04. However, improvement in productivity growth could not be sustained in the post GFC period. In fact, TFP growth decelerated slightly to 3% per annum during 2009–14, reflecting policy stasis. However, with the formation of new government in the year 2014, several measures, which are discussed in detail in the next section, were introduced to reduce the transaction costs in the economy. The various initiatives led to an increase in productivity growth to 5.5% per annum during 2015–18. Thus, the improvements in the resource use efficiency and productivity growth in the post-2014 period lends credence to a 10% per annum growth.

We now briefly discuss some of the key pro-growth initiatives which have been taken by the government in the recent past which augurs well for improving productivity of the economy in the coming years and makes the 10% per annum growth in the next two decades feasible. Broadly, the initiatives can be seen in six dimensions encompassing Governance, Inclusion, entrepreneurship, infrastructure, resolution, and sustainability.

III Pro-growth initiatives

First, the online governance framework has been strengthened in the last few years. Digital India, a flagship programme of the Government, was launched in 2014 with a vision to transform India into a digitally empowered society and knowledge economy (GoI, 2014). Digital India aims to deliver government services digitally and achieve universal digital literacy. UMANG, a Unified Mobile Application, has been developed to access to central and state government services such as Aadhaar, Digital Locker, PAN, Employee Provident Fund services (GoI, 2019a). Digital Locker allows to store important documents like mark sheets, PAN, Aadhaar, and degree certificates digitally. This reduces the need for physical documents and facilitates easy sharing of documents. Introduction of the faceless assessment of taxation using technology, digitisation of land record, faster processing of government documents like passport and driving license, has reduced the discretion of government officials in availing essential services. Aadhaar, a unique identification number issued by the Unique Identification Authority of India (UIDAI) which serves as proof of identity and address on the basis of biometric data, is being used extensively by the government to extend benefits of welfare schemes. Aadhaar is also used to E-sign documents like filing of income tax returns. The emphasis on online governance along with several innovations by fin-tech companies for cashless transactions has reduced transaction cost in the economy. Apart from reducing transaction cost, several socio-economic interventions have been designed to improve the efficiency of the Indian economy.

Second, government launched a massive financial inclusion initiative known as Pradhan Mantri Jan Dhan Yojana (PMJDY) in August 2014 to expand account ownership among unbanked people through 'biometric identification or AADHAAR cards'. In the first year of its launching, 17. 90-crore PMJDY accounts were opened. The number of PMJDY Accounts have grown three-fold from 14.72 crore in Mar 2015 to 43.04 crore on Aug 2021(GoI, 2021c). More importantly, the number of operative[3] accounts increased form 76% in Aug 2017 to 85.6% in Aug 2021. Further, India has declared 'National strategy for financial inclusion 2019–2024' and 'National strategy for financial education 2020–2025' showing a path for strengthening financial inclusion in the country. The findings from the latest Global Findex database (2017) show significant progress in access to finance between 2011 and 2017 for India. For instance, the share of adults with a bank account has increased from less than 40% in 2011 to 80% in 2017 for India. The progress made by India in financial inclusion from a comparative perspective can be appreciated from the fact that account ownership among rural adults at 33% in 2011 more than doubled to 79% by 2017. The importance of bank accounts opened under PMJDY is derived from the fact that they provide the platform for direct benefits transfer (DBT). DBT which allows directly crediting the account of the beneficiary was started on January 1, 2013. DBT got a major impetus with the opening of bank accounts of the poor under the PMJDY. The blend of PMJDY, Aadhaar, and a rise in mobile usage and communication, popularly known as the *'Jan Dhan-Aadhaar-Mobile (JAM)' Trinity* has facilitated DBT. The extensive use of DBT has helped in better targeting of welfare schemes and helps to plug leakages in the delivery of funds to the poor under the various welfare schemes.

Third, in an attempt to harness the latent potential of entrepreneurship in India, the government launched the Pradhan Mantri MUDRA Yojana (PMMY) in April 2015. The unique feature of the PMMY was to extend collateral free loans of up to Rs. 10 Lakh to non-corporate, non-farm small/micro enterprises from the formal financial institutions. The government has reported that PMMY has led to creation of 1.12 crore net additional employment during 2015–18 with women accounting for 69 lakh or 62% of the total increase (GoI, 2021b). Further, the government launched the Startup India initiative in 2016 to energise the startup ecosystem for nurturing innovation and promoting Startups. As part of the initiative, a number of steps were taken including financial assistance, fiscal concession, and easier compliance of labour and environmental laws through self-certification. Specifically, entrepreneurs were allowed to self-certify compliance under six labour and three environment laws for a period of three to five years from the date of incorporation. Further, the startups were exempted from meeting prior turnover and prior experience in public procurement, ceteris paribus. As a sign of its success, the government has asserted that more than 8-lakh jobs were created by startups during 2018–22 with more than 2-lakh jobs only in the year 2021. India achieved the feat of hosting 100 Unicorns in the year 2022, the third largest in the world. India's rank in the Global Innovation Index has also improved from 81 in 2015 to 46 in 2021 (GoI, 2021d). A lot of hope is pinned on the innovation eco system to drive higher sustainable economic growth and generate large-scale employment opportunities in India.

Fourth, the government has prepared a National Infrastructure Pipeline (NIP) in 2020 with a projected infrastructure investment of around Rs. 111 lakh crore during FY 2020–25 (GoI, 2020b). The Centre (39%) and state (40%) are expected to have an almost equal share in implementing projects, while the private sector has 21% share in 9,000 projects envisaged in the NIP. Already, 42% of the projects in the NIP are under implementation, 32% are in conceptualisation stage, and rests are under development. Further, the central government has launched the 'National Monetisation Pipeline' (NMP) in Aug 2021 to raise Rs. 6.0 lakh crores during the four-year period FY 2022 to FY 2025 from the existing infrastructure assets. The estimated revenue from NMP can fund around 14% of the proposed expenditure by the Centre of Rs. 43 lakh crore under NIP. Asset monetisation, based on the philosophy of 'Creation through Monetisation', will only transfer usufruct rights to the private sector for a specific period for creation of new infrastructure. The success of NMP will depend on a host of factors including nature of the assets, the terms of contract and private sector appetite.

In order to facilitate better coordination among the different Ministries for smooth implementation of the infrastructure projects, the PM GatiShakti National Master Plan was launched in October 2021 (GoI, 2021e). A technology platform has also been prepared for every mega project under the PM Gati Shakti to avoid logistic challenges and information sharing among the stakeholders. The Gati Shakti Master Plan is designed to enhance efficiency and have an integrated approach by use of latest satellite imagery for visual understanding, coordination among all the stakeholders; synchronisation in implementation of projects; planning tools for route planning, land acquisition, permissions and congestion reduction, and dashboard-based periodic monitoring for progress (PIB, 25.10.2021).

As far as financing of infrastructure projects is concerned, the government has finally recognised that banks lending to long-term infrastructure projects are not sustainable. Banks raising deposits of relatively shorter maturity if lend to long-duration infrastructure projects not only creates asset liability mismatch but exposes them to the concentration risk. Thus, the government decided in the year 2021 to set up a development financial institution for financing infrastructure projects. Subsequently, the national bank for financing infrastructure and development (NABFID) has been set up with a seed capital of Rs. 20,000 crore and an authorised capital of Rs. 1 lakh crore to achieve a lending portfolio of at least Rs. 5 lakh crore by 2025. The broader point that emerges from the government's plans and polices is that it is following its intentions through several action-oriented measures.

Fifth, the Insolvency and Bankruptcy Code (IBC) was enacted in May 2016 to facilitate a time-bound resolution mechanism for corporates. Lack of time-bound resolution of NPAs was a major stumbling block for banks. Though it provides for resolution within 330 days, critiques point out that the recovery rate of NPAs has been relatively low under the IBC. Much of these criticisms, however, are unfounded. It may be stressed that the primary objective of IBC is to preserve capital by rescuing a company in distress and recovery is incidental to the resolution process. Nonetheless, the recovery rate under IBC is the best compared to alternate[4] mechanisms. Critics often point out that IBC encourages liquidation of companies than resolution. This is because resolution was achieved for only 14% of the companies and as many as 47% of the companies were liquidated out of a total of 5,258 companies admitted for Corporate Insolvency Resolution Process between Dec 2016 and March 2022 (IBBI, 2022). However, it needs to be kept in mind that the high level of liquidation is on account of legacy issues. It is worthwhile to note that three-fourth of the corporates sent for liquidation were already either sick or defunct. The success of IBC needs to be measured from the fact that of the firms rescued, one-third were either sick or defunct. More success in resolution is expected once the legacy NPAs are sorted out. The RBI Governor has earlier remarked that 'The real impact of the IBC is to be seen in the fresh cases where I expect the law to provide an efficient avenue to effect a resolution' (Das, 2019). As the legacy NPAs issues are attended, the incremental increase in resolution of new NPAs through the IBC can act as guidance on its positive impact in preserving capital and in supporting higher growth in the economy.

Sixth, the government has committed to increase the production of renewable energy to 500 GW by 2030 at the 26th Conference of Parties (CoP26) at Glasgow in Nov 2021. Some of the other key commitments made by India at this forum are to meet 50% of its energy requirements from renewable energy, reduce India's total projected carbon emission by 1 billion tonnes and reduce the carbon intensity of the nation's economy by 45% by 2030, and achieve net-zero carbon emissions by 2070 (GoI, 2021f). Though India has not been a significant contributor to the greenhouse gases, it has displayed its responsibility to create a sustainable world. In order to promote the clean energy segment, government has allowed up to 100% FDI under the automatic route for renewable energy generation and distribution projects. The government is also encouraging the use of electric vehicles by providing fiscal concessions. The push to renewable energy will spur innovation and create new business opportunities.

IV Challenges

While being optimist, it pays to be cautious about the challenges in realising the growth ambitions. However, if India is not to charter the 5%

growth path, there is a need to spell out the pressing challenges and the course corrections in economic policy that are needed to tackle them. The three key structural challenges that face the Indian economy are: inadequate employment opportunities to absorb the working age population, increasing the manufacturing share in the total output and improving the share of investment in GDP. These three challenges are interrelated. Ideally, an expanding manufacturing sector should create employment opportunities. Further, developing a manufacturing base requires supportive physical, social, and financial infrastructure. As India deals with its structural challenges, it has to also protect its macro economy from the negative externalities arising from the three waves of COVID-19 during 2020–22 and the ongoing Russia–Ukraine war since Feb 2022. We will elaborate a bit on the challenges and the policy response to address them. We begin with the issues related to macroeconomic management.

Macroeconomic management

Supply disruptions from both COVID-19 and Russia–Ukraine war have created formidable price pressure in the major countries of the world including India. The central banks across countries seem to be behind the curve in raising interest rates to control inflation. With inflation touching 8.5% in March 2022, US Fed increased the policy rates by 75 basis points in just two months over Mar–May 2022. The US Fed has conveyed its intentions to increase interest rates aggressively as well as pursue quantitative tightening to tame inflation. Increasing interest rates in the US amidst global uncertainty can lead to capital outflow from emerging economies including India. This may trigger a depreciation of the Indian rupee. Further, a prolonged war will have implication for major commodity prices including that of oil. India being an oil-dependent country, elevated oil prices can have adverse implication for inflation, current account deficit, and the exchange rate. Increasing interest rates to curb inflation as well as inflationary implications can nullify to some extent the tendency for rupee depreciation. Higher interest rates in India will offset the interest rate differential between the United States and India to some extent. However, it may not be material in preventing the rupee depreciation in a global risk-off environment. In case such an eventuality arises, the RBI must resist the temptation to prevent the depreciation of the rupee. The rupee depreciation can act as a shock absorber for the Indian economy as the liquidity impact can be neutralised through the standing deposit facility of the central bank. The real exchange rate of Indian rupee has also appreciated in the last few years creating price disadvantage for Indian goods and services in the international market. Depreciation can lead to the much-needed correction to promote exports.

Protecting the MSMEs

Even in an environment of rising interest rates, there may be a need to protect the MSMEs, the most vulnerable segment of Indian industry. It is a standard stance of the monetary policy to ensure that productive sectors of the economy should not be deprived of credit while keeping a vigil on inflation. Adopting a tight monetary stance to control inflation makes credit expensive for all sectors. In fact, the risk premium is higher for the SME sectors compared to large corporates. As such, the impact of a tighter credit regime conveyed through elevated interest rates affects these fringe sectors more. In this context, the selective credit control measures can be used to encourage credit flow to some of the sectors which, otherwise, will be deprived of credit in a tighter policy environment. Selective credit controls which are appropriate in the current times of high inflation, however, are hardly considered an option in the current policy discussions. Thus, the central bank should deploy selective credit control measures to protect the MSMEs.

Creating employment opportunities

The unemployment rate in India shot up from 2.2% in 2011–12 to 6.1% in 2017–18 reflecting deterioration in the employment scenario. The unemployment rate has successively declined in the next two years to 5.8% in 2018–19 and 4.1% in 2019–20 (Table 1.2). These unemployment rates pertain to the entire population irrespective of the age of the unemployed. If we consider the most active age group 15–29 years in the population, unemployment rate of around 15% in 2020 notwithstanding the decline from 17–18% observed during 2018 and 2019 is quite worrisome. The unemployment rate of around 10% for the entire population and 22.5% in the 15–29 age group points to the inadequate labour absorptive capacity of the Indian economy.

The grim unemployment scenario needs to be weighed against the policy intent of the government to increase employment opportunities by introducing several initiatives such as Make in India, Skill India, and Start up India in the initial years of assuming office. These initiatives have met only limited success. Recently, the government has launched the production-linked incentive[5] (PLI) scheme in the year 2020 to give a boost to manufacturing sector so as to create more employment opportunities. Will such an attempt be effective? One can assess the effectiveness of PLI by pitching it in the broader context of India's approach to promote manufacturing output.

Table 1.2 Major Characteristics of Labour Market in India During 2012–20

(%)										
		LFPR			*WPR*			*UR*		
Year	*Age Group*	*Male*	*Female*	*Persons*	*Male*	*Female*	*Persons*	*Male*	*Female*	*Persons*
2011–12	All Ages	55.6	22.5	39.5	54.4	21.9	38.6	2.1	2.4	2.2
2017–18	15+	75.8	23.3	49.8	71.2	22	46.8	6.1	5.6	6
	15–29	58.8	16.4	38.2	48.3	13.5	31.4	17.8	17.9	17.8
	15–59	80.2	25.3	53	74.9	23.8	49.5	6.6	6	6.5
	All Ages	55.5	17.5	36.9	52.1	16.5	34.7	6.2	5.7	6.1
2018–19	15+	58.8	16.2	38.1	71	23.3	47.3	6	5.1	5.8
	15–29	80.3	26.5	53.6	48.6	13.3	31.5	17.2	17.7	17.3
	15–59	75.5	24.5	50.2	75.1	25	50.3	6.5	5.5	6.2
	All Ages	55.6	18.6	37.5	52.3	17.6	35.3	6	5.2	5.8
2019–20	15+	76.8	30	53.5	73	28.7	50.9	5	4.2	4.8
	15–29	60	20.6	40.9	51	17.6	34.7	15.1	14.6	15
	15–59	81.2	32.3	56.9	76.7	30.9	53.9	5.5	4.5	5.2
	All Ages	56.8	22.8	40.1	53.9	21.8	38.2	5.1	4.2	4.8

Source: National Statistical Office.
Note: The figures pertain to usual status taking principal and subsidiary activities together.

Increasing the share of manufacturing

Increasing the share of manufacturing in GDP has been an avowed objective of the government. Notwithstanding the policy intention, share of manufacturing in value added has hovered around 17–18% in the last 15 years during 2005–20. PLI scheme is designed to extend incentive of 4% to 6% on incremental sales over a base year and is applicable for a period of six years subsequent to the base year. The outlay for the scheme is pegged at Rs. 1.97 lakh crore (USD 26 Billion) for five years (GoI, 2021a). The scope of the PLI scheme[6] which was initially applicable for three sectors has been expanded to cover 13 sectors by Nov 2020. It may be noted that the central government had slashed the corporate tax rates from 30% to 22% for domestic companies and 15% for new domestic manufacturing companies and provided a host of tax reliefs to attract fresh investment in manufacturing in Sep 2019. Thus, PLI is on the back of tax concessions extended to the corporate sector. The PLI scheme though noble in its intention counters the principle of 'Minimum Government – Maximum Governance' espoused by the central government on many occasions. Apart from its adverse fiscal implications, implementation of a scheme-like PLI involves political and bureaucratic discretion. Already pressure groups have been formed to expand the scope of PLI, to avail exemptions for meeting the PLI targets on account of exogenous developments and seeking addition incentives beyond what is provided in the PLI. India's experience with schemes to promote industrialisation in the pre-reform decades only led to entrenchment of vested interests without the expected benefits. The PLI scheme is likely to create similar perverse incentives and may not be very effective. Thus, it would be prudent to phase out the PLI scheme in an orderly manner.

Building human capital

Another worrying feature of government policy has been to ignore the importance of education, in general, and that of higher education, in particular. The central Government's budget allocation for education which had increased from 0.39% of nominal GDP to 0.62% during the 2005–14 period has declined to 0.47% during 2015–20. Further, the government has accorded relatively low importance to higher education in the recent times. This is evident from the fact that the budget allocation for higher education increased by 4.5% per annum compared to 6% per annum for school education during 2015–20. The higher education system can play a pivotal role in shaping the innovation ecosystem and lack of due importance accorded to this sector can compromise India's long-term growth prospects.

Health too does not receive attention from the government in terms of budget allocation by the central government. However, the government-funded health insurance scheme Ayushman Bharat Pradhan Mantri Jan Arogya Yojana (AB-PMJAY) launched on September 23, 2018 provides a major relief to the poor. Healthcare spending by the central government though much less than that on education has increased from 0.26% of GDP in 2016 to 0.31% in 2021. Thus, the traction observed in health-care spending by the government seems to be missing for education. The willingness of the government to spend on the PLI scheme with doubtful efficacy and its reluctance to spend on creating better education and health infrastructure is indicative of misplaced priorities. The misplaced priorities if reinforced instead of being corrected can adversely impact the medium-term growth prospects of the country.

Reversing protectionism

The reliance on protectionist measures by the government in the last six years may also act as a drag on the medium-term growth prospects of the country. In a globalised world, inward-looking policies may not be in the best interest of a country that aspires to achieve a sustainable growth rate of 10%. Consumers bear the burden of protection by paying higher prices for similar or worse products and services. Experience of countries that have maintained growth rates in excess of 8% per annum for around three decades suggests that exports played a key role in achieving higher growth. Openness to trade forces domestic producers to improve their productivity so as to retain their competitiveness in the face of competition from foreign producers. India adopted a series of reforms in the early 1990s to improve the efficiency of its production system by encouraging competition, both internal and external. Internal controls on production were done away with the abolition of industrial licensing system. Reducing tariffs and non-tariff barriers as an integral part of the reform process contributed to infusing external competition. Indian pursued with tariff reduction between 1991 and 2016. However, tariffs as a part of policy to support the domestic industry has again surfaced after 2016. It is appealing that higher tariff for imported products will give space for domestic industries to grow. However, such growth comes at the expense of the consumer. Tariff can at best provide temporary relief to Indian business and may not contribute to their global competitiveness even after prolonged periods of protection. India's own experience with trade protection measures suggests that such polies hardly work in practice.

V Reforms that are work in progress

Strengthening agricultural markets

The Indian Parliament on Nov 29, 2021 repealed the three farm laws that were enacted in Sep 2020. The three agricultural laws dealt with different aspects of agricultural marketing. Together, they were designed to create a unified national market by connecting agriculture–food supply chain players directly with farmers, reducing reliance on traditional intermediaries. Farmers in India are required to sell their produce to the Mandis or markets designated under the agricultural produce market committees (APMCs). Majority of farmers, however, sell their products in the APMC Mandis not directly but through traders on account of long distances to the Mandis, lack of information about mandi prices, poor infrastructure (weighing and storage facilities), and high marketing fees. Lack of direct interface often led to collusion among the traders and the buyers resulting in poor price realisation by farmers. The Farmers Produce Trade and Commerce (Promotion and Facilitation) Act, 2020 permitted framers to sell their produce outside the APMC (agricultural produce market committee) market. Just like farmers can sell their produce within the state or anywhere else in the country, this law permitted traders to purchase agricultural produce outside the APMC Mandi without a license, thus can lead to better price discovery. The Farmers (Empowerment and Protection) Agreement on Price Assurance and Farm Services Act, 2020 provided a framework for contract farming through an agreement between a farmer and a buyer before the production of any farm produce.

Contract farming assures procurement of a pre-determined quantity of the crop at a pre-determined prices. Contract farming can also help in technology dissemination and extension services while reducing the risk of production and marketing cost. However, the contract also creates vulnerability when the agricultural product does not meet the quality requirement for procurement. Policymakers acknowledged that it may be difficult to implement contract farming in the presence of many small land-holder famers. Thus, the Farmer Producer Organisation (FPOs) as collectives of farmers were considered an alternative mechanism to promote contract farming. It is also easier to deal with vulnerabilities associated with contract farming as a group than as an individual farmer. The Essential Commodities (Amendment) Act, 2020 was enacted to promote investment in agriculture. Given that seasonal nature of agricultural production, ensuring round-the-clock supply requires sufficient inventories for the whole year in cold storages and warehouses. Earlier, private players were reluctant to invest in post-harvest facilities due to abrupt stock limits imposed through Essential Commodities Act. The new bill on 'Essential Commodities (Amendment) Bill, 2020' envisaged investment in storage and warehouses by the corporate sector. There were apprehensions amongst a section of farmers in Punjab whether the procurement of food grains by the government will be discontinued once the role of APMCs is downplayed. There were also concerns whether the farmer will be more vulnerable on account of contact farming.

The quick implementation and subsequent repeal of the three progressive agriculture laws suggests the need to build consensus for reforms through stakeholder consultation. A government that enjoys absolute majority needs to also show magnanimity while introducing changes through broad-based consultation.

Flexible labour laws

Labour which is a variable cost in production is often perceived as a fixed cost in India on account of restrictive labour laws. The labour laws are applicable once business employs people beyond a threshold. Thus, business purposefully remained small to avoid the constraining labour laws. Thus, the very rules and regulations which were designed to protect the interest of workers were serving against them. In a bid to rationalise the labour laws so that interest of both business and employees are served, the central government enacted four labour codes by consolidating 29 of the existing labour laws during 2019–20.

The four labour codes are (a) Code on Wages, 2019, that consolidates the laws on payment of wages and bonus; (b) Code on Social Security, 2020, consolidating the laws on social security benefits; (c) the Occupational Safety, Health & Working Conditions Code, 2020 (September, 2020) that consolidates the laws on safety, health and working conditions of workers at factory/establishment; and (d) Code on Industrial Relations, 2020, that consolidates the laws relating to trade unions, retrenchment, lay-offs and settlement of industrial disputes. Labour being in concurrent list of the Constitution, both the Centre and states are required to notify rules under the four codes to enforce these laws in the states. The Centre has already finalised the draft rules of these Codes in February 2022. Further, 27 States/UTs have also pre-published the draft rules under the Code on Wages, 23 States/UTs under Industrial Relations Code, 21 States/UTs under Code on Social Security, and 18 States/UTs under OSH & WC Code by Jan 2022 (GoI, 2022b).

Some of the key features in the Codes that will have implication for employees and business are (a) The Wage Code empowers the central government to fix the minimum floor wage for each region and there is a statutory obligation on the state governments to fix minimum wages above the floor wage. (b) The threshold of obtaining prior permission from government for winding up business with associated lay-offs and retrenchment of workmen has been increased to establishments employing 300 or more workmen from the existing 100 or more workmen, thereby making it easier for business to adapt to the evolving macroeconomic and business environment. (c) Fixed-term employment was not defined under previous labour legislations. The Code recognises fixed-term employment and defines it as an engagement of an employee based on a written contract of employment for a fixed period. The concept of fixed-term employment is now extended to all the sectors. As a social security measure, the Code places fixed-term employees on an equal footing with permanent workers on working hours, statutory benefits including gratuity. The Social Security Code allows payment of gratuity upon completion of at least one year of service.

The government should make all effort to implement the Labour Codes at an early date. The Labour Codes will not only protect the interest of the workers but will also improve the ease of doing business in India.

Stabilisation of GST

GST considered as one of the efficiency-enhancing tax reform with the ability to increase GDP growth rate by 2–4% in the medium-term was implemented by the Government on July 1, 2017. Considered as a game-changer initiative, GST was implemented much after it was mooted in the Budget Speech of 2006–07. The government used its political capital to develop the consensus for GST amongst the states. Termed as a good and simple tax by the prime Minister, GST envisaged to unify the country as a common market by removing barriers across states. Under GST, both the central and state taxes will be levied on a single commodity at the same rate across the country. India adopted a four slab tax rate structure of 5%, 12%, 18%, and 28% for GST. In the initial years of its implementation, it took some time to develop familiarity with the new system of filing tax returns. Once adaptability improved, tax payers faced technical problems in the GST network (GSTN) while reconciling information furnished by the seller and the buyer in processing the input tax credit (ITC). The mechanism for matching of input tax credit as per GST requires filing three forms viz, GSTR-1, GSTR-2A, and GSTR-3B. GSTR-1 is submitted on a monthly basis by the taxpayers that contains outward supplies of goods and services. GSTR 2-A is auto-populated from the GSTR-1s filed by the suppliers of goods and services of a Taxpayer. GSTR 3-B contains the summary of all outward and inward supplies that is furnished by taxpayers on monthly basis. Reconciliation between GSTR-2A and GSTR-3B ensures that ITC is being availed for the tax which has been paid to the supplier. The process of availing refund of unutilised input tax credit was not only cumbersome but also involved inordinate delays. The COVID-19 pandemic further delayed the stabilisation of GST. The states were quite upbeat about the revenue potential of the GST. However, as a safeguard mechanism and to encourage states to adopt GST by surrendering their rights to levy indirect taxes, a mechanism for compensating the states for possible revenue loss was instituted. This mechanism was for initial five years of implementation of GST. The states were entitled compensation for shortfall of indirect tax revenue keeping 14% per annum revenue growth as the benchmark.

Consequently, the Goods and Services Tax Compensation Fund was created from the compensation cess levied on certain goods such as luxury cars, aerated drinks, pan masala, and tobacco products, over and above the GST rate of 28% for payment of compensation to the states identified by the GST council. Assured of compensation, the GST council has pitched for reducing the tax slab for several commodities and services since its existence leading to a reduction in effective tax rate under GST. Against the revenue neutral rate of 15.3% which was recommended by the Arvind Subramanian Committee, weighted average GST rate has been falling continuously and was just 11.6% in the year 2019. An IMF analysis of GST, which was done on behalf of the 15th Finance Commission, indicated that the current effective tax rate is around 11.8%. States seem to have missed the woods for the trees as the compensation was applicable only for the initial five years of implementation of GST. On account of lower effective tax rate, the revenue mobilised from GST has been rather low that what was estimated. In addition, due to COVID-19, the revenue mobilised form compensation cess was not adequate to compensate the states for revenue loss. As such, the centre had to borrow Rs. 1.1 lakh crore and Rs. 1.5 lakh crore under a special window in FY21 and FY 22, respectively. Given initial teething troubles and the technical glitch in transitioning to the new system followed by COVID-19, the revenue from GST was not adequate and many states have asked for the compensation system to continue for another five years. With implementation of GST, both the centre and the states have given up their discretionary power to levy indirect taxes to the GST council. Decisions in the GST council are taken on the basis of 75% majority vote where centre has one-third of the total voting rights and all the states accounting for the rest. The GST council is in the process of further rationalising the tax structure under GST. Thus, in the years ahead, the political economy will have a major bearing on the efficacy of GST as a game-changer initiative.

VI Overall assessment

The preceding discussions have a few implications. First, the government has been steadfast in rolling out several measures to address the structural challenges in the Indian economy. However, it has often ignored the merits of the consultative process in its enthusiasm for quick implementation of reform initiatives leading to policy reversals. A case in point is the three legislations for improving the productivity of the agriculture sector. The opposition to the policies was not as much on the content but the manner in which they were adopted (Aakar Patel, Times of India).

Second, some observes might suggest that the high unemployment rates, notwithstanding the policy intent, is a failure of the government. A realistic assessment should also take note of the fact that the economy went through a number of transitions on account of an attempt to clean the balance sheet of banks, implementation of two long pending reform measures, and demonetisation, an exercise in natural experiment. Notwithstanding its well-intentioned objective, demonetisation led to disruption in economic activity causing higher incidence of unemployment. The situation has been made only more difficult with the global COVID-19 pandemic. While it is debatable whether the intended objective of demonetisation was met, a certain positive spinoff was the adoption of digital mode of payments. Both demonetisation and GST fast paced the formalisation of the Indian economy.

Third, the introduction of a time bound resolution mechanism through the enactment of the IBC code in May 2016 and the implementation of GST from July 1, 2017 were two long pending second-generation reforms. However, many of the reform initiatives like the GST, IBC, Labour codes, and the agricultural marketing reforms are work in progress. The adoption of the GST system caused some dislocation in economic activity as it went through several round of iterations coupled with delay in availing input tax credits. The IBC since its introduction has gone through several amendments to improve its efficacy. Thus, adoption of a new system of taxation and a new resolution framework coupled with dislocation caused by demonetisation must have contributed their bit to the deterioration of unemployment scenario.

Fourth, the increase in tariff for a host of goods pursued since 2016 to protect the domestic industry runs counter the logic of reform pursued since 1991. Tariff protection to domestic industry coupled with PLI may breed inefficiency instead of increasing the share of manufacturing. Tax cuts serves as a better incentive for corporates to improve their profitability by adopting productivity and efficiency enhancing measures than protectionist measures. A country aspiring to increase its global economic prowess cannot rely on protectionism. Having said that, one can hardly deny the need to create employment opportunities in manufacturing by increasing its share in the GDP. What is the way out in such a scenario? Perhaps, effort to improve the ease as well as cost of doing business instead of higher tariffs can be more useful to promote manufacturing. Though India has made some progress in the ease of doing business, much more needs to be done to encourage entrepreneurship. A country cannot pursue protectionism and attain higher sustainable growth. The sooner this fact is appreciated by its policymakers, the better it is for the India.

Fifth, policymaking in the developed countries is guided by changes in the employment scenario. The unemployment problem though is acknowledged by the policymakers in India, it does not figure prominently in macroeconomic management. The lack of high frequency data on the labour markets is partly responsible for such a situation. At present, unemployment rate for India is available only on an annual basis and the urban unemployment rate on a quarterly basis. When daily unemployment rate for India is published by CMIE, a private agency, there is no reason why unemployment data at monthly intervals cannot be generated by the official statistical system. It is often said that 'Only What Get Measured Gets Managed' (Kalus, 2015). In the similar vein, it can be said that what is not measured is often ignored. In the absence of high-frequency employment data, the unemployment challenge is often ignored in policy formulation. Thus, there is a need to bring employment into the public discourse for effective policymaking. India can assure a dignified living to its growing working age population only through creation of adequate employment opportunities. The government and the central bank must bring employment to the forefront in policymaking.

Sixth, estimates suggest that 28% of the Indian population belong to the middle class (Aslany, 2019). Thus, from the demand side, around 40 crore people are charging the economy forward. For achieving economic growth of 10% and sustaining it for around two decades, the size of the middle class must grow. There is a need to create an employment policy which will map the existing skill profile of the working age population, identify sectors that have growth potential, assess the knowledge and skills needed to absorb people in those sectors and most importantly, allocate funds to meet the skill gap. The 'Make in India' and the 'Skill India' initiatives introduced in the year 2015 were designed in this sprit and were steps in the right direction but government lost focus on them in the maze of initiatives. Bringing employment to the mainstream policy discourse will create accountability and force the government to prioritise investment in human capital. Such an approach will expand the size of the middle class, fuel growth and also meet the rising aspirations of an expanding working age population. The subsequent Chapters in the book also bring out the importance of human capital formation in improving productivity, reducing inequality, and ensuring political accountability in the Indian states.

Lastly, political stability, strong leadership, improved governance, and willingness to introduce reforms augur well for the Indian economy. The challenges are formidable and it will take dedicated efforts from both the political leadership and the bureaucracy to create a virtuous cycle of a booming manufacturing sector that absorb significant proportion of the working population. The faith of the people on the government is reflected in it being voted back to power in the year 2019 with a greater majority. As already discussed, the present government in its first term during 2014–19 and in the ongoing second term has already launched several reform measures and initiatives which will take time to stabilise. It will be useful to take stock and consolidate the various initiatives, and if needed, make course corrections so as to derive the intended benefits instead of launching more initiatives.

In short, Indian economy grew at a fast pace during 2005–09 reflecting the lagged effect of the various policy initiatives introduced during 2000–2004. Neither those policy initiatives were consolidated nor were any major economic reforms introduced during 2005–09. The high growth observed before the financial crisis had created a sense of complacency. The expansionary polices post-GFC and macroeconomic mismanagement coupled with failure in governance adversely impacted growth during 2010–14. The digital push by the government coupled with mission mode urgency to increase financial access reduced the transaction cost in the Indian economy in the post-2015 period. Thus, notwithstanding several setbacks and legacy NPAs, growth of the Indian economy improved during 2015–20. Though small in percentage terms, the middle class in terms of absolute numbers provide a large domestic market. Even if the middle class does not expand in a significant manner, the aspirations of the people to lead a better life will ensure a minimum of 5% economic growth. One may recall that 5% economic growth was reflective of a scenario of policy logjam, in the 12th Five-year plan. The government in the last eight years has shown great resolve in taking series of measures to improve India's growth potential. Investment in human capital must receive as much priority as the investment in building physical and digital infrastructure. There is no reason why the growth rate cannot surpass 10% with growth supportive policies.

VII Change in approach to regional development

There has been a paradigm change in the Centre–State relationship in India after the abolition of planning commission in the year 2015. Planning commission was created through an executive order in the year 1950 to formulate Five year Plans for the Country. Though a non-statutory entity, the planning commission was vested with financial powers, and it was one of the significant sources of fund transfer from the Centre to the states. With NITI Aayog replacing the planning commission, the financial devolution from the planning commission has now been subsumed under the transfers recommended by the Finance Commission.

The approach to regional development of the government after 2014 has been to promote competitive federalism in addition to cooperative federalism. There are statutory mechanisms in India to promote cooperative federalism. For instance, the Constitution of India mandates that the Centre must appoint a Finance Commission in every five years that will prescribe a method for devolution of funds from the Centre to the states to meet horizontal and vertical imbalances in the fiscal position of Centre and the states. The NITI Aayog and the erstwhile Planning Commission provided a collaborative platform to address the pressing problems of the states. Further, the central ministries provide funds to the states to implement centrally sponsored schemes. The GST compensation and GST council are instances of cooperative federalism.

In addition to cooperative federalism, the government is also stressing on competitive federalism in the post 2015 period. Competitive federalism has been pursued by presenting the comparative position of states in the form of progress made in ease of doing business, better governance, achieving sustainable development goals, and creating dashboards to track the progress made by the aspirational districts spread across states. Campaigns launched by different states such as 'Vibrant Gujarat', 'Happening Haryana', and 'Magnetic Maharashtra' are also indicative of the competitive spirit among Indian states. Competitive federalism creates a greater sense of accountability amongst the states. However, the downside is that it can prompt states to play to the gallery and paint a rosy picture of progress which is far from the ground reality. For instance, the improvement in rank of Uttar Pradesh from 12 in the Ease of Doing Business 2019 to 2 in 2020 has raised concerns about their genuineness (Chhibber, 2021).

Notwithstanding, the pressure created on the lagging states to perform, the outcome is yet to improve significantly. This is reflected from an analysis of the progress made by states in achieving the SDGs. The correlation between the underdevelopment index as on 2013 and the scores in the SDG index for the state for the year 2017, 2018, and 2019 suggest that it is the better-off states which have been able to make relatively better progress in achieving the SDGs. Though there is progress in the right direction, it is yet to gain traction (Table 1.3).

While it has a broader coverage and the philosophy behind the SDG index is laudable, it has limited practical utility for several reasons (Ghosh

Table 1.3 State of Underdevelopment and Progress in SDG-Experience of Indian States

State/UT	*Under Development Index*	*Composite SDG Score 2017–18*	*Rank 2018*	*Composite SDG Score 2018–19*	*Rank 2019*	*Composite SDG Score 2019–20*	*Rank 2020*
Goa	0.05	64	**4**	65	**6**	72	**4**
Kerala	0.09	69	**1**	70	**1**	75	**1**
Tamil Nadu	0.34	66	**3**	67	**3**	74	**2**
Maharashtra	0.35	64	**4**	64	7	70	**8**
Punjab	0.35	60	**9**	62	**10**	68	**10**
Uttarakhand	0.38	60	**9**	64	7	72	**4**
Haryana	0.4	55	**14**	57	**15**	67	**11**
Himachal Pradesh	0.4	69	**1**	69	**2**	74	**2**
Karnataka	0.45	64	**4**	66	**5**	72	**4**
Gujarat	0.49	64	**4**	64	7	69	**9**
Andhra Pradesh	0.52	64	**4**	67	**3**	72	**4**
West Bengal	0.55	56	**13**	60	**11**	62	**13**
Rajasthan	0.63	59	**11**	57	**15**	60	**17**
Uttar Pradesh	0.64	42	**20**	55	**18**	60	**17**
Chhattisgarh	0.75	58	**12**	56	**17**	61	**15**
Jharkhand	0.75	50	**18**	53	**19**	56	**19**
Bihar	0.76	48	**19**	50	**20**	52	**20**
Madhya Pradesh	0.76	52	**16**	58	**13**	62	**13**
Odisha	0.8	51	**17**	58	**13**	61	**15**
Sikkim	0.43	58	**3**	65	**1**	71	**1**
Tripura	0.47	55	**4**	58	**3**	65	**3**
Mizoram	0.49	59	**1**	56	**5**	68	**2**
Nagaland	0.55	51	**6**	57	**4**	61	**5**
Manipur	0.57	59	**1**	60	**2**	64	**4**
Meghalaya	0.69	52	**5**	54	7	60	**6**
Assam	0.71	49	**8**	55	**6**	57	**8**
Arunachal Pradesh	0.73	51	**6**	53	**8**	60	**6**
India		57		60		66	
Target		100		100		100	

Source: Report of the Committee for Evolving a Composite Development Index of States 2013, *Ministry of Finance*, New Delhi, for the Underdevelopment Index and Niti Aayog for the SDG Index.

et al. 2019; Nair, 2021). The major limitation of the SDG index is that it cannot be used for inter-temporal comparison. This is because the indicators underlying the SDG index are not common across the years. Further, the SDG index is computed by assigning equal weight to all the underlying indicators. As such, we rely on the per capita income as the indicator of development of the state.

Notes

1 2015 refers to the financial year 2014–15.
2 As per the Second Advance Estimates of National Income released on February 28, 2022.
3 As per RBI guidelines, a PMJDY account is treated as inoperative if there are no customer induced transactions in the account for over a period of two years.
4 For the financial year 2019–20 scheduled commercial banks (SCBs) have been able to recover 45.5% of their claims through IBC, which is the highest as compared to recovery under other modes and legislations.
5 The guidelines for PLI were published in June 2020
6 The initial three sectors were (i) Mobile Manufacturing and Specified Electronic Components, (ii) Critical Key Starting materials/Drug Intermediaries & Active Pharmaceutical Ingredients, (iii) Manufacturing of Medical Devices has been expanded to cover 13 sectors by Nov 2020. The other ten sectors which were covered under PLI are (i) Automobiles and Auto Components, (ii) Pharmaceuticals Drugs, (iii) Specialty Steel, (iv) Telecom & Networking Products, (v) Electronic/Technology Products, (vi) White Goods (ACs and LEDs), (vii) Food Products, (viii) Textile Products: MMF segment and technical textiles, (ix) High efficiency solar PV modules, and (x) Advanced Chemistry Cell (ACC) Battery.

References

Acharya, S. (2022). *An Economist at Home and Abroad* . Harper Collins India, New Delhi.

Aslany, M. (2019). The Indian Middle Class, Its Size, and Urban-Rural Variations, *Contemporary South Asia*, Vol. 27, pp. 1–18. https://doi.org/10.1080/09584935.2019.1581727.

Chhibber, A. (2021, July 22). Ease vs cost of doing business in India, Business Standard, July 22, 2021, available at https://www.business-standard.com/article/opinion/ease-vs-cost-of-doing-business-in-india-121072200013_1.html.

Das, S. (2019, November 16). *Indian Banking at Crossroads – Some Reflections, Speech by Governor of the Reserve Bank of India, at the First Annual Economics Conference, Amrut Mody School of Management.* Ahmedabad University, Ahmedabad.

Economic Times (2022), India on Course to Become USD 5 Trillion Economy by FY26: CEA, *Economic Times,* Feb 1, 2022, available at: https://economictimes.indiatimes.com/news/economy/finance/india-on-course-to-become-usd-5-trillion-economy-by-fy26-cea/articleshow/89281393.cms?utm_source=contentofinterest&utm_medium=text&utm_campaign=cppst.

Ghosh, N., Saha, R., and Bhomick, S. (2019). *SDG Index and Ease of Doing Business in India: A Sub-National Study, Occasional Papers.* Observes Research Foundation June 2019, New Delhi.

GoI. (2014). *Report of the 14th Finance Commission, 2015–2020.* Finance Commission of India.

GoI. (2014, August 20). *Digital India A Programme to Transform India into Digital Empowered Society and Knowledge Economy.* Press Information Bureau Press Release.

GoI. (2015). *Report of the Sub-Group of Chief Ministers on Rationalisation of Centrally Sponsored Schemes.* NITI Aayog, New Delhi, India.

GoI. (2016a). *Economic Survey 2015–2016. Delhi: Ministry of Finance, Department of Economic Affairs.* Economic Division, New Delhi.

GoI. (2016b). Spreading JAM Across India's Economy, *Economic Survey 2015–2016*, Chapter 3, Vol. 1, published by Government of India, Ministry of Finance, New Delhi, India.

GoI. (2017). The Festering Twin Balance Sheet Problem, *Economic Survey 2016–2017,* Chapter 4, Vol. 1, published by Government of India, Ministry of Finance, New Delhi, India.

GoI. (2019a). *India's Trillion Dollar Digital Opportunity, Ministry of Electronics and Information Technology.* Government of India, New Delhi, India.

GoI. (2019b). *Report of the 15th Finance Commission, 2020–2021.* Finance Commission of India.

GoI. (2020a). *Report of the 15th Finance Commission, 2021–2026.* Finance Commission of India.

GoI. (2020b, April 29). *Task Force on National Infrastructure Pipeline Presents its Final Report to Finance Minister Smt. Nirmala Sitharaman.* Press Information Bureau, Ministry of Finance press release.

GoI. (2021a, February 1). *Commitment of Financial Outlay of Rs 1.97 Lakh Crore in the Next 5 years Starting Fy 2021–2022 for PLI Schemes in 13 Sectors.* Press Information Bureau, Ministry of Finance press release.

GoI. (2021b, April 7). *PMMY Helped in Generation of 1.12 Crore Net Additional Employment from 2015 to 2018.* Press Information Bureau, Ministry of Finance Press Release.

GoI. (2021c, August 28). *Pradhan Mantri Jan-Dhan Yojana (PMJDY) -National Mission for Financial Inclusion, Completes Seven Years of Successful Implementation.* Press Information Bureau Press Release.

GoI. (2021d, September 21). *India Scores 46th Rank in the Global Innovation Index 2021.* Press Information Bureau Press Release.

GoI. (2021e, October 25). *PM GatiShakti – National Master Plan. Press Information Bureau.* Ministry of Information and Broadcasting Press Release.

GoI. (2021f, November 1). *National Statement by Prime Minister Shri Narendra Modi at COP26 Su*mmit in *Glasgow.* Press Information Bureau, Prime Minister's Office Press Release.

GoI. (2022a, January 5). *Direct Benefit Transfer.* Press Information Bureau, Ministry of Information and Broadcasting Press Release.

GoI. (2022b, March 21). *Implementation of New Labour Codes.* Press Information Bureau, Ministry of Labour & Employment Press Release.

IBBI. (2022). *Insolvency and Bankruptcy News Jan–Mar 2022.* Quarterly Newsletter of the Insolvency and Bankruptcy Board of India, New Delhi, India.

Klaus, P. (2015). *The Devil Is in the Details – Only What Get Measured Gets Managed. In: Measuring Customer Experience.* Palgrave Macmillan, London. https://doi.org/10.1057/9781137375469_7.

Mundra, S.S. (2016, April 29). *Asset Quality Challenges in India: Diagnosis and Prognosis.* Speech Delivered by Deputy Governor, Reserve Bank of India at the Edelweiss Credit Conclave, Mumbai.

Nair, R.(2021, June 5), State of the states: NITI Report Shows Who's Rising, Who's Lagging and the Gap in Between, *The Print*, available at: https://theprint.in/india/state-of-the-states-niti-report-shows-whos-rising-whos-lagging-and-the-gap-in-between/672171/.

NSSO (2014). Employment and Unemployment Situation in India, 2011–12, NSS Report No. 554, NSS 68th Round (July 2011–June 2012), NSSO, Ministry of Statistics and Programme Implementation Government of India, Jan 2014.

NSO (2019). Annual Report, Periodic Labour Force Survey 2017–18 (July 2017–June 2018), National Statistical Office, Ministry of Statistics and Programme Implementation Government of India, May 2019

Rajan, R.R. (2016a, February 11). *Issues in Banking Today, Speech at CII's First Banking Summit by Dr. Raghuram Rajan.* Governor, Reserve Bank of India at Mumbai on February 11, 2016.

Rajan, R.R. (2016b, June 22). *Resolving Stress in the Banking System, Speech by Dr. Raghuram G. Rajan, Governor, Reserve Bank of India.* at ASSOCHAM – Interactive Meet with Industry & Trade, June 22, 2016, Bengaluru.

Reserve Bank of India (2022). *Report on Currency and Finance, 2021–2022.* Published on April 29, 2022.

2 Growth performance of Indian States

I Introduction

This chapter chronicles the growth performance of Indian states during the period 2001–20. For this purpose, we have categorised states[1] as 'large' and 'small' depending on their share in the country's population. Large states (LS) have a share of more than 1% in India's population. States that have less than 1% share in the population are termed as small. Besides, the category of 'small' and the 'large' states, we have taken into account the union territories as another category.[2]

The growth of the Indian economy in the post-2000 period has been analysed in four different phases. The phases correspond to the tenure of the governments at the Centre. The Bharatiya Janata Party (BJP) and the Indian National Congress (INC) are the two major political parties which have led the United Progressive Alliance (UPA) and the National Democratic Alliance (NDA), respectively, that formed government at the Centre in the post-2000 period. The NDA formed the government after the 1999 general elections and was in power during 1999–2004. In the 2004 and 2009 general elections, the UPA was voted to power and formed the government. The tenure of the governments during 2004–09 and 2009–14 is popularly referred to UPA-1 and UPA-II. Subsequently, the NDA received popular mandate in the 2014 and 2019 general elections and formed the government at the Centre. Thus, the phases considered for our study are 2001–04, 2005–09, 2010–14, and 2015–20.

The rest of this chapter is structured as follows. Section II briefly discusses India's growth performance in the four phases. The growth performance of states as well as their share in the combined output and population of all states under study is described in Section III. Section IV presents the contribution of the states to the growth of the Indian economy. The sectoral shares in output for the country as well as for the different category of states are discussed in Section V. Section VI discusses

DOI: 10.4324/9781003278351-2

the volatility of output in the four sub periods for the different category of states.

II Growth performance during 2001–20

Subdued growth 2001-04

As India entered the 21st century, the country grew by a subdued 5.3% per annum during 2001–04. During this period, a number of reforms were undertaken like the disinvestment of public sector enterprises (PSUs), enactment of Fiscal Responsibility and Budget Management (FRBM) Act, allowing FDI in insurance sector, reforms in the telecom sector and launching of the Sarva Shiksha Abhiyan[3] in the year 2001. Notwithstanding the various reform initiatives by the Government, the relatively lower growth was due to multiple of factors. First, the Indian economy was in the midst of implementing several banking sector reform measures which prompted banks to invest in risk-free government bonds to than lending which intrinsically involves risk. This phase of low credit growth has been dubbed as lazy banking (Mohan, 2006). Second, the United States imposed sanctions on India following nuclear tests conducted by it in the year 1998. Third, the negative externalities emanating from the terrorist attack on the United States in Sep 2001 adversely impacted the Indian information technology (IT) industry. Lastly, the uncertainties associated with the dotcom bubble were a set back. Nonetheless, the foundation for higher growth in the subsequent period was laid down during the 2001-04 period (Acharya, 2022). For instance, government pursued a massive road connectivity programme called the golden quadrilateral programme for faster connectivity between major cities and ports, improved access to markets, reduce agricultural wastage in transport, drive economic growth, and promote road transport.

Growth acceleration 2005–09

The lagged and cumulative effect of the various initiatives led to an acceleration of GDP growth to 6.9% during 2005–09. This period also benefited from robust growth in world trade and the ultra cheap monetary policy pursed by the US Fed. The 8% plus growth during 2005–08 before the GFC had created a euphoria about the bright growth prospects in India. In the initial days of the GFC, it was thought that India was decoupled from the rest of the world because it had a relatively lower share of trade in GDP. However, it was soon found that India is very much coupled with the global economy through the trade, capital, and the confidence channels

(Misra, 2013b). Nonetheless, India could protect itself for some time from the after effects of the GFC with huge monetary and fiscal stimulus.

Growth slowdown 2010–14

The adverse consequences of stimulus created a high inflationary situation by early 2010 when inflation[4] exceeded 10% leading to a contractionary monetary policy for almost two years between March 2010 and April 2012. Rising interest rates coupled with governance issues faced by the Indian economy culminated in growth decelerating to 6.2% in the 2010–14 period. Several financial scams were also reported during this period which dented the image of the government. As discussed in Chapter 1, inability of the government to issue land and environmental clearances and delayed commissioning of several infrastructure projects which were financed by public sector banks contributed their bit to the growth slowdown. The time and cost overruns associated with the infrastructure projects adversely impacted the performance of banks as well as companies that had taken up bank financing for infrastructure projects. The situation was popularly described as the twin balance sheet challenge for the Indian economy (GoI, 2016). The hands off approach of the Reserve Bank of India in the forex market after the GFC when India received substantial amount of FIIs not only led to the over valuation of the Indian rupee but also relatively lower forex reserves. The vulnerabilities of the Indian economy were apparent when it faced a mini BoP crisis during 2014 (Acharya, 2013).

Growth revival 2015–20

The popular discontent with the UPA government was reflected in the 2014 general elections when the BJP-led NDA alliance was voted to power. The NDA alliance was again elected to form the government in 2019. The 2015–20 phase corresponds to the period when the BJP-led NDA government was in power. Though the government is formed by a coalition, its leading party received absolute majority in the Parliament and could have formed the government on its own. Absolute majority by one political party was observed successively in the 2014 and 2019 general elections after two and half decades. Having the political mandate, this government introduced a number of game changing reforms. Some of the long pending reforms were the introduction of the GST and enactment of a time-bound resolution process. Besides, several initiatives were undertaken including the launch of a major financial inclusion drive, leveraging the JAM trinity for efficient delivery of public services and the MUDRA initiative to promote entrepreneurship. The government finances also improved due to the subdued oil prices during 2015–18. Instead of transmitting the reduced oil prices to the consumers, the government used the additional revenue to finance several social welfare schemes. In 2016, the Government launched a demonetisation initiative, which helped accelerate digital payments in the Indian economy. The growth during the 2015–20 period accelerated to 6.8% per annum on account of the various reform initiatives of the government already discussed in Chapter 1.

When the price momentum is also taken into account, we find that both growth in output and inflation were rather subdued at 5.31% and 3.61% during 2001–04. The 2005–09 was a phase which witnessed higher inflation at 7.18% per annum along with higher growth of 6.90% per annum. Growth decelerated to 6.18% during 2010–14 period. However, price pressure reflected through the annual inflation rate further escalated to more than 8% during 2010–14. The phase of 2015–20 was much better in terms of inflationary containment with growth-gaining momentum. Growth accelerated to 6.84% with inflation averaging 3.35%. Overall, per annum growth of 7.25% and average inflation of 5.54% was observed during the period 2001–20. Thus, except the 2010–14 period, India broadly experienced acceptable level of inflation. However, growth of 7.25% when seen in conjunction with the low base of GDP leaves much scope for improvement.

In this backdrop, we discuss the change in the relative importance of the different states in India's growth during the study period by computing the share of individual as well as different categories of states in the combined output and population of all the state sunder study.

III Growth of SDP

Aggregate output for the different categories of states viz, LS, SS, and UTs grew in sync with that of GDP growth across the sub periods. As discussed in the preceding section, aggregate output grew at an accelerated pace during 2005–09 as compared to the period 2001–04. Growth, however, decelerated in the post GFC period 2010–14 when compared to period 2005–09. However, growth has again accelerated in the most recent phase 2015–20 compared to 2010–14.

The industrial as well as services sector output in all the three categories of states have followed a growth trajectory similar to that of aggregate output.

As far as agricultural output is concerned, we find that the different categories of states traversed a growth trajectory different from that observed at the all-India level. All-India agricultural output grew at a successively faster pace during 2005–09 and 2010–14 compared to the period

2001–04. However, in the most recent phase, there has been deceleration in the growth of all-India agricultural output. However, agricultural output in the LS has grown successively at a faster pace in the three subsequent periods beginning with the period 2001–04. Agricultural output growth has been rather volatile across the sub periods for the SS. For the UTs, agriculture accounted for a very small share in total output and the growth of agricultural output has decelerated successively during 2005–09 and 2010–14 before growing at a fast pace during 2015–20.

The growth trajectory of aggregate and sectoral output for the states is provided in Annexures 2.1–2.5 corresponding to different periods. We next discuss the relative importance of different categories of states by analysing their share in combined output and population of all states across the different time periods.

III Share of states in combined output and population

The following points are worth noting when we analyse the share of individual states as well as different groups of states in the combined output and population for all the states under study (Table 2.1).

- The share of LS in the combined SDP of all states was 91.15% during the entire study period followed by that of union territories (UTs) at 5.34% and smaller states (SS) at 3.5%, respectively. The share of LS in the combined population at 94.61% was greater than their share in combined output during 2001–20. The SS and UTs accounted for 2.74% and 2.65% in combined population during 2001–20. In contrast to the LS, the SS and UTs had a share in combined output which is larger than their share in combined population.
- The shares of both UTs and SS have marginally increased and that for the LS have undergone a slight decline in the combined SDP between 2001–04 and 2015–20. However, the share of LS and SS in the combined population has marginally declined and that of UTs have slightly increased during 2015–20 as compared to 2001–04. Notwithstanding their changing share over the years, LS, SS, and UTs accounted for 90.89%, 3.68%, and 5.42%, respectively in the combined SDP during 2015–20, the last phase of our study period. The share of LS, SS, and UTs in the combined population were 94.53%, 2.73%, and 2.74% respectively, during 2015–20.
- Amongst the LS, Maharashtra (14.58%), Uttar Pradesh (8.70%), Andhra Pradesh (8.45%), Tamil Nadu (8.35%), and Gujarat (8.21%) accounted for the bulk of output in combined SDP during

Annexure 2.1 Sectoral Growth and Sectoral Share in Output during 2001–04

(%)

State	Growth: Agriculture	Growth: Industry	Growth: Services	Growth: Output	Growth: Population	Growth: Prices	Shares: Agriculture	Shares: Industry	Shares: Services
Andhra Pradesh	0.54	6.51	7.20	5.12	1.16	3.89	30.31	28.64	41.05
Assam	0.75	13.22	5.41	5.40	1.68	3.28	27.60	34.37	38.03
Bihar	−2.86	1.86	4.34	1.44	2.03	3.05	36.56	11.90	51.54
Chhattisgarh	11.78	10.14	5.68	8.64	1.81	3.38	23.79	42.67	33.54
Gujarat	16.48	9.63	8.30	10.17	1.77	4.58	24.29	41.62	34.09
Haryana	1.75	9.68	10.83	7.90	2.07	4.27	34.47	32.75	32.77
Jharkhand	2.02	9.73	2.80	5.44	1.81	3.78	15.82	54.74	29.44
Karnataka	-10.23	8.85	7.94	3.69	1.32	3.51	19.11	30.07	50.82
Kerala	0.74	7.53	7.93	6.34	0.88	3.03	27.49	25.25	47.26
Madhya Pradesh	7.79	1.63	2.77	3.78	2.00	4.73	33.98	28.32	37.69
Maharashtra	5.76	5.84	6.71	6.33	1.62	4.00	19.28	34.95	45.77
Orissa	3.19	6.70	7.33	5.97	1.17	4.41	27.61	37.97	34.42
Punjab	1.44	2.65	5.84	3.53	1.68	3.82	44.13	19.32	36.55
Rajasthan	8.91	6.38	5.00	6.70	2.07	1.79	33.79	29.06	37.16
Tamil Nadu	-10.10	2.43	5.13	1.99	0.91	3.85	18.62	36.28	45.10
Uttar Pradesh	1.68	4.34	4.93	3.71	2.03	3.27	37.20	24.48	38.32
West Bengal	2.86	7.86	6.21	5.56	1.30	3.30	33.12	27.12	39.76
Large States	**2.30**	**6.48**	**6.30**	**5.23**	**1.64**	**3.71**	**28.05**	**30.82**	**41.13**
Arunachal Pradesh	−0.79	17.35	5.15	5.91	2.34	2.80	55.22	12.47	32.31
Goa	5.64	7.14	5.97	6.43	2.84	6.20	10.23	69.57	20.20
Himachal Pradesh	6.86	6.53	4.93	6.00	1.73	3.70	26.07	42.25	31.68

Manipur	3.91	13.32	1.68	5.00	2.08	2.56	26.04	17.77	56.19
Meghalaya	4.03	7.45	5.41	5.60	1.37	4.26	23.70	31.34	44.96
Mizoram	1.41	11.06	7.59	7.02	2.58	4.20	24.32	20.12	55.55
Nagaland	10.55	13.06	6.50	8.69	5.13	3.56	37.39	12.23	50.37
Tripura	7.25	12.18	7.56	8.49	1.18	3.38	30.53	20.24	49.23
Sikkim	6.90	11.14	6.41	7.65	1.77	4.40	16.09	30.31	53.60
Uttaranchal	1.44	14.89	7.88	7.90	1.70	3.74	30.20	35.66	34.14
Small States	**4.17**	**9.58**	**6.01**	**6.84**	**2.01**	**3.67**	**26.78**	**36.92**	**36.31**
A&N Islands	1.16	29.99	5.71	7.76	0.67	4.54	34.43	11.44	54.13
Chandigarh	4.07	13.97	9.89	10.64	3.17	4.32	1.76	13.40	84.84
Delhi	−0.87	4.88	6.22	5.87	3.05	3.98	1.62	24.03	74.35
Jammu and Kashmir	5.41	1.77	4.56	4.18	1.61	4.99	23.25	31.30	45.45
Puducherry	−1.64	10.46	5.40	7.48	1.90	4.68	7.20	62.33	30.46
Union Territories	**3.85**	**4.88**	**6.16**	**5.78**	**2.43**	**4.28**	**6.90**	**26.61**	**66.49**
NE States	**2.07**	**12.70**	**5.47**	**5.86**	**1.86**	**3.34**	**28.89**	**29.65**	**41.46**
India	**2.38**	**6.53**	**6.28**	**5.31**	**1.67**	**3.74**	**26.95**	**30.81**	**42.25**

Source: Estimates by the Author.
Notes: All-India figures are proxied through that for all states and union territories taken as a group. Bold values are used to denote 'groups of states'. Growth rates are compounded annual growth rates.

Annexure 2.2 Sectoral Growth and Sectoral Shares in Output during 2005–09

(%)

State	*Growth*						*Shares*		
	Agriculture	*Industry*	*Services*	*Output*	*Population*	*Prices*	*Agriculture*	*Industry*	*Services*
Andhra Pradesh	6.96	11.91	10.94	10.23	1.04	5.41	26.53	30.96	42.51
Assam	2.32	0.81	7.87	4.66	1.35	5.34	23.44	35.00	41.55
Bihar	5.43	15.74	8.82	8.87	1.60	5.23	31.40	14.95	53.65
Chhattisgarh	4.39	13.32	9.99	10.34	1.96	5.54	19.30	48.84	31.86
Gujarat	5.08	10.27	11.75	10.13	1.50	4.55	22.74	43.02	34.24
Haryana	5.11	7.12	12.88	9.37	1.84	5.50	28.31	33.96	37.72
Jharkhand	9.39	0.88	9.71	5.45	1.51	4.45	15.34	51.95	32.71
Karnataka	5.10	10.98	11.63	10.28	1.15	5.41	15.41	30.84	53.75
Kerala	−0.95	6.37	11.04	8.12	0.48	5.18	20.87	27.73	51.40
Madhya Pradesh	3.36	11.36	7.93	7.69	1.77	5.82	33.07	29.86	37.08
Maharashtra	6.41	11.61	10.68	10.54	1.51	4.57	15.91	36.95	47.15
Orissa	3.01	12.95	10.62	9.79	1.32	5.30	21.54	44.53	33.93
Punjab	2.59	14.31	8.10	8.10	1.85	4.76	38.57	23.41	38.02
Rajasthan	3.60	9.06	9.97	8.17	1.82	5.68	31.08	31.19	37.73
Tamil Nadu	4.50	7.40	12.65	10.19	0.76	4.92	15.31	36.50	48.19
Uttar Pradesh	3.01	8.93	9.02	7.31	1.89	5.32	31.37	28.85	39.78
West Bengal	2.43	4.91	−0.20	6.90	1.06	5.74	29.35	29.74	40.91
Large States	**4.18**	**9.49**	**9.90**	**9.05**	**1.46**	**5.21**	**23.72**	**33.39**	**42.89**
Arunachal Pradesh	4.42	9.18	8.59	7.43	2.34	6.63	45.73	20.67	33.60
Goa	−2.03	7.88	10.07	8.16	3.29	6.12	8.69	69.99	21.32
Himachal Pradesh	3.44	10.43	9.62	8.46	1.09	4.66	23.08	43.14	33.78

Manipur	4.73	3.54	6.37	4.95	2.21	5.12	25.37	21.28	53.34
Meghalaya	1.91	11.91	8.09	7.81	2.49	4.61	20.62	34.67	44.71
Mizoram	6.88	12.86	8.21	8.74	2.57	4.42	21.30	22.54	56.17
Nagaland	2.46	13.93	9.46	7.84	1.64	5.02	35.51	13.94	50.55
Tripura	9.23	7.81	7.16	7.84	1.22	3.86	28.79	21.56	49.65
Sikkim	2.87	13.98	8.51	9.26	1.25	6.10	13.83	33.99	52.18
Uttaranchal	0.59	20.86	16.41	14.89	1.58	4.56	19.84	47.29	32.87
Small States	**2.93**	**13.22**	**10.78**	**10.10**	**1.71**	**4.81**	**21.71**	**42.02**	**36.27**
A&N Islands	4.92	16.01	11.80	12.25	0.67	4.25	20.21	27.70	52.09
Chandigarh	2.14	5.32	11.22	10.30	5.39	5.60	1.24	15.75	83.01
Delhi	–1.33	5.92	13.00	11.66	1.92	4.65	1.06	23.15	75.79
Jammu and Kashmir	1.32	5.95	9.73	6.15	1.44	5.66	20.41	32.75	46.84
Puducherry	9.98	7.24	13.19	10.04	1.88	4.78	6.04	58.16	35.81
Union Territories	**1.43**	**6.10**	**12.46**	**10.49**	**1.86**	**4.91**	**5.21**	**25.92**	**68.87**
NE States	**3.35**	**3.29**	**7.87**	**5.67**	**1.53**	**5.26**	**25.12**	**31.05**	**43.83**
India	**3.42**	**9.04**	7.57	**6.90**	**1.46**	**5.54**	**21.11**	**31.74**	**47.15**

Note: Growth rates are compounded annual growth rates. Bold values are used to denote 'groups of states'.
Source: Estimates by the Author.

Annexure 2.3 Sectoral Growth and Sectoral Shares in Output during 2010–14

(%)

State	*Growth*						*Shares*		
	Agriculture	*Industry*	*Services*	*Output*	*Population*	*Prices*	*Agriculture*	*Industry*	*Services*
Andhra Pradesh	4.96	0.93	9.77	6.19	0.76	5.41	22.82	29.46	47.72
Assam	5.09	1.39	5.60	4.28	1.91	5.34	22.08	31.83	46.09
Bihar	6.93	7.30	8.57	8.18	3.46	5.23	25.12	18.52	56.36
Chhattisgarh	7.34	7.80	6.90	7.31	2.15	5.54	17.78	47.60	34.63
Gujarat	5.95	7.77	10.27	8.76	2.06	4.55	18.00	45.64	36.36
Haryana	3.29	6.74	9.97	7.90	1.39	5.50	22.63	32.24	45.14
Jharkhand	9.64	6.51	6.54	7.18	3.00	4.45	15.01	46.03	38.96
Karnataka	0.77	4.83	9.43	6.85	1.92	5.41	13.51	29.01	57.48
Kerala	–0.76	5.57	7.35	5.86	0.48	5.18	14.30	27.56	58.14
Madhya Pradesh	10.92	3.27	8.24	7.99	1.84	5.82	31.08	30.03	38.88
Maharashtra	5.36	4.83	8.21	6.78	1.13	4.57	13.04	35.82	51.14
Orissa	3.83	5.50	7.66	6.24	0.85	5.30	18.63	43.12	38.25
Punjab	1.81	3.56	9.33	6.18	–0.12	4.76	31.05	25.52	43.43
Rajasthan	8.85	6.61	8.51	8.08	1.82	5.68	28.66	31.20	40.14
Tamil Nadu	4.08	6.61	9.02	7.94	s2.73	4.92	12.11	37.09	50.80
Uttar Pradesh	3.87	3.83	7.79	5.81	1.46	5.32	26.63	28.06	45.31
West Bengal	0.93	2.01	6.73	4.42	1.57	5.74	23.89	26.95	49.16
Large States	**4.70**	**5.01**	**8.50**	**6.84**	**1.72**	**5.21**	**19.85**	**32.90**	**47.25**
Arunachal Pradesh	7.62	5.14	3.23	4.88	1.16	6.63	40.59	19.95	39.46
Goa	2.06	–12.43	15.83	1.09	–4.21	6.12	6.21	60.99	32.79
Himachal Pradesh	6.51	5.23	10.05	7.28	1.23	4.66	17.28	44.67	38.05

Manipur	0.37	–1.57	10.84	4.59	2.20	5.12	22.16	16.23	61.60
Meghalaya	5.80	5.96	7.75	6.39	2.27	4.61	16.26	37.40	46.34
Mizoram	2.88	7.77	7.70	7.76	0.99	4.42	19.36	20.81	59.84
Nagaland	7.08	–3.07	10.00	7.50	1.34	5.02	31.54	12.58	55.88
Tripura	8.44	7.39	8.64	8.26	1.56	3.86	27.89	20.70	51.41
Sikkim	13.26	6.48	4.98	6.82	1.01	6.10	7.70	60.90	31.40
Uttaranchal	2.40	10.57	8.62	8.68	1.82	4.56	12.27	53.44	34.29
Small States	**5.12**	**4.78**	**9.33**	**6.95**	**1.34**	**4.81**	**16.16**	**44.44**	**39.39**
A&N Islands	3.96	5.57	7.61	6.87	0.51	4.25	15.07	20.62	64.31
Chandigarh	–7.10	2.02	5.83	5.38	–6.47	5.60	0.71	12.55	86.74
Delhi	–6.71	1.66	6.74	6.44	2.18	4.65	0.84	16.99	82.18
Jammu and Kashmir	1.77	2.13	8.10	5.45	3.53	5.66	17.21	29.03	53.76
Puducherry	1.77	2.46	8.32	5.76	4.27	4.78	5.29	50.11	44.60
Union Territories	**0.48**	**1.90**	**6.90**	**6.21**	**2.41**	**4.91**	**4.02**	**20.12**	**75.86**
NE States	**5.62**	**2.72**	**6.63**	**5.21**	**1.84**	**5.26**	**22.73**	**29.88**	**47.39**
India	**5.20**	**4.39**	**7.35**	**6.18**	**1.76**	**5.54**	**18.13**	**32.31**	**49.56**

Source: Estimates by the Author

Note: Growth rates are compounded annual growth rates. Bold values are used to denote 'groups of states'.

Annexure 2.4 Sectoral Growth and Sectoral Shares in Output during 2015–20

(%)

	Growth						Shares		
State	Agriculture	Industry	Services	Output	Population	Prices	Agriculture	Industry	Services
Andhra Pradesh	10.49	7.99	7.91	8.86	0.76	5.41	21.35	26.00	52.65
Assam	1.26	11.28	4.27	7.33	1.07	5.34	18.33	38.44	43.23
Bihar	4.32	6.84	9.51	8.15	1.91	5.23	20.71	20.44	58.85
Chhattisgarh	4.04	6.45	5.53	6.41	1.61	5.54	17.39	47.79	34.81
Gujarat	4.63	10.15	9.01	9.50	1.62	4.55	14.61	49.59	35.79
Haryana	6.10	7.66	8.59	8.32	1.42	5.50	17.84	32.08	50.07
Jharkhand	–2.40	6.17	8.19	6.26	1.52	4.45	14.15	42.37	43.49
Karnataka	5.28	7.50	8.96	8.99	1.09	5.41	9.84	27.21	62.95
Kerala	–1.87	6.75	6.42	6.39	0.50	5.18	9.85	28.37	61.78
Madhya Pradesh	7.01	8.89	8.05	8.40	1.47	5.82	32.24	28.37	39.40
Maharashtra	4.37	5.64	7.37	6.79	0.98	4.57	10.21	34.70	55.09
Orissa	2.79	10.90	6.27	8.99	0.45	5.30	15.13	44.82	40.05
Punjab	3.67	5.29	6.66	5.97	1.31	4.76	25.79	25.05	49.16
Rajasthan	4.35	3.05	7.21	5.55	1.44	5.68	26.30	31.29	42.41
Tamil Nadu	5.40	9.46	5.79	7.49	0.52	4.92	11.18	36.79	52.03
Uttar Pradesh	4.02	9.24	7.33	6.98	1.53	5.32	21.91	29.50	48.59
West Bengal	2.76	10.91	6.30	6.48	1.00	5.74	20.70	27.02	52.27
Large States	**4.91**	**7.95**	**7.44**	**7.59**	**1.24**	**5.21**	**16.90**	**32.97**	**50.13**
Arunachal Pradesh	1.41	3.80	7.35	4.70	1.01	6.63	33.84	25.99	40.17
Goa	3.58	7.39	5.34	6.15	0.67	6.12	5.24	58.67	36.09
Himachal Pradesh	2.01	7.88	6.26	6.54	0.65	4.66	14.05	46.32	39.63

Manipur	11.12	1.46	5.22	6.18	2.18	5.12	20.40	16.40	63.20
Meghalaya	0.67	–2.66	8.71	4.60	2.15	4.61	18.26	22.12	59.63
Mizoram	0.90	17.28	9.27	9.68	0.19	4.42	24.95	24.65	50.40
Nagaland	–1.33	9.51	5.97	4.74	0.55	5.02	27.92	12.36	59.72
Tripura	6.63	5.98	11.11	9.03	1.02	3.86	25.37	27.79	46.84
Sikkim	9.85	8.66	7.72	8.85	1.05	6.10	7.89	62.89	29.21
Uttaranchal	1.45	7.03	8.29	7.36	1.32	4.56	8.67	53.57	37.77
Small States	**2.77**	**7.11**	**7.50**	**6.92**	**1.18**	**4.81**	**13.72**	**44.61**	**41.67**
A&N Islands	0.95	5.68	8.58	9.27	0.45	4.25	11.87	21.27	66.86
Chandigarh	3.28	6.76	5.18	6.27	1.28	5.60	0.50	10.97	88.53
Delhi	2.38	9.78	6.59	7.15	2.00	4.65	0.40	15.74	83.86
Jammu and Kashmir	5.37	7.21	6.16	7.25	1.21	5.66	15.39	27.63	56.98
Puducherry	1.43	10.48	6.45	6.57	2.69	4.78	4.70	47.19	48.11
Union Territories	**4.62**	**9.11**	**6.48**	**7.13**	**1.69**	**4.91**	**3.06**	**18.48**	**78.46**
NE States	**2.38**	**9.42**	**5.94**	**7.16**	**1.17**	**5.26**	**20.09**	**33.93**	**45.98**
India	**4.52**	**5.63**	**7.58**	**6.84**	**1.14**	**5.54**	**15.35**	**31.06**	**53.59**

Source: Estimates by the Author.

Note: Growth rates are compounded annual growth rates. Bold values are used to denote 'groups of states'.

Annexure 2.5 Sectoral Growth and Sectoral Share in Output during 2001–20

(%)

State	*Growth*						*Shares*		
	Agriculture	*Industry*	*Services*	*Output*	*Population*	*Prices*	*Agriculture*	*Industry*	*Services*
Andhra Pradesh	5.30	6.77	9.53	7.98	0.90	5.41	24.80	28.63	46.56
Assam	2.91	6.29	6.48	5.89	1.46	5.34	22.40	35.11	42.48
Bihar	3.22	10.89	8.18	7.41	2.12	5.23	27.65	16.88	55.46
Chhattisgarh	5.26	7.81	7.60	7.30	1.91	5.54	19.24	46.98	33.77
Gujarat	5.63	10.70	9.89	9.78	1.65	4.55	19.43	45.37	35.21
Haryana	3.49	7.76	11.12	8.73	1.62	5.50	24.98	32.73	42.29
Jharkhand	5.56	4.68	9.28	6.78	1.91	4.45	15.00	48.15	36.85
Karnataka	3.15	6.91	9.27	7.78	1.33	5.41	14.00	29.14	56.85
Kerala	−0.82	6.99	8.29	6.94	0.47	5.18	17.25	27.39	55.37
Madhya Pradesh	6.78	7.10	7.57	7.50	1.74	5.82	32.51	29.15	38.35
Maharashtra	3.38	7.48	9.06	7.99	1.29	4.57	14.16	35.59	50.25
Orissa	3.41	8.45	8.71	7.78	0.98	5.30	20.10	42.95	36.95
Punjab	1.89	7.25	7.85	6.25	1.21	4.76	33.97	23.61	42.42
Rajasthan	5.50	7.49	8.20	7.44	1.73	5.68	29.58	30.80	39.62
Tamil Nadu	4.32	8.05	8.93	8.28	1.20	4.92	13.93	36.69	49.37
Uttar Pradesh	2.60	7.21	7.98	6.39	1.70	5.32	28.51	27.98	43.51
West Bengal	2.22	5.37	7.55	5.76	1.18	5.74	26.14	27.71	46.15
Large States	**3.77**	**7.59**	**8.73**	**7.59**	**1.47**	**5.21**	**21.57**	**32.63**	**45.80**
Arunachal Pradesh	2.95	10.55	7.84	7.01	1.70	6.63	42.77	20.45	36.78
Goa	1.61	4.83	10.95	7.56	0.40	6.12	7.34	64.26	28.40
Himachal Pradesh	3.03	8.18	9.12	7.56	0.99	4.66	19.52	44.30	36.18

Manipur	4.38	4.79	7.24	5.79	2.21	5.12	23.21	17.85	58.93
Meghalaya	3.78	3.23	7.86	5.84	2.40	4.61	19.44	30.92	49.64
Mizoram	9.27	10.79	8.81	9.90	1.70	4.42	22.51	22.26	55.23
Nagaland	4.20	6.25	7.81	6.65	0.34	5.02	32.62	12.79	54.60
Tripura	7.32	10.55	8.31	8.73	1.26	3.86	27.89	22.95	49.16
Sikkim	7.12	18.50	7.62	12.30	1.12	6.10	10.97	48.65	40.38
Uttaranchal	2.01	13.52	11.66	10.70	1.58	4.56	16.67	48.38	34.95
Small States	**3.65**	**9.61**	**9.52**	**8.62**	**1.41**	**4.81**	**18.94**	**42.38**	**38.68**
A&N Islands	1.34	11.06	10.08	9.10	0.60	4.25	19.27	20.75	59.98
Chandigarh	-1.55	5.17	7.47	7.36	1.14	5.60	0.99	13.05	85.96
Delhi	-1.03	4.97	9.14	8.62	1.97	4.65	0.92	19.56	79.52
Jammu and Kashmir	2.56	4.32	7.14	5.56	1.95	5.66	18.67	29.99	51.33
Puducherry	3.05	4.12	9.18	6.45	2.68	4.78	5.68	53.69	40.63
Union Territories	**2.03**	**4.78**	**8.79**	**7.93**	**1.95**	**4.91**	**4.60**	**22.38**	**73.02**
NE States	**3.86**	**7.18**	**7.08**	**6.55**	**1.50**	**5.26**	**23.77**	**31.34**	**44.89**
India	**4.26**	**7.42**	**5.96**	**7.25**	**1.48**	**5.54**	**18.10**	**30.01**	**51.89**

Source: Estimates by the Author.

Note: Growth rates are compounded annual growth rates. Bold values are used to denote 'groups of states'.

Table 2.1 Share of States in Combined SDP and Population

(%)

State	*Share in Combined SDP*					*Share in Combined Population*				
	2001–04	*2005–09*	*2010–14*	*2015–20*	*2001–20*	*2001–04*	*2005–09*	*2010–14*	*2015–20*	*2001–20*
Andhra Pradesh	8.26	8.43	8.36	8.68	8.45	7.38	7.24	7.01	6.78	7.07
Assam	2.13	1.86	1.66	1.65	1.80	2.59	2.58	2.57	2.57	2.58
Bihar	2.88	2.60	2.77	2.68	2.72	8.09	8.17	8.46	8.83	8.42
Chhattisgarh	1.80	1.86	1.84	1.72	1.80	2.02	2.07	2.11	2.16	2.10
Gujarat	6.04	6.79	7.27	8.21	7.18	4.93	4.95	4.98	5.04	4.98
Haryana	3.19	3.31	3.48	3.71	3.45	2.06	2.10	2.11	2.12	2.10
Jharkhand	1.86	1.76	1.74	1.64	1.74	2.62	2.64	2.70	2.78	2.69
Karnataka	7.45	7.47	7.14	7.62	7.43	5.12	5.05	5.02	5.00	5.04
Kerala	4.33	4.38	4.24	3.97	4.21	3.07	2.92	2.77	2.64	2.83
Madhya Pradesh	4.00	3.62	3.71	3.80	3.77	5.89	5.98	6.04	6.13	6.02
Maharashtra	13.81	14.72	14.92	14.69	14.58	9.42	9.43	9.34	9.18	9.33
Odisha	2.62	2.81	2.72	2.72	2.72	3.56	3.53	3.46	3.32	3.45
Punjab	3.55	3.27	3.10	2.90	3.17	2.38	2.41	2.35	2.30	2.36
Rajasthan	5.05	4.82	4.94	4.85	4.91	5.52	5.61	5.68	5.73	5.64
Tamil Nadu	7.86	8.15	8.62	8.61	8.35	6.02	5.84	5.82	5.74	5.84
Uttar Pradesh	9.74	8.89	8.40	8.08	8.70	16.22	16.53	16.66	16.79	16.58
West Bengal	7.01	6.58	6.04	5.38	6.17	7.77	7.65	7.52	7.43	7.57
Large States	**91.60**	**91.33**	**90.93**	**90.89**	**91.15**	**94.67**	**94.67**	**94.60**	**94.53**	**94.61**
Arunachal Pradesh	0.13	0.13	0.13	0.12	0.13	0.11	0.11	0.11	0.11	0.11
Goa	0.40	0.40	0.41	0.40	0.40	0.14	0.14	0.13	0.12	0.13
Himachal Pradesh	0.85	0.84	0.84	0.84	0.85	0.60	0.58	0.57	0.55	0.57

Manipur	0.18	0.17	0.15	0.14	0.16	0.22	0.23	0.24	0.25	0.24
Meghalaya	0.23	0.22	0.22	0.18	0.21	0.22	0.24	0.25	0.26	0.24
Mizoram	0.09	0.08	0.09	0.11	0.09	0.09	0.09	0.09	0.09	0.09
Nagaland	0.15	0.14	0.14	0.13	0.14	0.20	0.16	0.16	0.16	0.17
Tripura	0.22	0.22	0.23	0.26	0.23	0.31	0.31	0.30	0.30	0.30
Sikkim	0.07	0.07	0.13	0.13	0.10	0.05	0.05	0.05	0.05	0.05
Uttarakhand	0.90	1.06	1.33	1.37	1.19	0.83	0.83	0.83	0.84	0.83
Small States	**3.22**	**3.35**	**3.66**	**3.68**	**3.50**	**2.76**	**2.74**	**2.74**	**2.73**	**2.74**
Andaman and Nicobar Islands	0.04	0.04	0.05	0.05	0.04	0.03	0.03	0.03	0.03	0.03
Chandigarh	0.22	0.24	0.23	0.22	0.23	0.09	0.10	0.10	0.09	0.09
Delhi	3.60	3.85	4.04	4.16	3.94	1.37	1.37	1.40	1.46	1.41
Jammu and Kashmir	1.11	1.00	0.90	0.82	0.94	0.99	0.98	1.02	1.05	1.01
Puducherry	0.21	0.19	0.20	0.17	0.19	0.09	0.10	0.10	0.11	0.10
Union Territories	**5.18**	**5.32**	**5.40**	**5.42**	**5.34**	**2.57**	**2.59**	**2.65**	**2.74**	**2.65**
North East	**3.20**	**2.89**	**2.75**	**2.72**	**2.86**	**3.79**	**3.77**	**3.77**	**3.79**	**3.78**
All States	**100.00**	**100.00**	**100.00**	**100.00**	**100.00**	**100.00**	**100.00**	**100.00**	**100.00**	**100.00**

Note: All States consists of Large States, Small States, and UTs. The North East states is a category of states comprising eight states. The eight states included Assam from large states and seven states viz, Arunachal Pradesh, Manipur, Meghalaya, Mizoram, Nagaland, Sikkim, and Tripura from the category of smaller states. Bold values are used to denote 'groups of states'.

2001–20. Likewise, Himachal Pradesh (0.85%) and Uttarakhand (1.19%) amongst SS and Delhi (3.94%) and Jammu and Kashmir (0.94%) under UTs had an appreciable share in combined SDP.

- Uttar Pradesh (16.58%) along with Bihar (8.42%) accounted for one-fourth of India's population during 2001–20. Maharashtra (9.33%), West Bengal (7.57%), and Andhra Pradesh (7.07%) were the other three states which had a relatively higher share in the combined population during 2001–20. Though Uttar Pradesh accounted for more than 16% in the combined population, its share in combined output was only 8.7%. Likewise, share of Bihar in combined output was only 2.72% compared to its share of 8.42% in combined population. More importantly, share of Bihar and Uttar Pradesh in combined population has increased and that in output has declined during 2015–20 when compared to 2001–04.
- Some other states which had a higher share in combined population than in combined output during 2001–20 were Assam, Chhattisgarh, Jharkhand, Madhya Pradesh, Odisha, Rajasthan, and West Bengal amongst the LS; Manipur, Meghalaya, Nagaland, and Tripura amongst the SS. These states have not been able to leverage their endowment of human resources to achieve higher growth. Except Delhi (1.41) and Jammu and Kashmir (1.01%) amongst UTs, no other states within SS had a population share exceeding 1% of the combined population during 2001–20.

IV Contribution of states to growth in combined output and population

As far as contribution of states to the growth in 'combined output of all states' and growth in 'combined population of all the states' under study is concerned, the following key inference can be drawn (Table 2.2)

- The LS contributed 90.49% to the growth in combined output and 93.91% to growth in combined population during 2001–20. As a group, the UTs (5.55%) contributed more than the SS (3.96%) to the growth in combined output during 2001–20. The contribution to the growth in combined population was also higher for UTs (3.47%) compared to that for SS (2.62%).
- Between 2001–04 and 2015–20, we find contribution of LS to the growth in combined output and growth in combined population have increased and that of SS and UTs have declined. Thus, while larger states as a group are getting more prominent in shaping the growth outcome the country, the SS and UTs are waning in importance.

Table 2.2 Contribution to Growth in Combined Output and Population

State	*Contribution to Combined Growth in Output*					*Contribution to Combined Growth in Population*				
	2001–04	*2005–09*	*2010–14*	*2015–20*	*2001–20*	*2001–04*	*2005–09*	*2010–14*	*2015–20*	*2001–20*
Andhra Pradesh	7.95	9.39	7.59	10.18	8.80	5.10	5.08	3.06	4.14	4.30
Assam	2.16	0.94	1.04	1.60	1.39	2.59	2.35	2.84	2.20	2.53
Bihar	0.78	2.51	3.32	2.90	2.64	9.81	8.82	16.90	13.48	12.02
Chhattisgarh	2.92	2.09	1.97	1.46	1.72	2.19	2.74	2.63	2.78	2.70
Gujarat	11.53	7.48	9.35	10.33	9.17	5.22	5.02	5.91	6.53	5.53
Haryana	4.73	3.38	4.03	4.08	3.93	2.56	2.61	1.70	2.39	2.30
Jharkhand	1.90	1.04	1.83	1.36	1.54	2.85	2.69	4.68	3.38	3.47
Karnataka	5.17	8.36	7.17	9.08	7.55	4.05	3.94	5.56	4.34	4.53
Kerala	5.16	3.87	3.64	3.36	3.81	1.63	0.95	0.77	1.05	0.89
Madhya Pradesh	2.84	3.03	4.34	4.23	3.70	7.06	7.15	6.41	7.18	7.05
Maharashtra	16.40	16.89	14.83	13.20	15.20	9.13	9.61	6.08	7.21	8.13
Odisha	2.94	3.00	2.49	3.24	2.76	2.49	3.14	1.71	1.18	2.29
Punjab	2.35	2.88	2.81	2.29	2.59	2.39	3.00	-0.16	2.41	1.92
Rajasthan	6.36	4.28	5.86	3.57	4.77	6.85	6.88	5.96	6.61	6.57
Tamil Nadu	2.93	9.04	10.04	8.55	9.03	3.27	2.98	9.17	2.38	4.74
Uttar Pradesh	6.79	7.08	7.15	7.47	7.26	19.72	21.14	14.06	20.53	18.94
West Bengal	7.31	4.94	3.91	4.62	4.64	6.03	5.47	6.84	5.93	6.03
Large States	**90.22**	**90.21**	**91.36**	**91.50**	**90.49**	**92.93**	**93.58**	**94.11**	**93.73**	**93.91**
Arunachal Pradesh	0.15	0.11	0.09	0.08	0.12	0.15	0.18	0.08	0.09	0.13
Goa	0.48	0.35	0.07	0.32	0.40	0.23	0.30	-0.32	0.06	0.03
Himachal Pradesh	0.96	0.78	0.90	0.73	0.83	0.62	0.43	0.40	0.29	0.38
Manipur	0.17	0.09	0.10	0.12	0.12	0.28	0.35	0.30	0.44	0.35
Meghalaya	0.24	0.19	0.21	0.11	0.16	0.18	0.40	0.32	0.45	0.39

(*Continued*)

State	*Contribution to Combined Growth in Output*					*Contribution to Combined Growth in Population*				
	2001–04	*2005–09*	*2010–14*	*2015–20*	*2001–20*	*2001–04*	*2005–09*	*2010–14*	*2015–20*	*2001–20*
Mizoram	0.11	0.08	0.10	0.15	0.12	0.13	0.16	0.05	0.01	0.10
Nagaland	0.24	0.12	0.15	0.08	0.12	0.61	0.18	0.13	0.07	0.04
Tripura	0.36	0.19	0.27	0.31	0.27	0.22	0.25	0.27	0.24	0.26
Sikkim	0.11	0.08	0.13	0.15	0.17	0.06	0.04	0.03	0.04	0.04
Uttarakhand	1.33	1.72	1.70	1.33	1.66	0.84	0.88	0.87	0.88	0.89
Small States	**4.15**	**3.70**	**3.72**	**3.38**	**3.96**	**3.33**	**3.17**	**2.15**	**2.57**	**2.62**
Andaman and Nicobar Islands	0.06	0.05	0.05	0.06	0.05	0.01	0.01	0.01	0.01	0.01
Chandigarh	0.44	0.27	0.18	0.18	0.22	0.17	0.37	-0.37	0.09	0.07
Delhi	3.97	4.89	3.81	3.94	4.43	2.50	1.78	1.77	2.34	1.87
Jammu and Kashmir	0.88	0.67	0.72	0.79	0.69	0.95	0.96	2.08	1.01	1.33
Puducherry	0.29	0.20	0.17	0.15	0.16	0.11	0.12	0.25	0.24	0.19
Union Territories	**5.63**	**6.09**	**4.92**	**5.12**	**5.55**	**3.74**	**3.25**	**3.74**	**3.69**	**3.47**
North East	**3.53**	**2.37**	**2.32**	**2.85**	**2.59**	**4.23**	**3.90**	**4.02**	**3.53**	**3.83**
All States	**100.00**	**100.00**	**100.00**	**100.00**	**100.00**	**100.00**	**100.00**	**100.00**	**100.00**	**100.00**

Source: Estimates by the Author

Notes: All States consists of Large States, Small States, and UTs. The North East states is a category of states comprising eight states. The eight states included Assam from large states and seven states viz, Arunachal Pradesh, Manipur, Meghalaya, Mizoram, Nagaland, Sikkim, and Tripura from the category of smaller states. Bold values are used to denote 'groups of states'.

Growth rates are compounded annual growth rates.

- Within the LS, Andhra Pradesh, Bihar, Karnataka, Madhya Pradesh, Odisha, Tamil Nadu, and Uttar Pradesh have increased their contribution to the growth in output of all states. However, unlike Andhra Pradesh, Karnataka, Tamil Nadu which contributed in the range of 8–10%, Bihar, Madhya Pradesh, and Odisha contributed less than 5% to the growth in combined output during 2015–20. Thus, the later three states though have improved their performance; they are yet to make a strong impact on the country's growth in output. Uttar Pradesh though increased its contribution the growth in the combined output to 7.47%, its performance has been relatively unsatisfactory given the fact it has the largest share in the country's population.
- The five states which contributed to about half of the growth in combined output of all states were Maharashtra (15.20%), Gujarat (9.17%), Tamil Nadu (9.03%), Andhra Pradesh (8.80%), and Karnataka (7.55%).
- As far as contribution to growth in population during 2001–20 is concerned, Uttar Pradesh (18.94%) contributed the largest followed by Bihar (12.02%), Maharashtra (8.13%), Madhya Pradesh (7.05%), and Rajasthan (6.57%).
- Nine large states viz, Andhra Pradesh, Haryana, Gujarat, Karnataka, Kerala, Maharashtra, Odisha, Punjab, Tamil Nadu contributed more to the growth in combined output than to combined population. As many as seven out of ten smaller states viz, Goa, Himachal Pradesh, Mizoram, Nagaland, Tripura, Sikkim, and Uttarakhand contributed more to the growth in combined output than combined population. All UTs, except, Jammu and Kashmir, contributed more to the growth in output than growth in combined population.

V Sectoral shares in output

During the entire period of study viz, 2001–20, we find services accounted for the largest share in output (51.9%) followed by industry (30%) and agriculture (18.1%) at the all-India level (Annexure 2.5). This pattern of relative importance of the different sectors in all-India output is also observed across the different sub-periods. Nonetheless, the relative importance of the three sectors in the GDP has undergone certain changes which are noteworthy (Annexures 2.1–2.5).

First, compared to 2001–04, the share of both agriculture and industry increased and that of services declined during 2005–09. Second, the increase was rather sharp for industry by 8.3% points. Third, the share of industry which was 23.4% during 2001–04 increased successively to

31.7% and 32.3% during 2005–09 and 2010–14, respectively. However, the share of industry in output fell marginally but remained above 31% during 2015–20. Share of agriculture which had slightly increased during 2005–09 declined in successively the subsequent two time periods and was slightly above 15% during 2015–20.

For the LS, the share of agriculture in SDP has declined successively from 28% during 2001–04 to 16.9% during 2015–20. The share of services, in contrast, has increased successively from 41.1% during 2001–04 to 50.1% during 2015–20. Industry's share in SDP has hovered in the range of 30–33% across the different sub periods.

The share of agriculture in SDP has declined relatively more sharply for the SS from 26.7% during 2015–20 as compared to 13.7% during 2001–04. Compared to services, industry has gained from the 13% point decline in the share of agriculture. This is because the share of industry improved from 36.9% to 44.6% and that for services increased from 36.3% to 41.6%. Thus, unlike for the LS, industry accounted for the largest share in SDP followed by services and agriculture during 2015–20 for the SS.

Contribution of Sectors to growth in Output

The share of a sector in the output along with its growth rate gives us the contribution of that sector to the output growth during a period. During 2001–20, we find that agriculture, industry, and services contributed 12.7%, 36.6%, and 50.8% to the growth of GDP. The pattern of contribution of different sectors to GDP growth for India is also broadly observed for the LS. In contrast, industry (48.2%) contributed more than services (43.6%) to the growth in SDP of the SS. Contribution of agriculture to growth was much less at 8.2% for the SS. For the UTs, about 85% of the growth is contributed by services followed by about 14% by industry and only 1% by agriculture.

As far as contribution of different sectors to growth in output across different time period is concerned, we find the following noticeable patterns. First, services sector contributed to slightly less than three-fourth, industries another one-fourth, and agriculture slightly more than 1% of the GDP growth during 2001–04. Second, the contribution of industry increased substantially to more than 42% and that of services declined to about 53% during the high growth phase of 2005–09. In the subsequent phases, contribution of industry declined to 23% and that of services increased to 68.7%. During 2015–20, the contribution of industry increased slightly to about 27% and that of services fell to 62.5% during 2015–20. The contribution of agriculture to GDP growth has increased successively to 10.7% during 2015–20.

VI Variability in output

Stability of output is as important as its growth. We present the broad findings from an analysis of the stability of growth measured through co-efficient of variation (CV) in output across the regions in the different sub periods. A lower value of CV is desirable. Taking all the states as one group, we find that CV of output increased during 2005–09 compared to that in 2000–04. The variability in aggregate output declined in the subsequent period viz 2010–14 before rising again during 2015–20 (Table 2.3). This pattern is observed for all the three categories of states. Thus, at an aggregate level, relatively higher growth is accompanied with higher volatility.

Amongst the LS, all states except Jharkhand, Madhya Pradesh, and Rajasthan exhibited the pattern observed at the aggregate level. While for Jharkhand and Madhya Pradesh, volatility has increased in the three successive periods compared to 2001–04. In Rajasthan, the CV of SDP increased between 2005–09 and 2001–04. However, in the subsequent two periods, the volatility has successively declined. The pattern of volatility observed in Rajasthan is also found in Meghalaya and Nagaland amongst the SS. Tripura amongst the SS exhibited the same pattern of volatility as observed for Jharkhand and Madhya Pradesh across the sub periods. In Goa, the volatility of output increased successively during 2005–09 and 2010–14 as compared to 2001–04 before declining during the period 2015–20.

When we consider the volatility of sectoral output in industry and services, a pattern similar to that for segregate output aggregate output is observed for all states and the three categories of states. Volatility of agricultural output, however, increased successively in three sub periods following 2001–04 at the level of all states as well as LS as a group. For the UTs as a group, volatility of agricultural output declined during 2005–09 compared to 2001–04. However, the CV of agricultural output increased successively in the sub periods 2010–14 and 2015–20. The volatility of agricultural output for the LS dipped during 2005–09 compared to 2001–04. However, it had again increased during 2010–14 before declining in the 2015–20 period (Annexures 26–2.8).

During the entire period of study, services sector had the highest volatility in output followed by that for industry and agriculture when we consider all states as one group as well as the three groups of states.

Gujarat, Haryana, Tamil Nadu, Andhra Pradesh, and Karnataka had the highest volatility in SDP in the descending order during the entire study period. The volatility in these states is primarily contributed by the industry and services sector. Amongst the SS, Sikkim, Mizoram, and Uttarakhand had the highest volatility in SDP in the descending order during the entire study period. In these three estates, industry output had the highest volatility compared to output form agricultural and industry.

Table 2.3 Variability in State Domestic Product

(%)

State	*2001–04*	*2005–09*	*2010–14*	*2015–20*	*2001–20*
Andhra Pradesh	6.78	15.32	9.58	15.64	44.57
Assam	6.94	7.28	6.62	13.11	35.08
Bihar	4.59	14.29	12.4	14.82	41.99
Chhattisgarh	11.44	15.72	11.21	11.69	39.34
Gujarat	12.85	15.05	13.27	16.8	52.92
Haryana	9.9	14.05	12.04	14.76	47.87
Jharkhand	6.97	10.24	11.07	12.16	37.97
Karnataka	4.7	15.39	10.6	15.82	44.34
Kerala	7.97	12.24	8.96	11.5	37.89
Madhya Pradesh	6	12.01	12.21	14.99	43.14
Maharashtra	8.07	15.68	10.35	12.17	42.9
Odisha	8.54	14.83	9.71	15.88	42.85
Punjab	4.68	12.32	9.47	10.78	35.17
Rajasthan	12.29	12.42	12.2	10.04	40.97
Tamil Nadu	3.36	15.15	11.98	13.43	44.96
Uttar Pradesh	4.83	11.15	8.89	12.49	36.55
West Bengal	7	10.52	6.82	11.71	32.31
Large States	**6.81**	**13.6**	**10.4**	**13.54**	**42.1**
Arunachal Pradesh	8.55	11.87	7.77	9.17	38.35
Goa	8.14	12.44	13.56	12.17	42.1
Himachal Pradesh	7.64	12.78	11.05	11.76	41.73
Manipur	6.88	7.77	7.57	11.24	33.32
Meghalaya	7.07	12.14	10.05	8.54	31.83
Mizoram	8.83	13.82	12.84	17.34	57.75
Nagaland	10.7	11.82	11.35	8.79	36.17
Tripura	10.51	12.06	12.61	16.62	49.83
Sikkim	9.51	14.54	10.44	15.75	61.98
Uttarakhand	9.9	21.88	13.07	13.14	53.87
Small States	**8.56**	**15.24**	**10.59**	**12.4**	**46.17**
Andaman and Nicobar Islands	10.05	18.56	10.49	16.4	49.39
Chandigarh	13.11	15.32	8.92	11.28	39.23
Delhi	7.44	17.5	9.89	12.78	46.32
Jammu and Kashmir	5.42	9.46	8.39	13.06	32.19
Puducherry	9.3	15.09	9.12	11.98	35.67
Union Territories	**7.33**	**15.79**	**9.54**	**12.74**	**43.27**
All States	**6.88**	**13.76**	**10.36**	**13.45**	**42.3**

Note: Variability is measured through coefficient of variation. Bold values are used to denote 'groups of states'.

Annexure 2.6 Variability in Agricultural Output 2001–20

State	*2001–04*	*2005–09*	*2010–14*	*2015–20*	*2001–20*
Andhra Pradesh	5.81	11.25	7.93	18.93	32.89
Assam	1.16	3.63	8.87	3.63	17.72
Bihar	11.34	11.7	13.31	8.44	20.32
Chhattisgarh	21.29	9	11.55	9.22	30.47
Gujarat	22.48	10.1	12.89	9.94	31.23
Haryana	3.42	8.48	5.61	11.07	20.77
Jharkhand	12.48	14.84	15.39	12.01	32.87
Karnataka	13.89	8.41	5.9	12.04	20.14
Kerala	1.33	3.01	3.35	4.21	6.48
Madhya Pradesh	15.92	5.77	17.5	13.5	40.12
Maharashtra	7.58	13.29	9.73	9.18	20.13
Odisha	10.34	4.73	7.32	9.06	20.23
Punjab	2.61	4.13	2.89	6.82	11.34
Rajasthan	25.96	5.77	14.52	8.52	31.49
Tamil Nadu	14.66	9.27	8.68	10.56	26.71
Uttar Pradesh	2.36	4.74	6.18	7.37	15.59
West Bengal	4.31	4.2	2.08	5.18	13.09
Large States	**5.23**	**6.59**	**7.35**	**9.2**	**22.1**
Arunachal Pradesh	2.8	8.53	11.62	11.49	19.5
Goa	8.77	9.64	5.17	8.35	12.53
Himachal Pradesh	8.88	5.78	10.73	6.58	18.03
Manipur	6.78	8.54	8.61	22.46	29.24
Meghalaya	5.18	3.31	9.28	2.19	22.37
Mizoram	2.2	11.95	6.48	4.12	59.38
Nagaland	12.85	4.33	10.92	4.38	23.98
Tripura	10.04	14.49	13.7	12.49	41.43
Sikkim	8.63	4.63	20.26	17.83	42.94
Uttarakhand	3.7	2.42	4.1	2.91	12.01
Small States	**5.52**	**4.76**	**7.97**	**5.65**	**21.16**
Andaman and Nicobar Islands	3.43	12.85	6.33	3.3	13.49
Chandigarh	5.35	3.77	13.06	7.26	13.86
Delhi	1.41	2.35	13.85	6.17	14.98
Jammu and Kashmir	7.01	2.32	4.13	11.06	16.11
Puducherry	3.28	21.15	8.44	4.24	19.73
Union Territories	**5.08**	**2.77**	**3.92**	**9.21**	**12.8**
All States	**5.17**	**6.47**	**7.3**	**9.05**	**21.95**

Note: Variability has been measured through Coefficient of Variation. Bold values are used to denote 'groups of states'.

Annexure 2.7 Variability in Industrial Output 2001–20

State	*2001–04*	*2005–09*	*2010–14*	*2015–20*	*2001–20*
Andhra Pradesh	8.2	17.6	6.78	14.16	36.8
Assam	16.33	3.22	3.48	19.96	41.73
Bihar	3.49	23.49	15.1	12.48	55.64
Chhattisgarh	13.13	20.61	12.62	12	40.6
Gujarat	12.71	15.23	12.56	17.76	57.79
Haryana	11.95	10.81	10.47	13.68	42.77
Jharkhand	13.28	11.53	10.8	13.56	27.8
Karnataka	10.9	16.37	7.68	13.82	38.45
Kerala	9.7	9.86	8.77	12.17	37.85
Madhya Pradesh	2.63	17.68	5.44	15.9	39.99
Maharashtra	8.07	17.35	7.79	10.31	39.56
Odisha	10.5	19.59	9.46	19.12	45.28
Punjab	4.27	20.94	5.6	9.63	38.19
Rajasthan	8.5	13.76	10.98	8.11	40.55
Tamil Nadu	6.63	11.95	10.27	16.54	44.4
Uttar Pradesh	5.93	13.52	6.29	17.04	40.9
West Bengal	9.9	7.95	3.57	19.15	32
Large States	**8.61**	**14.26**	**7.76**	**14.11**	**41.46**
Arunachal Pradesh	25.99	16.77	8.88	8.15	53.62
Goa	8.92	12.06	23.93	15.84	31.88
Himachal Pradesh	8.23	15.62	8.15	14.14	45.12
Manipur	17.25	5.59	7.59	4.91	28.11
Meghalaya	9.79	18.21	11.94	9.9	32.07
Mizoram	13.48	19.39	16.68	29.73	67.15
Nagaland	15.72	20.4	9.52	17.54	35.4
Tripura	14.81	11.96	11.95	11.59	61.47
Sikkim	13.49	23.31	10.71	15.55	77.94
Uttarakhand	17.81	28.9	15.64	12.6	60.64
Small States	**11.77**	**19.4**	**7.78**	**12.86**	**49.11**
Andaman and Nicobar Islands	37.09	26.08	9.46	11.2	48.97
Chandigarh	17.51	19.39	5.32	12.88	29.36
Delhi	7.39	9.08	6.56	17.65	30.37
Jammu and Kashmir	2.68	9.3	3.95	13.56	25.39
Puducherry	12.71	12.82	8.99	18.84	26.15
UTs	**6.65**	**9.33**	**5.74**	**16.25**	**28.61**
All States	**8.62**	**14.27**	**7.57**	**14.1**	**41.37**

Note: Variability has been measured through coefficient of variation. Bold values are used to denote 'groups of states'.

Annexure 2.8 Variability in Services Output

State	*2001–04*	*2005–09*	*2010–14*	*2015–20*	*2001–20*
Andhra Pradesh	8.98	16.28	14.54	14.09	51.72
Assam	6.92	11.93	8.6	8.32	35.51
Bihar	5.53	13.91	12.9	17.27	46.03
Chhattisgarh	7.26	15.24	10.73	10.32	40.84
Gujarat	10.29	17.52	15.28	16.23	52.66
Haryana	13.2	18.97	15.06	15.29	57.58
Jharkhand	4.41	14.74	10.11	14.9	49.76
Karnataka	9.89	17.33	14.42	15.8	51.31
Kerala	9.86	16.37	11.24	11.6	43.82
Madhya Pradesh	3.54	12.28	12.44	14.59	43.27
Maharashtra	8.4	15.86	12.44	13.29	48.41
Odisha	9.34	16.01	11.62	11.41	46.09
Punjab	7.34	12.39	13.97	12.02	43.88
Rajasthan	7.22	15.18	12.88	13.25	45.24
Tamil Nadu	6.6	18.51	13.52	10.56	46.82
Uttar Pradesh	6.27	13.85	11.77	13.28	44.59
West Bengal	7.76	14.3	10.23	11.49	42.28
Large States	**7.92**	**14.78**	**12.8**	**13.38**	**47.38**
Arunachal Pradesh	6.5	13.26	7.11	13.43	43.34
Goa	7.53	15.54	23.17	9.71	56.51
Himachal Pradesh	6.38	14.45	14.98	11.35	48.65
Manipur	3.34	9.9	16.31	9.57	41.01
Meghalaya	6.81	12.57	11.68	15.69	44.19
Mizoram	9.5	13.05	12.3	16.93	49.08
Nagaland	8.11	14.13	14.91	11.3	42.48
Tripura	9.45	11.27	12.98	20.99	47.48
Sikkim	8.08	12.89	8.69	16.01	42.16
Uttarakhand	9.79	24.34	13.14	14.69	59.04
Small States	**7.53**	**16.3**	**13.94**	**13.51**	**50.78**
Andaman and Nicobar Islands	7.25	22.11	11.55	15.23	54.07
Chandigarh	12.16	17.07	9.47	9.46	39.68
Delhi	7.82	19.4	10.24	11.89	48.24
Jammu and Kashmir	6.17	14.82	12.23	11.29	39.44
Puducherry	7.05	19.14	12.69	11.92	47.84
Union Territories	**7.76**	**18.61**	**10.47**	**11.7**	**46.69**
All States	**7.89**	**15.13**	**12.64**	**13.25**	**47.42**

Note: Variability has been measured through Coefficient of Variation. Bold values are used to denote 'groups of states'.

Notes

1 States were often classified as 'general category' and 'special category' for analysing comparative growth performance as the later received cheaper financial assistance from the central government (Misra, 2013b). The fourteenth finance commission (FFC), however, dropped the distinction between general category states and special category states. The FFC was guided by the philosophy that states be given more freedom to choose their development initiatives by endowing them with greater resources. As such, it increased the share of states in the divisible pool of funds of the central government from 32% to 42%.
2 In the tables where growth numbers are reported, we have included the eight north eastern states viz Arunachal Pradesh, Assam, Manipur, Meghalaya, Mizoram, Nagaland, Sikkim and Tripura as another category.
3 The Sarva Shiksha Abhiyan later culminated in the Right to Education Act in the year 2008.
4 Inflation measured through whole sale price index. Whole sale price inflation was the headline inflation in India before 2012.

References

Acharya, S. (2013, August 8). *5 Policy Missteps that Have Led India to Economic Crisis*, available at: https://www.business-standard.com/article/opinion/5-policy-missteps-that-have-led-india-to-economic-crisis-113080701462_1.html.

Acharya, S. (2022). *An Economist at Home and Abroad*. Harper Collins India, New Delhi.

GoI. (2016). *Economic Survey 2015–16*. Ministry of Finance, Government of India, New Delhi, India.

Misra, B.S. (2013a, September 1). The Price of Not Stocking Forex, *Business Line*, available at: https://www.thehindubusinessline.com/opinion/the-price-of-not-stocking-forex/article64597095.ece.

Misra, B.S. (2013b). *Revisiting Regional Growth Dynamics in India in the Post-Economic Reforms Period*. Palgrave Macmillan, London.

Mohan, R. (2006). *Economic Growth, Financial Deepening and Financial Inclusion*. Speech by Rakesh Mohan, Deputy Governor, RBI at the Annual Bankers' Conference 2006, at Hyderabad on Nov 3, 2006.

3 Inequality in Indian States

I Introduction

In addition to achieving higher growth rates for the Indian economy, balanced region development has been a concern of Indian policymakers throughout the planning period. Notwithstanding India's adoption of economic reforms in 1991 when market forces were given a bigger role in resource allocation, development of the lagging states continued to be a policy priority. This chapter analyses the efficacy of several interventions in reducing regional inequality during 2001–20. The chapter is structured as follows. Section II discusses the policy initiatives in the post-2000 period for promoting equitable development across states. The impact of the development intervention on per capita income of the lagging states is discussed in Section III. We couch our analysis in terms of how the per capita income (PCI) has evolved in the different category of states. In addition to analysing the PCI differential between the states, we have undertaken a rank analysis of the states on the basis of their PCI. Section IV discusses the widely used Gini coefficient for aggregate as well as sectoral income. We have attempted the decomposition of Gini to understand the implication of different income sources for inequality in Section V. This chapter concludes in Section VI which discusses the broad findings from the recent literature on convergence of income across Indian states.

II Policy initiatives for reducing inter-state disparity

Inter-state disparity gained added significance in the 10th Five-Year Plan (2002–07) when the central government launched the Rashtriya Sam Vikas Yojana (RSVY), a new initiative to reduce regional disparity (Misra, 2013). The RSVY was launched as an independent programme in 2003–04. Under the RSVY, the Backward Districts Initiative (BDI) was launched in 2003–04 which identified 147 backward districts across states

DOI: 10.4324/9781003278351-3

using a backwardness measure (Misra, 2013). Under the BDI, states were given dedicated funds to address issues such as low agricultural output and unemployment as well as to fill critical gaps in physical and social infrastructure. However, only two years following the Tenth Plan's ratification, a new government was formed in 2004. Based on the first two years of experience in administering the BDI, the new government established the Backward Regions Grant Fund (BRGF) in 2005–06 to make the BDI implementation process more participatory and holistic.

The scope of RSVY which was limited to 147 districts in 27 states was expanded under the BRGF to include 250 districts. The majority of the 250 districts were in low-income states. The BRGF was restructured in the 12th Five Year Plan (2012–17) to reinforce the institutional framework of governance. To ensure efficiency and accountability in the utilisation of funds, it was proposed that local governments need to play a key role in service delivery. To that end, the 12th Five-Year Plan emphasised local government capacity augmentation in terms of human resources and implementation procedures (GoI, 2013). Each of the identified 250 districts receives INR 10 crores (a crore denotes 10 million) per annum (USD 2.19 million at the 2010–11 yearly average exchange rate) for development activities as well as INR 1 crore (equivalent to USD 0.21 million at the 2010–11 yearly average exchange rate) for local government capacity building.

The BRGF Programme, however, was discontinued in 2015–16 with the abolition of planning commission. Instead, states were assigned a higher proportion in net proceeds of the Union taxes by the Fourteenth Finance Commission so that they can design their own development schemes for backward regions. It may be noted that the share of States in the net proceeds of the Union taxes was significantly enhanced from 32% to 42% by the Fourteenth Finance Commission.

The NITI Aayog which replaced the planning commission has a Governing Council comprising the Prime Minister of India, Chief Ministers of all the States and Union Territories with Legislature, Lt Governors of other UTs, Ex-Officio Members, and Special Invitees. The Governing Council is a forum to discuss inter-sectoral, inter-departmental, and federal issues to accelerate the implementation of the national development agenda. Guided by the principle that strong States build a strong nation, the NITI Aayog is entrusted with the responsibility of developing a shared vision of national development priorities, sectors, and strategies, with states actively participating in the development narrative. It seeks to design and assist in the implementation of strategic and long term policy frameworks. The NITI Aayog monitors the progress and efficacy of development programmes.

The Government of India has launched the 'Transformation of Aspirational Districts' initiative in January, 2018 with a vision of a New India by

2022 where the focus is to improve India's ranking under Human Development Index, raising living standards of its citizens and ensuring inclusive growth of all. The broad strategy of the Aspirational Districts Programme rests on the 3 Cs – Convergence (between Central and State Schemes), Collaboration (between Centre, State, District Administration, Development Partners and Citizens), and Competition (between Districts).

The Aspirational Districts Programme encompasses 115 districts that were identified from 28 states, using a composite index of key data sets that included deprivation enumerated under the Socio-Economic Caste Census, key health and education sector performance and state of basic infrastructure. While NITI Aayog is steering the initiative in 30 districts, various central ministries oversee 50 districts besides the Ministry of Home Affairs, which focuses on 35 Left Wing Extremism (LWE) affected districts. Officers at the level of Joint Secretary/Additional Secretary have been nominated to become the 'Central Prabhari Officers' of each district. States have appointed state-nodal and Prabhari officers. An Empowered Committee under the Convenorship of the CEO, NITI Aayog will help in the convergence of various government schemes and streamlining of efforts. Performance of these districts is monitored on a monthly basis which is made available in the public domain on the Champions of Change Dashboard. The progress of aspirational districts is assessed through a composite score which is based on 49 indicators from the 5 identified thematic areas viz, 'Education' and 'Health & Nutrition' with a weight of 30% each, 'Agriculture & Water Resources' with a weight of 20% and 10% weight each to 'Financial Inclusion & Skill Development' and 'Basic Infrastructure' (10%). Every month, districts are ranked on the basis of progress made on the key performance indicators mentioned above, and this instills in them with a sense of competition which results in rapid improvement.

We assess the effectiveness of the initiatives to improve the growth prospect of the relatively underdeveloped states by studying the behaviour of per capita income during 2001–20. We begin with the analysis of the changes in the per capita income differential across the states which is a simple way to assess interstate inequality.

III Impact of development interventions on per capita income

The range of per capita income and the evolution of PCI differential over time can give a broad idea whether the different states have grown at similar pace. We will base our discussion separately for the LS, SS, and UTs.

The PCI of India increased by 2.8 times from Rs. 38,958 to Rs. 108,645 between 2001 and 2020 (Table 3.1). When we consider all the states under study, the lowest PCI across states increased by a smaller multiple than

Table 3.1 SDP Per Capita 2001–20

(Figures are in Indian Rupees)

States	*2001*	*2002*	*2003*	*2004*	*2005*	*2006*	*2007*	*2008*
Large States								
Andhra Pradesh	42,003	43,489	44,003	47,562	50,866	55,131	60,652	67,257
Assam	31,230	31,439	33,115	34,600	35,388	36,088	37,258	38,539
Bihar	14,429	13,336	14,707	13,700	15,103	14,600	16,691	17,346
Chhattisgarh	31,506	35,322	34,477	39,443	40,676	41,249	47,868	51,108
Gujarat	43,447	46,019	49,069	55,398	59,358	67,178	71,722	78,449
Haryana	56,299	59,148	61,940	66,714	70,951	76,028	83,019	88,425
Jharkhand	26,485	27,711	27,938	29,680	33,647	32,066	32,329	38,389
Karnataka	55,701	56,402	58,259	59,517	64,587	70,529	76,668	85,359
Kerala	51,597	53,898	57,242	60,281	66,710	73,089	78,485	84,959
Madhya Pradesh	26,043	27,353	25,753	28,147	28,477	29,447	31,598	32,511
Maharashtra	54,662	55,854	58,789	62,490	66,871	74,636	83,469	91,496
Odisha	27,376	28,741	28,231	32,149	35,824	37,367	41,622	45,575
Punjab	57,858	58,226	58,799	61,237	63,102	65,614	70,982	76,000
Rajasthan	34,128	36,860	32,654	41,195	396,60	415,25	45,536	47,037
Tamil Nadu	51,634	50,373	50,779	53,355	58,973	66,668	76,220	80,298
Uttar Pradesh	23,323	23,285	23,717	24,478	25,301	26,435	28,033	29,532
West Bengal	33,265	35,308	36,107	37,879	40,023	42,070	44,860	47,844
Small States								
Arunachal Pradesh	44,577	50,390	47,133	51,094	58,134	58,380	60,035	65,733
Goa	110,802	112,466	117,168	122,532	139,368	145,298	155,328	158,605
Himachal Pradesh	53,498	55,321	57,122	60,706	65,751	70,498	76,054	81,692
Manipur	30,771	32,170	31,385	34,090	36,456	37,929	37849	39,226
Meghalaya	38,293	39,921	41,184	43,429	44,027	46,354	48,722	49,689
Mizoram	36,120	37,494	40,345	40,593	41,236	43,013	43,914	47,533
Nagaland	27,236	28,851	30,049	30,025	39,825	43,193	45,804	48,366
Tripura	24923	28,380	29,652	30,997	33,100	34,603	37,011	39,380
Sikkim	51,172	53,227	56,807	60,391	64,742	70,213	73,395	78,186
Uttarakhand	39,504	40,949	44,285	46,868	52,089	58,610	65,533	76,211
UTs								
Andaman and Nicobar Islands	42,034	42,988	46,724	51,304	52,815	55,197	64,716	70,799
Chandigarh	87,993	91,843	101,499	107,435	112,833	118,653	129,475	131,703
Delhi	100,723	100,876	105,690	108,510	122,248	131,996	145,541	158,782
Jammu and Kashmir	43,531	43,310	45,078	46,685	48,389	50,433	526,69	55,256
Puducherry	80,090	84,266	90,521	93,402	81,771	100,234	102,011	108,758
India	38,958	40,013	40,906	43,463	50,325	53,478	56,964	60,466

2009	*2010*	*2011*	*2012*	*2013*	*2014*	*2015*	*2016*
71,180	73,700	81,524	86,966	87,697	92,406	99,048	109,974
40,224	43,293	44,994	45,538	46,264	47,900	50,558	57,735
19,573	20,324	23,057	23,525	24,068	24,874	25,379	26,504
54,246	55,186	59,813	61,305	63,348	68,577	68,685	69,328
82,578	90,596	98,323	101,075	110,617	117,429	128,068	139,327
93,973	103,196	108,994	116,408	123,799	132,182	138,975	152886
37,185	40,389	46,155	45,318	48,230	48,200	53,347	49,210
90,424	90,618	98,774	98,567	103,463	112,128	117,844	129,489
89,250	96,962	103,164	108,665	115,159	119,106	123,574	132,114
35,954	38,746	40,532	43,023	47,153	48,159	49,827	53,485
92,491	99,650	109,330	113,192	118,716	125,511	131,977	139,960
48,466	50,008	53,307	54,855	57,478	62,460	63,238	67,910
78,985	82,432	86,210	95,378	99,157	104,367	107,381	112,080
50,427	52,903	59,546	62,907	64,825	68,354	72,270	76,955
84,080	92,556	104,017	103,743	108,566	116,021	120,914	130,000
31,018	32,466	34,403	35,917	37,044	38,596	39,548	42,397
49,702	53,190	55,746	56,693	58,472	59,635	60,722	63,803
69,838	74,680	75,743	79,530	80,364	86,829	100,088	98,075
167,963	178,314	201,518	289,192	243,052	212,582	268,338	306,252
86,840	92,942	100,145	105,376	111,152	117,965	125,720	134,706
40,905	42,777	41,610	44,641	43,954	46,723	49,384	52,056
54,752	56,917	60,279	66,304	66,320	66,111	62,899	63,095
52,525	57,577	65,746	65,335	68,528	77,985	96,166	103,386
50,590	53,210	57,590	61,159	63,956	67,810	70,067	70,585
42,592	46,573	49,768	51,999	55,900	60,464	70,701	69,504
89,769	154,036	16,5525	181,842	183,916	193,207	206,492	224,523
84,547	98,389	106,680	113,456	120,084	128,515	133,507	142,390
80,409	90,420	96,870	104,147	108,242	116,280	121,893	130,232
134,510	134,058	128,591	176,227	187,652	201,501	205,482	220,639
175,919	186,841	196,494	202,139	210,876	221,182	236,112	256,816
580,06	59,795	62,342	61,852	62,878	65,268	62,219	72,168
115,394	131,722	137,247	132,739	133,055	143,597	132,798	135,467
61,468	65,394	69,994	71,609	74,599	78,348	83,091	88,616

(Figures are in Indian Rupees)

States	*2017*	*2018*	*2019*	*2020*
Large States				
Andhra Pradesh	118,774	129,568	137,931	145,922
Assam	60,270	65,138	67,680	68,916
Bihar	28,054	29,405	32,109	33,971
Chhattisgarh	76,506	77,556	82,413	85,258
Gujarat	150,862	163,090	175,132	185,398
Haryana	166542	175209	183323	195660
Jharkhand	53,480	57,465	61,666	63,210
Karnataka	145,112	155,910	164,247	170,609
Kerala	141,397	149,651	158,563	163,215
Madhya Pradesh	59,225	61,670	64,757	70,014
Maharashtra	151,353	158,844	167,108	173,757
Odisha	78,028	83,270	88631	94199
Punjab	118,228	124,208	129850	133322
Rajasthan	80,359	82,943	85804	88839
Tamil Nadu	138,529	14,9717	159457	168449
Uttar Pradesh	46,505	47,897	50129	51255
West Bengal	67,718	71,312	75087	78904
Small States				
Arunachal Pradesh	101,525	105,159	111096	118573
Goa	338,056	344,811	373740	343687
Himachal Pradesh	142,933	151,260	160,124	166,895
Manipur	52,984	56,924	57,339	60,106
Meghalaya	65,041	66,113	68,021	70,718
Mizoram	111,987	125,598	135,526	150,531
Nagaland	75,349	79,152	80,361	85,415
Tripura	78,422	84,141	92,509	100,217
Sikkim	237,979	270,235	282,197	295,355
Uttarakhand	154,295	164,345	171,519	176,838
UTs				
Andaman and Nicobar Islands	146,360	163,657	173,409	180,865
Chandigarh	235,085	245,726	252,319	263,138
Delhi	270,804	281,172	291,583	306,385
Jammu and Kashmir	73,427	76,934	82,730	85,219
Puducherry	141,716	150,325	150,384	159,804
India	94,751	100,035	105,526	108,645

highest PCI across states between 2001 and 2020. For instance, the lowest PCI increased by 2.4 times between 2001 and 2020 compared to 3.4 times for the highest PCI amongst 17 states. This suggests that inequality across the states has increased during the study period. We now discuss how the PCI has changed for states classified under three broad categories.

LS: Bihar had the lowest PCI in the beginning year as well as the last year of the study. Punjab had the highest PCI in 2001. However, by 2020,

Haryana had replaced Punjab as the state having highest PCI. The PCI of Punjab was four times that of Bihar in 2000. By 2020, the PCI of Haryana was 5.75 times that of Bihar. Thus, the gulf between the richest and the poorest state has increased over the study period.

The average PCI of LS has increased 2.9 times between 2001 and 2020. Eight out of the 17 states viz, Andhra Pradesh, Gujarat, Haryana, Karnataka, Kerala, Maharashtra, Odisha, and Tamil Nadu, had an increase in PCI by a higher multiple than the average between 2001 and 2020. Gujarat had the increase in PCI by the highest multiple of 4.27 between 2001 and 2020.

SS: Goa and Tripura had the highest and lowest PCI positions, respectively, in the year 2001. The PCI in Goa was 4.45 times that of Tripura. Goa continued to have the highest PCI in the year 2020, but Manipur had replaced Tripura as having the lowest PCI. In 2001, the PCI of Goa was as much as 5.7 times that of Manipur. Thus, the 'PCI multiples' between the states having the highest and lowest PCI was of a higher order for the SS compared to LS between 2001 and 2020. The average PCI of the SCS increased by 3.4 times between 2001 and 2020. Only Mizoram, Sikkim, Tripura, and Uttarakhand had an increase in PCI by a higher multiple than that of the SCS average. Sikkim had the increase in PCI by the highest multiple between 2001 and 2020.

UTs: Delhi had the highest PCI and Andaman & Nicobar Islands had the lowest PCI in 2001. The PCI of Delhi was 2.4 times that of Andaman & Nicobar Island. In 2020, Delhi continued to have the highest PCI. However, Jammu and Kashmir had replaced Andaman and Nicobar Islands as the UT having the lowest PCI by 2020. In 2020, the PCI of Delhi was 3.6 times that of Jammu and Kashmir. The average PCI of the UTs increased by 2.8 times between 2001 and 2020. Except Jammu and Kashmir and Puducherry, the other three UTs had an increase in PCI by a higher multiple than that of the average.

In addition to studying PCI differential, we have undertaken a rank analysis of the states under the LS, SS, and the UTs to get a holistic perspective on the income mobility of the states.

Rank analysis

The evolution of ranks of the states under the LS, SS, and the UTs during 2001–20 has been depicted in Table 3.2. The states have been ranked in descending order of PCI, that is the state having the highest PCI gets rank 1 and the state having the second highest PCI gets rank 2 and so on.

When we consider all states as one group, the small state of Goa and Bihar belonging to the LS category occupy the first and the last rank, respectively, both in 2001 and 2020. As Goa being a small state with the highest

Table 3.2 Ranking of Per-Capita Income of States 2001–20

States	*2001*	*2002*	*2003*	*2004*	*2005*	*2006*	*2007*	*2008*	*2009*	*2010*	*2011*	*2012*	*2013*	*2014*	*2015*	*2016*	*2017*	*2018*	*2019*	*2020*
Large States																				
Andhra Pradesh	8	8	8	8	8	8	8	8	8	8	8	8	8	8	8	8	7	7	7	7
Assam	12	12	11	12	13	13	13	13	13	13	14	13	15	15	14	13	13	13	13	14
Bihar	17	17	17	17	17	17	17	17	17	17	17	17	17	17	17	17	17	17	17	17
Chhattisgarh	11	10	10	10	9	11	9	9	9	9	9	10	10	9	10	10	11	11	11	11
Gujarat	7	7	7	6	6	5	6	6	6	6	6	5	4	4	3	3	3	2	2	2
Haryana	2	1	1	1	1	1	2	2	1	1	2	1	1	1	1	1	1	1	1	1
Jharkhand	14	14	14	14	14	14	14	14	14	14	13	14	13	13	13	15	15	15	15	15
Karnataka	3	3	4	5	4	4	4	3	3	5	5	6	6	6	6	6	4	4	4	4
Kerala	6	5	5	4	3	3	3	4	4	3	4	3	3	3	4	4	5	6	6	6
Madhya Pradesh	15	15	15	15	15	15	15	15	15	15	15	15	14	14	15	14	14	14	14	13
Maharashtra	4	4	3	2	2	2	1	1	2	2	1	2	2	2	2	2	2	3	3	3
Odisha	13	13	13	13	12	12	12	12	12	12	12	12	12	11	11	11	10	9	9	9
Punjab	1	2	2	3	5	7	7	7	7	7	7	7	7	7	7	7	8	8	8	8
Rajasthan	9	9	12	9	11	10	10	11	10	11	10	9	9	10	9	9	9	10	10	10
Tamil Nadu	5	6	6	7	7	6	5	5	5	4	3	4	5	5	5	5	6	5	5	5
Uttar Pradesh	16	16	16	16	16	16	16	16	16	16	16	16	16	16	16	16	16	16	16	16
West Bengal	10	11	9	11	10	9	11	10	11	10	11	11	11	12	12	12	12	12	12	12
Small States																				
Arunachal Pradesh	4	4	4	4	4	5	5	5	5	5	5	5	5	5	5	6	6	6	6	6
Goa	1	1	1	1	1	1	1	1	1	1	1	1	1	1	1	1	1	1	1	1
Himachal Pradesh	2	2	2	2	2	2	2	2	3	4	4	4	4	4	4	4	4	4	4	4
Manipur	8	8	8	8	9	9	9	10	10	10	10	10	10	10	10	10	10	10	10	10

Meghalaya	6	6	6	6	6	6	6	6	6	7	7	6	7	8	9	9	9	9	9	9
Mizoram	7	7	7	7	7	8	8	8	7	6	6	7	6	6	6	5	5	5	5	5
Nagaland	9	9	9	10	8	7	7	7	8	8	8	8	8	7	8	7	8	8	8	8
Tripura	10	10	10	9	10	10	10	9	9	9	9	9	9	9	7	8	7	7	7	7
Sikkim	3	3	3	3	3	3	3	3	2	2	2	2	2	2	2	2	2	2	2	2
Uttarakhand	5	5	5	5	5	4	4	4	4	3	3	3	3	3	3	3	3	3	3	3
UTs																				
Andaman and Nicobar Islands	5	5	4	4	4	4	4	4	4	4	4	4	4	4	4	4	3	3	3	3
Chandigarh	2	2	2	2	2	2	2	2	2	2	3	2	2	2	2	2	2	2	2	2
Delhi	1	1	1	1	1	1	1	1	1	1	1	1	1	1	1	1	1	1	1	1
Jammu and Kashmir	4	4	5	5	5	5	5	5	5	5	5	5	5	5	5	5	5	5	5	5
Puducherry	3	3	3	3	3	3	3	3	3	3	2	3	3	3	3	3	4	4	4	4

PCI can distort the analysis of movement in PCI during the study period. For instance, two small states figured in the top ten PCI ranks in 2001. However, by 2020, three small states were found within the top ten ranks in PCI. To exclude the impact of smaller population in influencing PCI ranks, we have undertaken the analysis for different state groups. The key findings from the rank analysis for the different category of states are provided below.

LS

- Gujarat has improved its rank from 7th in 2001 to 2nd in 2020, the best improvement recorded by any state during the study period.
- Haryana moved up from 2nd rank in 2001 to 1st during 2002–06 and again from 2012 till 2020.
- Andhra Pradesh, Madhya Pradesh, Maharashtra, and Odisha also recorded some improvement of in their PCI rank.
- Punjab has slid in its PCI rank from 1st in 2001 to 8th in 2020, the sharpest decline witnessed by any state.
- Assam, Jharkhand, Rajasthan, and West Bengal also experienced a decline in their PCI rank between 2001 and 2020.

SS

- Goa had the 1st rank among SCS during the entire period of the study.
- Mizoram, Tripura, Uttarakhand, Sikkim, and Nagaland also improved their rank to some extent between 2001 and 2020
- The PCI rank of Arunachal Pradesh, Himachal Pradesh, Manipur, and Meghalaya declined during 2001 and 2020.
- The PCI rank of Meghalaya notched up and that of Tripura declined by three points.

UTs

- Delhi and Chandigarh have maintained their PCI rank of one and two, respectively, all through the study period.
- While Jammu and Kashmir and Puducherry have gone down in the PCI rank among UTs, that of Andaman & Nicobar improved in 2020 compared to 2001.

In order to ascertain the stability of the ranks over time, we have computed Kendall's coefficient of concordance. Kendall's coefficient of concordance ranges from 0 to 1, with values closer to one signifying stability of ranks. The value of coefficient of concordance suggests that the PCI rank of the

Table 3.3 Kendall's Coefficient of Concordance 2001–20

Large States	0.969 (0.00)
Small States	0.965 (0.00)
Union Territories	0.965 (0.00)

Notes: The null hypothesis is that there is no agreement between ranks.
The figures in parenthesis indicate the p-values.

states has been quite stable during the study period for all the three categories of states (Table 3.3). This indicates lack of mobility of states in their per capita income or persistence of inequality during the study period.

IV Inequality measures

To add robustness to our findings based on rank analysis and for a better understanding of the dynamics of inequality in income over time, we use several other measures of inequality of per capita income across the states under the 'large' and 'small' category. We have also computed the inequality measures for the north eastern (NE) states as a group, given that Ministry of Development of North Eastern Region was established in 2001 as a nodal agency for their all-round development.

We have computed the Gini coefficient and a series of other summary inequality measures, viz, Entropy Index, Kakwani Index, Theil Index, and Mehran Index. These measures reflect several inequality attributes of the income distribution. The Gini coefficient is sensitive to changes across the distribution. It meets the criteria of mean independence, symmetry, independence from sample size, and the Pigou-Dalton transfer sensitivity (Misra, 2013). Gini and Theil indices rank the distribution of income with equal weights above and below the average. The Entropy Index is highly sensitive to changes at the lower end of the distribution. The Theil Index is more balanced in giving weight across the distribution and so is closer to the Gini in that regard. The Mehran Index also assigns higher weights to low incomes. The Kakwani Index is similar to the Gini, which is one minus the area under the Lorenz Curve measuring the inequality in the distribution of income, except that the Kakwani Index squares the area under the Lorenz Curve so that larger values are given greater weights.

Inequality between all the states under study has increased during the study period as suggested by the evolution of various inequality measures (Table 3.4). The inequality measures also suggest deterioration in inequality for all the three groups of states.

Table 3.4 Inter-state Inequality Measure 2001–20

State	*All States*				*Large*				*Small*				*North East*			
Year	*EI*	*KI*	*MI*	*TI*	*EI*	*KI*	*MI*	*TI*	*EI*	*KI*	*MI*	*TI*	*EI*	*KI*	*MI*	*TI*
2001	0.085	0.046	0.303	0.083	0.077	0.037	0.290	0.061	0.090	0.056	0.312	0.107	0.027	0.016	0.187	0.027
2002	0.087	0.044	0.298	0.080	0.083	0.037	0.291	0.061	0.082	0.052	0.298	0.098	0.026	0.016	0.180	0.027
2003	0.089	0.046	0.307	0.084	0.084	0.039	0.301	0.065	0.083	0.053	0.298	0.100	0.025	0.015	0.174	0.026
2004	0.094	0.046	0.307	0.083	0.092	0.039	0.300	0.064	0.085	0.053	0.305	0.100	0.028	0.017	0.185	0.029
2005	0.096	0.048	0.310	0.088	0.092	0.040	0.304	0.067	0.086	0.055	0.304	0.106	0.026	0.016	0.173	0.027
2006	0.108	0.052	0.326	0.093	0.111	0.047	0.327	0.078	0.086	0.055	0.305	0.103	0.027	0.017	0.178	0.029
2007	0.109	0.053	0.332	0.095	0.112	0.048	0.334	0.080	0.091	0.057	0.315	0.108	0.027	0.017	0.177	0.029
2008	0.112	0.053	0.334	0.093	0.118	0.050	0.338	0.083	0.090	0.055	0.315	0.102	0.030	0.019	0.184	0.032
2009	0.109	0.053	0.335	0.093	0.111	0.049	0.335	0.081	0.091	0.055	0.320	0.100	0.035	0.022	0.203	0.039
2010	0.126	0.061	0.358	0.108	0.114	0.050	0.339	0.083	0.120	0.068	0.366	0.121	0.085	0.057	0.289	0.110
2011	0.129	0.063	0.365	0.113	0.112	0.050	0.340	0.083	0.133	0.074	0.382	0.132	0.091	0.060	0.305	0.115
2012	0.154	0.078	0.391	0.150	0.116	0.051	0.343	0.085	0.179	0.101	0.429	0.191	0.098	0.065	0.313	0.125
2013	0.141	0.069	0.378	0.126	0.119	0.053	0.347	0.088	0.150	0.083	0.399	0.150	0.097	0.063	0.313	0.122
2014	0.136	0.064	0.371	0.112	0.126	0.055	0.354	0.091	0.126	0.069	0.373	0.121	0.098	0.063	0.316	0.121
2015	0.150	0.071	0.385	0.127	0.130	0.056	0.358	0.094	0.145	0.078	0.395	0.140	0.105	0.065	0.334	0.122
2016	0.163	0.077	0.399	0.141	0.138	0.059	0.367	0.099	0.168	0.090	0.420	0.163	0.108	0.069	0.333	0.132
2017	0.166	0.078	0.402	0.144	0.139	0.059	0.367	0.099	0.177	0.093	0.430	0.171	0.111	0.070	0.342	0.133
2018	0.170	0.080	0.406	0.145	0.143	0.061	0.371	0.102	0.180	0.094	0.433	0.170	0.124	0.078	0.359	0.150
2019	0.172	0.081	0.410	0.148	0.141	0.061	0.371	0.102	0.190	0.097	0.442	0.176	0.130	0.080	0.369	0.152
2020	0.165	0.076	0.403	0.136	0.142	0.062	0.374	0.103	0.170	0.085	0.422	0.152	0.134	0.080	0.377	0.152

Notes: EI, KI, MI and TI stand for Entropy Index, JKakwani Index, Mehran Index and Thheil Index respectively.

When looking at the evolution of Gini for aggregate and sectoral SDP, the following patterns emerge for all states as one group and for the groups of LS, SS, and NE (Graphs 3.1–3.4).

All States

- Between the beginning and end year of our analysis, the Gini of overall income has deteriorated (increased) from 0.22 in 2001 to 0.28 in 2020.

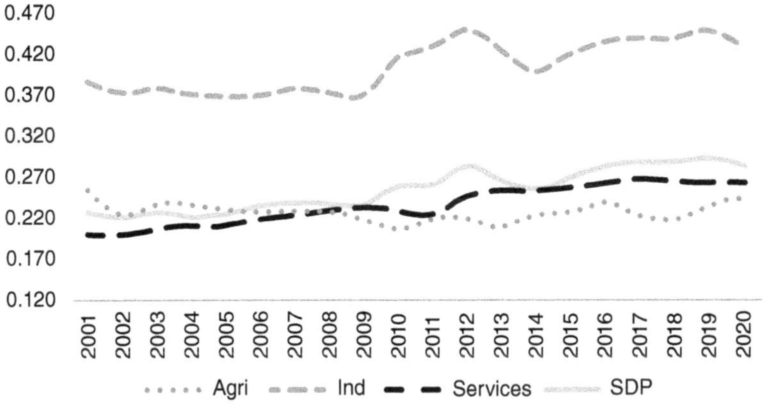

Graph 3.1 Evolution of Sectoral Gini 2001-2020: All States.

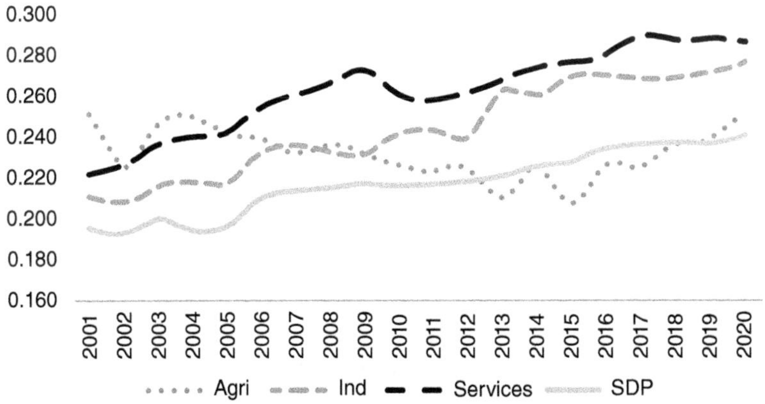

Graph 3.2 Evolution of Sectoral Gini 2001-2020: Large States.

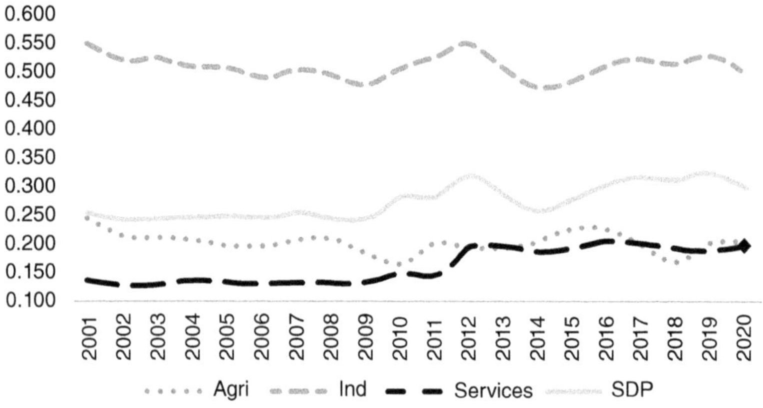

Graph 3.3 Evolution of Sectoral Gini 2001-2020: Small States.

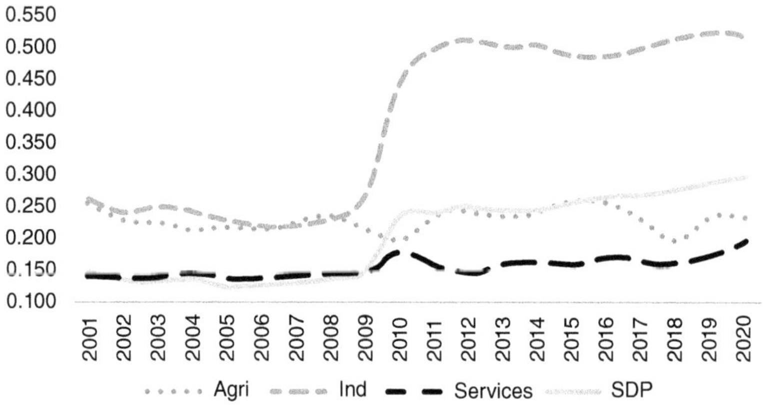

Graph 3.4 Evolution of Sectoral Gini 2001-2020: North Eastern States.

- Seen in terms of sub-periods, we find that the Gini coefficient was stable during 2001–04. It increased in the subsequent period with a major spike observed during the low growth phase of 2010–14 when it reached 0.28 in the year 2012. In the subsequent years, Gini has been fluctuating within a range of 0.25–0.29.

- Among the sectors, industry had the highest Gini coefficient in all the years. Till the year 2008, agriculture had slightly higher inequality than services. However, beginning with the year 2009 or roughly after the GFC, we find inequality in services has been consistently higher than that in agriculture.

LS

- Gini coefficient computed for overall income of the states has shot up from 0.19 in 2001 to 0.24 in 2020.
- The worsening of inequality is more pronounced for the industry and services sectors though Gini for the later has been consistently higher than that for the former.
- The Gini coefficient at two decimal value has not changed for the agriculture sector in the year 2020 compared to 2000. Though Gini coefficient had declined from 0.25 in 2001 to 0.21 in 2015, it increased in the subsequent years.

SS

- For this group if states, inequality too increased for overall income.
- Inequality was highest for Industry followed by agriculture and services.
- Gini coefficient for industry sector declined during the study period, albeit from very high levels of 0.54 in 2001 to 0.50 in 2020. Like in industry, Gini coefficient for agriculture also declined.
- Though Gini coefficient increased for the services sector during the study period, the coefficient value was relatively small compared to agriculture.
- Except for the year 2017, notwithstanding the decline in Gini coefficient value for agriculture, it was higher than that for services sector during the entire study period.

NE

- The inequality amongst the NE states has increased acutely in the post 2010 period to reach 0.29 in 2020 compared to 0.15 in 2001.
- As far as sectoral Gini is concerned, we find that it was the highest for industry followed by that for agriculture and services. Except for agriculture, the Gini coefficient increased during the study period for the other two sectors.

- Industry had a Gini coefficient higher than that for agriculture in 2001. However, in the subsequent years, Gini coefficient for agriculture has declined marginally and that for industry has increased significantly.

V Gini decomposition by income source

Given that income inequality has worsened over time, it would be instructive from a policy perspective to assess if inequality is prevalent across all sectors of the economy or confined to some specific sectors. Deciphering the sectoral pattern, in other words, can help in identifying the sources of income disparity. To ascertain the sectors which are contributing to inequality, we divide the economy into three major sectors: primary, secondary, and tertiary. Lerman and Yitzhaki (1985), Shorrocks (1982), and Stark, Taylor, and Yitzhaki (1986) have proposed methods to decompose the Gini coefficient according to the sources of income.

The decomposition approach can also be used to calculate the impact of a marginal change in one particular source of income on inequality. This type of decomposition has been operationalised by Lopez-Feldman (2005). Lerman and Yitzhaki (1985), building on Shorrocks' (1982) findings, show that when decomposed by income sources, the Gini coefficient for total income inequality, G, can be represented as the combined influence of the share of each source k (Sk) in total income, the source Gini (Gk) corresponding to the distribution of income from source k, and the Gini correlation of income from source k (Rk) with the distribution of total income.

The relationship between these three components has a clear and intuitive meaning (Stark et al., 1986). Even if a source of income accounts for a substantial share of overall income, it need not have a significant impact on inequality if it is entirely evenly distributed (Gk = 0). However, if the share of an income source is large and it is unequally distributed (Sk and Gk are large), it may increase or decrease inequality depending on where the income recipients fall in the income distribution. The contribution to inequality will be positive if the income source is unequally distributed and is tilted disproportionately towards those at the top of the income distribution (Rk is positive and large). The income source, on the other hand, may have an equalising influence on the income distribution if it is unequally distributed but favours the poor. Furthermore, Lerman and Yitzhaki (1985) show that using this approach of Gini decomposition, one may assess the effect on inequality of small changes in income from a specific sector while keeping income from all other sectors constant. We have attempted decomposition of Gini for all the states as group and also for the group of large, small and the north eastern states.

All states

When all states are treated as one group, the Gini decomposition for all the years under study indicates that increase in income from agriculture and services had a sobering effect on inequality (Table 3.5a). However, growth in industrial income accentuated inequality.

We find that industry had the highest share in income inequality followed by services and agriculture during the entire period of study. If we look at the Gini decomposition results for the year 2001, a 1% increase in income from industry increases the Gini coefficient of total income by 0.129%, all else being equal. In contrast, increase in income from agriculture and services lowers inequality by 0.017% and 0.112%, respectively. This was because industry accounted for the second largest share in SDP after services and the source Gini is highest for this sector (0.386). Moreover, the Gini correlation between industry and total income is also quite high (0.815) suggesting that income from industry benefits the wealthy more.

Even if an income source is unequally distributed, it might benefit the poor. This is the scenario for services income in the year 2001. In the year 2001, income from the services sector had an equalising influence on the distribution of total income. This was due to two reasons. The Gini coefficient for this sector is the lowest (0.20), and the Gini correlation between primary sector income and total income is also the quite low (0.275) when compared to that for industry. It is also observed that agriculture not only contributes the least to income disparity, but that its contribution has decreased over time. The services sector's contribution to income inequality has followed an increasing pattern.

LS

In contrast to all the states under study, for the group of LS, only income from industry has an ameliorating impact on inequality (Table 3.5a). Income from both agriculture and services sector accentuated inequality. If we take the year 2001, we find the source Gini was lowest for industry (0.212). The Gini correlation between industrial income and total income was also the lowest among the three sectors (0.721). In the same year, agriculture had the highest source Gini along with very high Gini correlation between agricultural income and total income. Thus, agricultural sector had an unequalising effect on total income in the year 2001. Like agriculture, services sector also had an unequalising effect as it accounted for the highest share in income, relatively higher source Gini and the highest Gini correlation between income from services and total income. As far as contribution of different sectors to income inequality is concerned, we find contribution of

Table 3.5a Gini Decomposition by Income Source for Indian States

		All States					*Large Sates*				
Source	*Year*	*Sk*	*Gk*	*Rk*	*Share*	*% Change*	*Sk*	*Gk*	*Rk*	*Share*	*% Change*
Agriculture	2001	0.281	0.251	0.847	0.264	−0.017	0.295	0.251	0.913	0.346	0.051
Industry	2001	0.332	0.386	0.815	0.461	0.129	0.315	0.212	0.721	0.246	−0.069
Services	2001	0.387	0.200	0.807	0.275	−0.112	0.390	0.222	0.917	0.408	0.018
SDP	2001		0.226					0.195			
Agriculture	2002	0.279	0.225	0.815	0.231	−0.047	0.299	0.227	0.896	0.314	0.016
Industry	2002	0.332	0.374	0.852	0.478	0.146	0.305	0.209	0.777	0.256	−0.049
Services	2002	0.390	0.199	0.830	0.291	−0.099	0.397	0.227	0.922	0.429	0.033
SDP	2002		0.221					0.193			
Agriculture	2003	0.259	0.239	0.739	0.202	−0.057	0.268	0.247	0.871	0.288	0.020
Industry	2003	0.346	0.378	0.845	0.487	0.142	0.325	0.217	0.770	0.270	−0.055
Services	2003	0.396	0.207	0.860	0.311	−0.085	0.407	0.237	0.916	0.441	0.034
SDP	2003		0.227					0.200			
Agriculture	2004	0.262	0.237	0.707	0.198	−0.065	0.276	0.250	0.790	0.279	0.004
Industry	2004	0.349	0.370	0.855	0.496	0.147	0.325	0.219	0.750	0.274	−0.051
Services	2004	0.389	0.209	0.838	0.307	−0.083	0.400	0.240	0.907	0.447	0.047
SDP	2004		0.223					0.195			
Agriculture	2005	0.247	0.230	0.698	0.176	−0.071	0.258	0.242	0.817	0.260	0.002
Industry	2005	0.361	0.369	0.852	0.504	0.142	0.338	0.218	0.733	0.275	−0.063
Services	2005	0.392	0.212	0.871	0.321	−0.071	0.404	0.243	0.930	0.465	0.061
SDP	2005		0.226					0.196			
Agriculture	2006	0.239	0.227	0.689	0.160	−0.079	0.251	0.239	0.797	0.226	−0.025
Industry	2006	0.362	0.370	0.883	0.504	0.142	0.336	0.233	0.818	0.304	−0.032

Services	2006	0.399	0.219	0.901	0.336	−0.063	0.413	0.255	0.939	0.470	0.057
SDP	2006		0.234					0.211			
Agriculture	2007	0.226	0.225	0.635	0.136	−0.090	0.238	0.233	0.729	0.188	−0.050
Industry	2007	0.373	0.378	0.887	0.525	0.153	0.345	0.236	0.881	0.334	−0.011
Services	2007	0.402	0.223	0.901	0.339	−0.063	0.417	0.261	0.940	0.478	0.060
SDP	2007		0.238					0.214			
Agriculture	2008	0.219	0.229	0.595	0.127	−0.092	0.228	0.237	0.701	0.175	−0.053
Industry	2008	0.375	0.373	0.875	0.519	0.144	0.349	0.234	0.864	0.326	−0.022
Services	2008	0.406	0.227	0.905	0.354	−0.052	0.423	0.267	0.952	0.499	0.075
SDP	2008		0.235					0.216			
Agriculture	2009	0.207	0.218	0.508	0.097	−0.110	0.220	0.232	0.691	0.162	−0.057
Industry	2009	0.377	0.371	0.891	0.526	0.149	0.344	0.232	0.847	0.312	−0.032
Services	2009	0.416	0.233	0.919	0.377	−0.039	0.436	0.273	0.958	0.526	0.090
SDP	2009		0.237					0.217			
Agriculture	2010	0.188	0.207	0.487	0.073	−0.114	0.206	0.226	0.689	0.148	−0.057
Industry	2010	0.393	0.417	0.919	0.584	0.191	0.344	0.243	0.846	0.326	−0.018
Services	2010	0.419	0.228	0.924	0.343	−0.077	0.450	0.261	0.967	0.526	0.075
SDP	2010		0.258					0.216			
Agriculture	2011	0.185	0.218	0.467	0.072	−0.113	0.204	0.224	0.678	0.143	−0.061
Industry	2011	0.391	0.429	0.930	0.600	0.209	0.342	0.244	0.896	0.344	0.002
Services	2011	0.424	0.224	0.898	0.328	−0.096	0.455	0.258	0.949	0.513	0.059
SDP	2011		0.260					0.217			
Agriculture	2012	0.178	0.219	0.533	0.073	−0.105	0.201	0.225	0.739	0.152	−0.049
Industry	2012	0.392	0.450	0.933	0.582	0.190	0.337	0.241	0.883	0.327	−0.010
Services	2012	0.429	0.248	0.916	0.345	−0.085	0.463	0.262	0.942	0.521	0.059
SDP	2012		0.283					0.219			
Agriculture	2013	0.179	0.210	0.451	0.064	−0.115	0.194	0.211	0.597	0.110	−0.084
Industry	2013	0.371	0.426	0.924	0.550	0.178	0.331	0.263	0.885	0.348	0.017
Services	2013	0.450	0.252	0.907	0.387	−0.063	0.475	0.268	0.942	0.542	0.067
SDP	2013		0.266					0.221			
Agriculture	2014	0.181	0.223	0.473	0.075	−0.106	0.191	0.226	0.648	0.123	−0.068

(Continued)

		All States					*Large Sates*				
Source	*Year*	*Sk*	*Gk*	*Rk*	*Share*	*% Change*	*Sk*	*Gk*	*Rk*	*Share*	*% Change*
Industry	2014	0.357	0.399	0.912	0.511	0.153	0.328	0.261	0.873	0.330	0.002
Services	2014	0.462	0.253	0.905	0.415	−0.047	0.481	0.274	0.939	0.547	0.066
SDP	2014		0.255					0.227			
Agriculture	2015	0.176	0.227	0.425	0.063	−0.113	0.183	0.208	0.605	0.100	−0.083
Industry	2015	0.369	0.422	0.940	0.543	0.174	0.324	0.269	0.906	0.346	0.022
Services	2015	0.456	0.257	0.906	0.394	−0.062	0.493	0.277	0.929	0.554	0.061
SDP	2015		0.269					0.229			
Agriculture	2016	0.162	0.239	0.434	0.059	−0.102	0.168	0.227	0.614	0.100	−0.068
Industry	2016	0.381	0.434	0.947	0.556	0.175	0.337	0.271	0.928	0.361	0.025
Services	2016	0.457	0.263	0.901	0.385	−0.073	0.495	0.281	0.908	0.539	0.044
SDP	2016		0.282					0.235			
Agriculture	2017	0.159	0.223	0.445	0.055	−0.104	0.171	0.226	0.573	0.093	−0.077
Industry	2017	0.390	0.440	0.948	0.568	0.178	0.342	0.269	0.915	0.357	0.015
Services	2017	0.451	0.268	0.896	0.377	−0.074	0.488	0.290	0.918	0.550	0.062
SDP	2017		0.287					0.236			
Agriculture	2018	0.154	0.219	0.478	0.056	−0.098	0.167	0.237	0.612	0.102	−0.065
Industry	2018	0.393	0.439	0.952	0.573	0.180	0.343	0.269	0.930	0.362	0.019
Services	2018	0.452	0.264	0.891	0.371	−0.082	0.491	0.288	0.900	0.536	0.045
SDP	2018		0.287					0.237			
Agriculture	2019	0.149	0.234	0.454	0.054	−0.095	0.159	0.239	0.576	0.093	−0.067
Industry	2019	0.398	0.449	0.955	0.585	0.187	0.345	0.272	0.921	0.364	0.019
Services	2019	0.453	0.263	0.882	0.361	−0.092	0.496	0.289	0.901	0.543	0.048
SDP	2019		0.292					0.237			
Agriculture	2020	0.151	0.245	0.458	0.060	−0.091	0.160	0.253	0.597	0.100	−0.060
Industry	2020	0.380	0.430	0.951	0.548	0.169	0.338	0.277	0.919	0.356	0.019
Services	2020	0.469	0.264	0.895	0.392	−0.077	0.503	0.287	0.907	0.544	0.041
SDP	2020		0.283					0.241			

Table 3.5b Gini Decomposition by Income Source for Indian States Continued

		Small States					*North Eastern States*				
Source	*Year*	*Sk*	*Gk*	*Rk*	*Share*	*% Change*	*Sk*	*Gk*	*Rk*	*Share*	*% Change*
Agriculture	2001	0.263	0.242	0.761	0.189	−0.074	0.324	0.256	0.878	0.500	0.176
Industry	2001	0.355	0.548	0.884	0.673	0.318	0.204	0.259	0.493	0.180	−0.024
Services	2001	0.381	0.137	0.674	0.138	−0.244	0.472	0.141	0.698	0.320	−0.152
SDP	2001		0.256					0.145			
Agriculture	2002	0.252	0.216	0.686	0.152	−0.099	0.309	0.229	0.790	0.415	0.106
Industry	2002	0.369	0.521	0.907	0.713	0.344	0.223	0.241	0.595	0.238	0.015
Services	2002	0.380	0.129	0.673	0.135	−0.245	0.468	0.137	0.732	0.347	−0.120
SDP	2002		0.245					0.135			
Agriculture	2003	0.246	0.212	0.475	0.101	−0.145	0.301	0.227	0.589	0.309	0.008
Industry	2003	0.374	0.525	0.937	0.751	0.378	0.227	0.249	0.664	0.288	0.061
Services	2003	0.380	0.132	0.717	0.148	−0.233	0.472	0.142	0.787	0.403	−0.069
SDP	2003		0.244					0.131			
Agriculture	2004	0.244	0.209	0.489	0.100	−0.143	0.295	0.213	0.527	0.249	−0.046
Industry	2004	0.381	0.510	0.962	0.756	0.375	0.241	0.241	0.742	0.324	0.083
Services	2004	0.375	0.136	0.697	0.144	−0.232	0.464	0.146	0.839	0.427	−0.037
SDP	2004		0.248					0.133			
Agriculture	2005	0.233	0.199	0.441	0.082	−0.151	0.287	0.217	0.531	0.266	−0.021
Industry	2005	0.392	0.508	0.965	0.771	0.379	0.249	0.229	0.675	0.309	0.060
Services	2005	0.375	0.135	0.727	0.147	−0.228	0.465	0.137	0.829	0.425	−0.039
SDP	2005		0.249					0.124			
Agriculture	2006	0.224	0.198	0.582	0.104	−0.120	0.272	0.208	0.606	0.270	−0.002
Industry	2006	0.397	0.493	0.940	0.743	0.346	0.255	0.220	0.655	0.290	0.035
Services	2006	0.379	0.132	0.758	0.153	−0.226	0.472	0.141	0.841	0.440	−0.033
SDP	2006		0.248					0.127			
Agriculture	2007	0.209	0.205	0.412	0.069	−0.140	0.267	0.223	0.693	0.317	0.051

(*Continued*)

		Small States					*North Eastern States*				
Source	*Year*	*Sk*	*Gk*	*Rk*	*Share*	*% Change*	*Sk*	*Gk*	*Rk*	*Share*	*% Change*
Industry	2007	0.411	0.506	0.959	0.782	0.371	0.254	0.221	0.602	0.260	0.006
Services	2007	0.380	0.134	0.744	0.149	−0.231	0.479	0.143	0.803	0.423	−0.056
SDP	2007		0.255					0.130			
Agriculture	2008	0.207	0.210	0.319	0.056	−0.152	0.267	0.234	0.598	0.272	0.005
Industry	2008	0.411	0.497	0.951	0.777	0.366	0.256	0.229	0.662	0.281	0.026
Services	2008	0.382	0.134	0.815	0.167	−0.215	0.478	0.147	0.877	0.447	−0.030
SDP	2008		0.250					0.138			
Agriculture	2009	0.191	0.186	0.124	0.018	−0.173	0.248	0.214	0.488	0.174	−0.075
Industry	2009	0.420	0.481	0.965	0.789	0.369	0.276	0.268	0.841	0.417	0.141
Services	2009	0.389	0.135	0.909	0.193	−0.196	0.475	0.147	0.873	0.410	−0.066
SDP	2009		0.247					0.149			
Agriculture	2010	0.165	0.166	0.009	0.001	−0.164	0.210	0.199	0.443	0.078	−0.132
Industry	2010	0.454	0.509	0.985	0.812	0.358	0.341	0.451	0.922	0.601	0.261
Services	2010	0.381	0.150	0.919	0.187	−0.194	0.449	0.178	0.948	0.321	−0.129
SDP	2010		0.281					0.236			
Agriculture	2011	0.162	0.203	0.122	0.014	−0.148	0.207	0.232	0.596	0.118	−0.089
Industry	2011	0.453	0.528	0.973	0.813	0.360	0.344	0.499	0.891	0.631	0.288
Services	2011	0.385	0.145	0.885	0.173	−0.212	0.450	0.157	0.858	0.251	−0.199
SDP	2011		0.286					0.242			
Agriculture	2012	0.153	0.196	0.218	0.020	−0.133	0.207	0.241	0.640	0.128	−0.078
Industry	2012	0.456	0.548	0.981	0.764	0.308	0.351	0.511	0.900	0.648	0.298
Services	2012	0.391	0.192	0.925	0.216	−0.175	0.443	0.146	0.858	0.224	−0.219
SDP	2012		0.321					0.249			
Agriculture	2013	0.161	0.198	0.212	0.024	−0.137	0.211	0.231	0.676	0.135	−0.076
Industry	2013	0.420	0.507	0.964	0.714	0.294	0.333	0.502	0.871	0.597	0.264
Services	2013	0.419	0.195	0.925	0.263	−0.157	0.456	0.161	0.892	0.268	−0.188

dSDP	2013		0.288					0.244			
Agriculture	2014	0.169	0.205	0.186	0.025	−0.144	0.210	0.241	0.643	0.132	−0.078
Industry	2014	0.395	0.475	0.941	0.678	0.283	0.331	0.502	0.883	0.596	0.265
Services	2014	0.437	0.189	0.939	0.298	−0.139	0.459	0.162	0.903	0.272	−0.187
SDP	2014		0.260					0.246			
Agriculture	2015	0.167	0.226	0.117	0.016	−0.151	0.222	0.261	0.730	0.165	−0.057
Industry	2015	0.422	0.487	0.979	0.713	0.291	0.342	0.485	0.916	0.592	0.250
Services	2015	0.412	0.196	0.951	0.271	−0.140	0.437	0.159	0.902	0.244	−0.193
SDP	2015		0.282					0.257			
Agriculture	2016	0.154	0.227	0.104	0.012	−0.142	0.209	0.256	0.707	0.144	−0.065
Industry	2016	0.434	0.510	0.987	0.716	0.282	0.352	0.487	0.921	0.599	0.248
Services	2016	0.412	0.208	0.973	0.272	−0.139	0.439	0.170	0.907	0.257	−0.182
SDP	2016		0.305					0.263			
Agriculture	2017	0.145	0.199	0.158	0.014	−0.131	0.199	0.229	0.750	0.127	−0.072
Industry	2017	0.448	0.523	0.996	0.735	0.287	0.361	0.498	0.945	0.631	0.270
Services	2017	0.407	0.202	0.967	0.250	−0.156	0.440	0.166	0.888	0.242	−0.198
SDP	2017		0.317					0.269			
Agriculture	2018	0.140	0.170	0.135	0.010	−0.129	0.189	0.194	0.781	0.104	−0.085
Industry	2018	0.453	0.515	0.998	0.744	0.290	0.375	0.513	0.948	0.660	0.286
Services	2018	0.407	0.195	0.973	0.246	−0.161	0.436	0.160	0.933	0.236	−0.200
SDP	2018		0.313					0.276			
Agriculture	2019	0.138	0.203	0.189	0.016	−0.121	0.189	0.231	0.801	0.121	−0.068
Industry	2019	0.460	0.529	0.999	0.752	0.292	0.372	0.522	0.951	0.640	0.268
Services	2019	0.402	0.193	0.964	0.231	−0.171	0.438	0.172	0.914	0.239	−0.200
SDP	2019		0.323					0.289			
Agriculture	2020	0.141	0.211	0.129	0.013	−0.128	0.186	0.242	0.769	0.117	−0.069
Industry	2020	0.430	0.501	1.000	0.715	0.285	0.355	0.518	0.959	0.597	0.242
Services	2020	0.430	0.200	0.953	0.272	−0.158	0.459	0.195	0.943	0.286	−0.173
SDP	2020		0.301					0.295			

agriculture has declined and that for industry and services has broadly increased during the study period, albeit with intermittent fluctuations.

SS

For the group of smaller states, we find that income from both agriculture and services sector contributed to lowering inequality for all the years under study. Only income from industry accentuated inequality. Among the three sectors, inequality was the highest for industry reflected through the source Gini in the range of 0.48–0.54 as compared to 0.16–0.24 for agriculture and 0.13–0.20 for services (Table 3.5b). As far as contribution to income inequality is concerned, industry contributed the most.

NE

The services sector had a sobering effect on inequality for all the years under study. Income from agriculture also contributed to lowering inequality for 15 out of 20 years under study. Except for the year 2001, we find income from industry increased inequality (Table 3.5b). In the post 2008 period, source Gini was highest for industry and the Gini correlation between industry and total income was also very high suggesting that income from industry benefits the wealthy more. Thus, industrial income had an adverse impact on income inequality.

Intra-state Inequality

The district level income is available for 12 states till the year 2011–12. The district income data were available in two different bases viz, 1999–00 and 2004–05. We have spliced the data to convert district income for all the years in the 2004–05 base. The Gini coefficient suggests that inter-district or intra state inequality worsened in 2012 as compared to 2001. The increase in inequality has been secular in nature for all the 12 states.

Thus, we find there has been deterioration in inter-state as well as intra-state inequality.

VI Convergence of income-select review of literature

Convergence among states

There is a vast body of literature to assess the convergence of income across Indian states. Recently, there has been an attempt to also study the convergence in the major sources of growth across Indian states

(Misra et al., 2022b). We discuss below the key findings from some of the recent studies that have investigated convergence of income. The analysis of the standard deviation of log of per capita income across states clearly indicates absence of sigma convergence in the post-2000 period (Misra, 2013). In addition to sigma convergence, most empirical studies employ the growth regression approach using either cross-section or panel data to analyse absolute and conditional convergence. Most studies find lack of absolute convergence. However, evidence is found in favour of conditional convergence by many studies. Conditional convergence is obtained by several studies after controlling for several factors including agriculture, infrastructure, investment, and political and institutional factors (Nagaraj et al., 1998; Aiyar, 2001); financial factors (Singh and Srinivasan, 2002); social and geographic variables (Sachs et al., 2002); educational and non-educational human capital and physical capital (Trivedi, 2002; Mallick, 2014); credit growth, male literacy, and share of agriculture (Nagaraj et al., 1998; Aiyar, 2001); the growth of production inputs and technology (Agarwalla and Pangotra, 2011); credit growth, male literacy, and share of agriculture (Cherodian et al., 2015). Misra et al. (2021) provide a comprehensive summary of the findings from different studies on convergence of income across Indian states. While majority of the studies have tested for conditional convergence, Ghosh et al. (2013) have explored the possibility of club convergence among Indian states. Using the notion of club convergence suggested by Phillips and Sul's (2007), Ghosh et al. (2013) find evidence in favour of convergence clubs among Indian states for the period 1969–2009.

We find that in the last decade, some studies have examined stochastic convergence of income for Indian states. Stochastic convergence is studied by investigating if the relative income series exhibits mean reversion from panel unit root tests. A key study in this context is by Das (2012) which analyses convergence in per capita real state domestic product (SDP), rural monthly per capita consumption expenditure (MPCE), and urban monthly per capita consumption expenditure (MPCE) in 14 large states for the period 1981 to 2007. Das (2012) finds convergence in urban MPCE and divergence in per capita SDP and rural MPCE using unit root tests with either cross-section dependency or structural breaks. The findings of Das (2012) were based on two different sets of unit root tests viz, one with cross-section dependency and another with structural breaks for these three variables. Not using a unified framework that addresses both cross-section dependency and structural breaks while testing for unit root tests was a limitation of the study by Das (2012).

Mishra and Mishra (2018) tried to overcome the limitations of Das (2012) by using unit root test developed by Bai and Carrion-i-Silverstre

(2009) that are robust to cross-section dependency and multiple endogenous structural breaks. This study found evidence in favour of divergence amongst 17 major Indian states over a fairly long period of 1960–2012 when only cross-section dependency was considered and structural breaks were ignored. However, when multiple break points that are determined endogenously along with cross-section dependency was considered, Mishra and Mishra (2018) found that relative per capita income amongst 17 states were converging. However, the findings of Mishra and Mishra (2018) that relative per capita income is converging have been contested in a recent study by Misra et al. (2022a). Both Das (2012) and Mishra and Mishra (2018) used a panel unit root testing methodology based on the assumption that structural breaks are sharp, meaning that income levels are subject to sudden breaks that are captured by dummy variables. The sharp breaks assumption also necessitates a priori knowledge of the number of structural breaks in the series (one or two). Misra et al. (2022) argues that a more realistic approach would be to model structural changes in the income series as a gradual or smooth process.

Recent works on unit root testing procedures contends that economic series may contain several smooth breaks at unknown dates that dummy variables may not represent properly and offer novel tests that allow for gradual structural shifts using a Fourier approximation (see Becker et al., 2006; Enders and Lee, 2012a, 2012b; Rodrigues and Taylor, 2012). Misra et al. (2022a) provide several reasons why it is appropriate to model structural breaks as smooth processes. For instance, growth-friendly policies may be announced on a particular date, but the announcement is often made after extensive consultation with stakeholders and after giving them ample lead time to make the necessary adjustments. Further, when growth is adversely impacted by external shocks such as floods and earthquakes, the rebuilding effort that follows mitigates the negative impact on growth. The impact of natural disasters can also be perceived in a staggered fashion. Moreover, data typically display spikes in a year, suggesting that the shift occurred during that year. Data jumps are frequently caused by constraints in data measurement and reporting. The rise in GDP owing to a change in the base year is a good example of the sudden jumps in the data. Because of a change in the base year as well as a change in the computing process, GDP data can show substantial jumps. A good example is the dramatic increase in India's GDP growth from 5% to 6.9% in 2013–14 after the base year was changed from 2004–05 to 2012–13. Because of the constraints of a country's statistical system, the base year is not altered regularly. However, this does not change the fact that the economy is always changing. Mishra et al. (2022a) explored the post-reform convergence behaviour of 19 Indian states during the period 1994–2018 by using a unit root test that controls for structural breaks as smooth shift. This study does not find evidence in favour of convergence. This study attributes the reason for divergence to insufficient funds earmarked for the development of lagging states.

Given that the recent literature indicates stochastic divergence in income across Indian states, Misra et al. (2022b) have attempted to study whether factors inputs such as labour and capital or total factor productivity are responsible for divergence in income. They have tested for stochastic convergence of factor inputs and TFP for 15 states of India for the period 2001–15. They find divergence in labour, capital, as well as TFP. Misra et al. (2022b) attributed the divergence in capital to the inability of the low-income states to attract capital because of their poor infrastructure and a discouraging business climate. This study finds that high-income states are able to attract capital as well as have a higher TFP. Hence, investment in a sense depicts the enabling provisions to achieve higher levels of TFP growth. Migration which could result in convergence of the labour input is primarily an intra-district phenomenon. Relatively, lower share of inter-state migration in total migration may be responsible for divergence in the labour input.

District level convergence

While most studies of convergence in India are undertaken at the state level, there have been a few attempts to investigate convergence of income between districts. In the absence of readily available income data at the district level, some studies have examined the evolution of consumption inequality using data from the National Sample Survey Organization's Consumer Expenditure Surveys (Chakrabarty, 2009; Dubey, 2009). Nonetheless, two studies have investigated the convergence of per capita district income in specific states. Shaban (2006) used a growth regression framework to examine the convergence behaviour of per capita net state domestic product (NSDP) at 1993–94 prices for 30 districts of Maharashtra during 1994–2003. When estimating the growth regressions, Shaban (2006) took into account spillover effects. This study finds support for both sigma and beta convergence. However, another study by Dadibhavi (2019) on income of 27 districts of Karnataka for the period 2000–13 found neither sigma nor unconditional beta convergence. Dadibhavi (2019), however, found evidence in favour of conditional convergence after taking into account several control variables such as literacy rate, infant mortality rate (IMR), surfaced road length, net irrigated area as a percentage of net sown area, per capita commercial bank credit, and share of urban population.

In addition to the state-specific studies, there have been several attempts to analyse convergence of per capita district income across multiple states. Singh et al. (2014), for example, looked at the convergence of per capita district domestic product (DDP) for nine states viz, Andhra Pradesh, Karnataka, Kerala, Maharashtra, Punjab, Rajasthan, Tamil Nadu, Uttar Pradesh, and West Bengal in the 1990s. Several control variables were used in this study including population, road kilometres, literacy rate, credit, and deposit levels. Neither absolute convergence nor absolute divergence was found by Singh et al. (2014). However, this study found support for conditional convergence across the districts. Another study, Das et al. (2015), looked at convergence behaviour using data from 575 districts in India spread over 28 states between 2001 and 2008. Das et al. (2015) found evidence of absolute beta convergence for districts in Assam, Chhattisgarh, Kerala, and Rajasthan, as well as significant divergence for districts within Haryana, Odisha, and Uttar Pradesh, using cross-sectional growth regression. The combined estimates for all 575 districts showed unconditional beta divergence.

Some research studies have used luminosity data to infer about income convergence across districts. For instance, Chakravarty and Deheja (2017) have used luminosity data to estimate intra-state income convergence in 12 Indian states. The authors extend the observed association between luminosity and income at the state level to estimate income convergence at the district level. Chakravarty and Deheja (2017) find evidence of income divergence among districts within a state by analysing the evolution of luminosity sigma. Inter-district disparity has risen in 10 of the 12 states studied between 1992 and 2013, according to their findings. Though the authors do not assert that higher income leads to greater intra-state inequality, they do suggest that such a link exists and it should be investigated.

Recently, Misra et al. (2020) have investigated stochastic convergence of district income in 12 large states of India during the period 2001–11. Districts within a state have structural similarities. As such, districts of a given states form a natural basis for clustering. Nonetheless, due to the enormous geographical size and population of some Indian states, it is possible that all districts within a state need not share similar initial conditions. Given the data constraints at the district level and the need to use relevant indicators to control for initial conditions, Misra et al. (2020) have clustered districts selected from different states that share similar attributes such as production structure, financial development, human capital, and educational infrastructure. Misra et al. (2020) find lack of convergence among districts with identical structural characteristics or initial conditions. The absence of convergence is a policy concern, given the policy focus on districts to promote balanced regional development. The lack of conditional stochastic convergence according to Misra et al. (2020) is due to deteriorating economic and social infrastructure in the backward districts of the states. The findings suggest that the post-2000 district-focused policies did not appear to have improved the capabilities of backward districts and, hence, did not serve the cause of balanced regional development.

References

Agarwalla, A., and Pangotra, P. (2011). *Regional Income Disparities in India and Test for Convergence-1980 to 2006.* Indian Institute of Management, Ahmadabad, Working Paper No. 2011-01-04.

Aiyar, S. (2001). Growth Theory and Convergence across Indian States: A Panel Study. *Chapter 8 in India at the Crossroads: Sustaining Growth and Reducing Poverty,* ed. Tim Callen, Patricia Reynolds and Christopher Towe, International Monetary Fund. Washington, pp. 143–69

Bai, J., and Carrion-I-Silvestre, J.L. (2009). Structural Changes, Common Stochastic Trends, and Unit Roots in Panel Data, *The Review of Economic Studies,* Vol. 76, No. 2, pp. 471–501.

Becker, R., Enders, W., and Lee, J. (2006). A Stationarity Test in the Presence of an Unknown Number of Smooth Breaks, *Journal of Time Series Analysis,* Vol. 27, pp. 381–409.

Chakravarty, P., and Dehejia, V. (2017). Will GST Exacerbate Regional Divergence?, *Economic & Political Weekly,* Vol. 52, No. 25–26, pp. 97–102.

Chakraborty, P. (2009). Intra-Regional Inequality and the Role of Public Policy: Lessons Learnt from Kerala, *Economic and Political Weekly,* Vol. XLIV, No. 26 and 27, pp. 274–281.

Cherodian, R., and Thirlwall, A.P. (2015). Regional Disparities in Per Capita Income in India: Convergence or Divergence? *Journal of Post Keynes Economics,* Vol. 37, No. 3, pp. 384–407.

Dadibhavi, R.V. (2019). Regional Disparities, Growth and Divergence in Income in Karnataka, *Review of Development and Change,* Vol. 24, No. 1, pp. 55–78.

Das, S. (2012). The Convergence Debate and Econometric Approaches: Evidence from India. In *The Oxford Handbook of the Indian Economy,* ed. C. Ghate, pp. 766–782, Oxford University Press, New York.

Das, S., Ghate, C., and Robertson, P.E. (2015). Remoteness, Urbanization and India's Unbalanced Growth, *World Development,* Vol. 66, No. C, pp. 572–587.

Dubey, A. (2009). Intra-state Disparities in Gujarat, Haryana, Kerala, Orissa and Punjab, *Economic and Political Weekly,* Vol. XLIV, No. 6, pp. 224–230.

Enders, W., and Lee, J. (2012a). A Unit Root Test Using a Fourier Series to Approximate Smooth Breaks, *Oxford Bulletin of Economics and Statistics,* Vol. 74, pp. 574–599.

Enders, W., and Lee, J. (2012b). The Flexible Fourier form and Dickey-Fuller Type Unit Root Tests, *Economics Letters,* Vol. 117, pp. 196–199.

Ghosh, M., Ghoshray, A., and Malki, I. (2013). Regional Divergence and Club Convergence in India, *Economic Modelling*, Vol. 30, pp. 733–742. https://doi.org/10.1016/j.econmod.2012.10.008.

Ghosh, N., Saha, R., and Bhomick, S. (2019). *SDG Index and Ease of Doing Business in India: A Sub-National Study*. Occasional Papers, Observes Research Foundation June 2019.

Government of India. (2013). Twelfth Five Year Plan 2012-17. Planning Commission, Government of India, New Delhi, available at: https://niti.gov. in/planningcommission.gov.in/docs/plans/planrel/fiveyr/welcome.html.

Lerman, R., and Yitzkaki, S. (1985). Income Inequality Effects by Income Source: A New Approach and Applications to the United States, *The Review of Economics and Statistics*, Vol. 67, No. 1, pp. 151–156.

Mishra, A., and Mishra, V. (2018). Re-examination of Convergence Hypothesis Among Indian States in Panel Stationarity Testing Framework with Structural Breaks, *Appl Econ*, Vol. 50, No. 3, pp. 268–286.

Misra, B.S. (2013). *Revisiting Regional Growth Dynamics in India in the Post-economic Reforms Period*. Palgrave Macmillan, London.

Misra, B.S., Kar, M., Nazlioglu, S., and Karul, C. (2020). Income Convergence in Indian Districts: New Evidence from Panel Stationarity Test with Finite Time Dimension, *Journal of International Development Coauthored*, Vol. 32, No. 8, pp. 2020. https://doi.org/10.1002/jid.3502.

Misra, B.S., Kar, M., Nazlioglu, S., and Karul, C. (2022a). Income Convergence of Indian States in the Post-reform Period: Evidence from Panel Stationarity Tests With Smooth Structural Breaks, *Journal of the Asia Pacific Economy*, https://doi.org/10.1080/13547860.2021.2022352.

Misra, B.S., Nazlioglu, S., and Kucukkaplan, I. (2022b). Sources of Divergence in Income in Indian States, 2001–2015. *Development Policy Review*, Vol. 40, pp. e12594. https://doi.org/10.1111/dpr.12594.

Mallick, J. (2014). Regional Convergence of Economic Growth during Post-Reform Period in India, *The Singapore Economic Review*, Vol. 59, No. 2, pp. 1–18.

Nagaraj, R., Varoudakis, A., and Veganzones, M-A. (1998). Long-Run Growth Trends and Convergence across Indian States, *OECD Technical Paper No. 131*.

Phillips, P. C., and D. Sul. 2007. Transition Modeling and Econometric Convergence Tests. *Econometrica*, Vol. 75, No. 6, pp. 1771–1855. https://doi.org/10.1111/j.1468-0262.2007.00811.x.

Rodrigues, P., and Taylor, A.M.R. (2012). The Flexible Fourier form and Local GLS de-Trending Unit Root Tests, *Oxford Bulletin of Economics and Statistics*, Vol. 74, pp. 736–759.

Sachs, J., Bajpai, N., and Ramiah, A. (2002). Understanding Regional Economic Growth in India, *Asian Economic Papers*, Vol. 1, No. 3, pp. 32–62.

Shaban, A. (2006). Regional Structures, Growth and Convergence of Income in Maharashtra, *Economic and Political Weekly*, Vol. 41, No. 18, pp. 1803–1815.

Singh, N., and Srinivasan, T.N. (2002). *Indian Federalism, Economic Reform and Globalization*. Paper Prepared for CREDPR Project on Globalization and Comparative Federalism.

Singh, N., Kendall, Jain, R.K., and Chander, J. (2014). Regional Inequality in India in the 1990s: A District Level View, *Economic and Political Weekly*, Vol. XLIX, No. 15, pp. 71–76.

Shorrocks, A.F. (1982). 'Inequality Decomposition by Factor Components, *Econometrica*, Vol. 50, pp. 193–211.

Stark, O., Taylor, J.E., and Yitzhaki, S. (1986). Remittances and Inequality, *The Economic Journal*, Vol. 383, pp. 722–740.

Trivedi, K. (2002). *Regional Convergence and Catch-up in India between 1960 and 1992*. Nuffield College, University of Oxford University Press, New York.

4 Sources of growth in Indian States

I Introduction

Indian economy has grown at a compounded annual growth rate of 7.25% in the last two decades. This growth rate is much better when compared to per annum growth rate of 5.1% in the last seven decades between 1951 and 2021. Though India's growth rate has improved in the post-2000 period, it lacks the necessary pace to break out of the middle-income trap in the foreseeable future. This is because India's nominal per capita gross national product (GNP) was US$1927 in the year 2020. At around 7% per annum growth, it will take India around three decades to attain the threshold per capita GNI or GNP of US$12,696 to become a high-income country. However, if the pace of growth can accelerate to 10% per annum, a decade can be saved. A 10% growth rate may appear very high but is attainable with the relatively lower GNP compared to several countries.

Growth in output or income can come about from either increase in inputs or from improvements in productivity. Productivity growth is widely acknowledged in the literature as critical to achieve higher rates of growth on a long-term basis (Hall and Jones, 1999; Hulten, 2000; Isaksson, 2007; Kim and Loyoza, 2017; Kim and Park, 2018). Given its importance, several attempts have been made to estimate TFP growth (TFPG) for the Indian economy (Sivasubramonian, 2001; Pallikara, 2004; Virmani, 2004; Bosworth and Virmani, 2007; Gupta, 2008; Das et al., 2010; Goldar, 2014; Saha, 2014). The Goldar (2014) study as a part of the KLEMS project is the most comprehensive effort to estimate India's TFP growth. Goldar (2014) has estimated that TFPG for India improved to 2.3% between 2000 and 2008, compared to 1.1% between 1980 and 1999. Notwithstanding the various attempts to estimate TFPG for the Indian economy, there are very few studies that have estimated TFPG for Indian states. The estimation of TFPG for Indian states, however, is crucial since it will reveal resource usage efficiency and, hence, their potential to achieve higher growth

DOI: 10.4324/9781003278351-4

rates. From a different perspective, TFPG estimates will also provide insight into the ability of the relatively underdeveloped states to catch up to the wealthier states given the large disparity in income levels. This should also help lift the national growth rate. Notwithstanding its extensive scope, the KLEMS project does not give state-wise estimates of TFPG.

In this backdrop, the present chapter has undertaken TFPG estimates for the Indian states for the period 2001–18. The chapter is structured as follows. We review the literature on TFPG estimates for Indian states with a focus on the methodology used by them in Section II. Section III deliberates on the methodology used by us to compute TFPG in view of the limitations of the existing studies. We discuss the TFPG estimates for the entire period as well as in four sub periods corresponding to the tenure of the central government in Section IV. We also evaluate the sustainability of the growth process in the states in this section. Section V assesses whether an underdeveloped region in a large state achieves higher productivity growth if it is accorded the status of a separate state drawing on the experience of two states created in 2001. The concluding observations are provided in Section VI.

II Review of literature

Given the data constraints, only a few studies have attempted to estimate TFPG for Indian states. We could find two papers viz, Agarwal (2011) and Kumar and Managi (2012), that have estimated aggregate TFPG for Indian states. These two studies, however, are based on restrictive assumptions.

Aggarwal (2011) used the growth-accounting framework to estimate TFP for 27 states over the period 1981–2007. This study computed the sectoral capital–output ratio (COR) at the national level for different years using all-India sectoral capital stock data and net domestic product. Aggarwal (2011) assumed that the sectoral CORs estimated at the state level were the same as those computed at the national level. To assess the net capital stock in different sectors of a state, sectoral CORs were applied to net state domestic product (NSDP). Sectoral CORs were assigned to 13 broad sectors. The state-level capital stock was obtained by adding the sectoral capital stocks in the 13 sectors. Assuming that all states have the same capital–output ratio ignores state-specific characteristics and to that extent makes the study less useful.

Kumar and Managi (2012) used the perpetual inventory accumulation method (PIAM) to estimate TFPG for 14 states for the period 1994–2005. They used the approach of Nehru and Dhareswar (1993) to compute the capital stock series, which involves information on gross fixed capital formation (GFCF) and the rate of depreciation. Kumar and Managi (2012) used GFCF estimates from Lakhchaura (2004) for the years 1994–2000. They extrapolated the Lakhchaura (2004) estimates to compute capital stock for the period 2001–05. The capital stock series used by Kumar and Managi (2012) is less representative of the actual investment trends in the states because they have used extrapolated data for GFCF and a uniform depreciation rate for all states.

Trivedi (2004) employed the PIAM approach to estimate capital stock in the registered manufacturing sector for Indian states. PIAM requires a capital stock estimate in a benchmark year as well as investment in succeeding years. The capital stock in the registered manufacturing sector for India published by the Central Statistical Organization (CSO) for the year 1980–81 is used to calculate state-level capital stock in the benchmark year. The share of the states in the all-India fixed capital in manufacturing given by ASI is used to allocate the all-India capital stock to different states in 1980–81. Investment figures from ASI were used to calculate the capital stock in succeeding years. Trivedi (2004) was unable to compute the aggregate TFPG at the state level since investment data for agriculture and services is not available at the state level.

Government sources do not publish statistics on capital stock for Indian states. As such, empirical studies have employed a variety of techniques to estimate the capital stock each with its own set of limitations. We have attempted to overcome the shortcomings of previous research by employing a novel approach to obtain state-level capital stock and labour data in order to estimate TFPG for 18 states.

III Methodology for computing TFPG

To calculate the TFPG, we have employed the growth accounting framework. After deducting the contributions of labour and capital to growth, the TPFG estimate is obtained as a residual.

Assuming a two-input neoclassical production function with constant returns to scale, TFPG can be calculated as follows:

$$\Delta \ln(\mathrm{TFP}) = \Delta \ln(\mathrm{Y}) - (1 - \alpha_1)\, \Delta \ln(\mathrm{K}) - \alpha_1\, \Delta \ln(\mathrm{L}) \quad (1)$$

where Y is output, K is capital stock, and L is the workforce engaged in production activity.

Output at the national level is represented through gross domestic product (GDP) and at the state level through state domestic product (SDP). Both GDP and SDP are measured at factor cost at 2011–12 prices. Capital stock is also measured at 2011–12 prices. The parameters α_1 and $1 - \alpha_1$ denote the shares of labour and capital, respectively, in the output.

The method used by us for obtaining the capital stock, labour force, and factor shares is discussed next.

Capital stock estimation

To overcome the limitations associated with capital stock estimation in the existing studies, we have distributed sectoral capital stocks at the all-India level to the different states using a state's share of all-India fixed assets in the relevant sectors. For this purpose, we considered three broad sectors: agriculture, industry, and services. The all-India sectoral capital stock data for the period 2001–18 is available in three different base years. We have first used forward splicing to convert the sectoral capital stock data at the all-India level available in three different base years to the 2011–12 base.

In the second step, we have used state-wise fixed assets data in the three sectors from various NSSO surveys which are available in public domain. To calculate the state-wise share of the all-India capital stock in agriculture, we have used information on state-wise assets of rural cultivator household from the Situation Assessment Survey of Agricultural Households conducted by the National Sample Survey Office (NSSO) between January and December 2003 (NSSO, 2005) and January and December 2013 (NSSO, 2016). Thus, the state-wise share in fixed assets of cultivators is available for the years 2002 and 2013. Linear interpolation is used to calculate the share for the years 2003–12, while linear extrapolation is used to get the share for the years 2001–02 and 2014–15. We apply this share to the total agricultural capital stock in India to derive state-wise estimates.

State-wise capital stock in industry has been computed by using the data on state-wise fixed capital in different years published in ASI. We have apportioned the share of a state in the all-India fixed capital to the net capital stock in industry at the India level to get the state-level estimate of net stock of capital in Industry.

We have considered both organised and unorganised services to obtain the share of a state in the all-India capital stock in the services sector. State-wise fixed assets in the unorganised services from NSSO Survey are available for two years viz, 2002 (NSSO, 2003) and 2011 (NSSO, 2013). However, the state-wise fixed assets in the organised services are published by NSSO only for the year 2007 (NSSO, 2009). We have linearly interpolated the fixed assets in unorganised services between 2002 and 2011 to obtain the values for 2007. As such, we have the state-wise value of fixed assets in both the organised and unorganised services for the year 2007. The observed proportionality of fixed assets between organised and unorganised services sector for each state in the year 2007 is assumed to hold for all the years under study.

This gives us an estimate of fixed assets in the services sector by taking into account the organised as well as unorganised segments in each state during the study period. In the next step, we have computed the share of each state in the combined fixed assets of services sector for all the states and have applied these shares to the all-India capital stock in services to get the state-wise estimates. The state-wise capital stocks obtained for agriculture, industry, and services in the above manner are added to obtain the state-wise aggregate capital stock.

Labour force estimation

The worker participation rate (WPR) multiplied by the population of a state is used to estimate the labour force employed in the production process. The Census provided state-wise population numbers between 2001 and 2011, and we have used an exponential growth rate to compute population for the in between years. This population growth rate is also used to extrapolate the population from 2012 to 2018. The worker participation rate is available for each state from NSSO surveys for the years 1999–00, 2004–05, 2007–08, 2009–10, and 2011–12. It may be noted that in the 1999–00 survey, the NSSO did not provide a single WPR for each state but instead provided separate WPRs for the rural and urban sectors of each state. The share of rural and urban population in each state was calculated using data from the 2001 Census. To compute the state-level WPR for 1999–00, the weighted average WPR for rural and urban areas with population proportion of rural and urban areas in the 2001 Census was used as weights. The NSSO surveys on employment–unemployment have been replaced by the periodic labour force survey (PLFS). The first PLFS was undertaken by the National Statistical Office during July 2017 to June 2018. We have the state-wise WPR for 2017–18 from the first PLFS. Thus, we have WPR data for six years viz, 2001, 2005, 2008, 2010, 2012, and 2018, during our study period. We have apportioned the change in WPR between two years equally for the intervening years. We have assumed that the change in WPR remains constant between years until the findings of a fresh survey became available.

Output shares of labour and capital

We assume that labour and capital consume the entire output. As a result, once we have computed the share of labour in output, the share of capital is obtained as a residual. The national accounts statistics (NAS) published by CSO were used to calculate the share of labour in output. Share of labour in income has two components. The first component is the share of payment to employees in the National Domestic Product, which is published in the NAS. The share of labour in mixed income is the second component. The share of compensation paid to employees in the states is taken to be same as it was at the national level during the study period. Because data on mixed income is not reported in the NAS after 2000, calculating labour share in mixed income presents additional challenges. However, the NAS has published mixed income data for the years 1991 to 2000.

To determine the state-wise share of labour in mixed income, we used a three-step technique. In the first step, we calculated the average share of mixed income in total income from 1991 to 2000. Second, to calculate the share of labour in mixed income, we utilised the 2/3 rule of thumb employed in empirical investigations (Johnson, 1954; Rosés and Prado's de la Escosura, 2003; Guscina, 2006; Guerriero, 2012). Using this rule of thumb, we find that the average share of labour is 31.62%. In the absence of actual information, we have used 31.62% to represent the share of labour in mixed income in the states for the period 2001–16.

We modified the share of revenue accruing to labour from mixed income in different states in the third step. The adjusted share for a state in a given year is calculated by multiplying the constant share of 31.62% by an adjustment factor that reflects the importance of the services sector in the concerned state relative to all other states in that year. Because the services sector is relatively labour intensive, we have used it to adjust the mixed income. The adjustment factor for a given year is calculated by dividing the state's sectoral output share of services by the average sectoral output share of services for all of the states under consideration. The distribution of labour in mixed income across states is such that the average adjusted share for all states is the constant share of mixed income of 31.62%. The share of compensation to employees combined with the adjusted share of labour in mixed income gives the share of labour in state income.

We have estimated two sets of TFPG for the states. The unadjusted TFPG estimates use the constant or unadjusted share of labour in mixed income. Using the adjusted share of labour in mixed income share, we obtain the adjusted TFPG estimates.

IV Findings

During the entire period of study, labour, capital, and productivity growth contributed about 8%, 33%, and 59%, respectively, to the growth of State output. Seen across sub periods, contribution of labour to growth has declined successively from 2001–04 to 2015–18 (Table 4.1). In fact, labour contributed negatively to the growth of output during 2015–18. In contrast, contribution of capital to growth increased significantly from about 9% in 2001–04 to 36% during 2005–08 and further to 45% during

Table 4.1 Sources of Growth during 2001–18

(%)

State	Adjusted				Unadjusted			
	Output	Productivity	Labour	Capital	Output	Productivity	Labour	Capital
Andhra Pradesh	7.88	3.86	0.15	3.87	7.88	3.65	0.15	4.09
Bihar	6.67	4.36	0.22	2.1	6.67	3.71	0.19	2.77
Chhattisgarh	7.54	0.98	1.4	5.16	7.54	1.65	1.57	4.32
Gujarat	9.93	5.93	0.36	3.65	9.93	6.41	0.39	3.13
Haryana	8.72	5.5	0.81	2.42	8.72	5.57	0.83	2.32
Himachal Pradesh	7.41	3.99	0.57	2.84	7.41	4.31	0.63	2.47
Jammu and Kashmir	5.45	1.86	1.33	2.27	5.45	1.57	1.23	2.66
Jharkhand	6.72	2.41	0.99	3.32	6.72	2.74	1.08	2.9
Karnataka	7.7	5.54	0.4	1.76	7.7	4.96	0.35	2.38
Kerala	7	6.06	-0.36	1.3	7	5.64	-0.32	1.68
Madhya Pradesh	7.14	1.93	0.92	4.28	7.14	2.28	0.98	3.88
Maharashtra	7.94	5.51	0.7	1.73	7.94	5.3	0.66	1.99
Orissa	7.92	2.16	0.2	5.57	7.92	2.78	0.21	4.93
Punjab	5.96	4.62	0.29	1.05	5.96	4.65	0.29	1.01
Rajasthan	7.48	3.85	0.48	3.15	7.48	4.06	0.5	2.93
Tamil Nadu	7.74	5.14	0.49	2.12	7.74	4.87	0.46	2.41
Uttar Pradesh	6.16	2.37	0.59	3.2	6.16	2.39	0.6	3.18
Uttaranchal	10.54	10.81	0.77	-1.04	10.54	10.57	0.86	-0.89
West Bengal	5.83	2.7	1.12	2.01	5.83	2.64	1.1	2.1
India					7.25	4.26	0.57	2.42

2010–14. Subsequently, during 2015–18, contribution of capital has declined significantly to 29%. Accordingly, productivity growth which is a residual contributed more than 70% of the total growth during 2015–18.

It may be noted that our estimates of TFPG are much higher than that estimated from the KLEMS project of the RBI. This is partly due to the fact that we have obtained TFPG estimates as a residual after subtracting the contribution of only two factors of production viz, labour and capital. In contrast and more appropriately, TFPG estimates from the KLEMS project are obtained after excluding the contribution of energy, material, and services in addition to labour and capital. In a way, the contribution of energy, material, and services is embodied in our TFPG estimates for the states. Further, the capital stock data we have used have been computed by making several of assumptions which would also have an effect the TFPG estimates. In a way, our TFPG estimates reflect the absence of state-level data on key inputs in the growth process. Notwithstanding the limitations, the TFPG estimates computed by us help compare productivity growth across time and between states.

Eight States viz, Gujarat, Haryana, Karnataka, Kerala, Maharashtra, Punjab, Tamil Nadu, and Uttaranchal, had a TFPG higher than that for India during the entire study period. It is pertinent to note that Gujarat had the highest TFPG during 2001–04. Notwithstanding the successive decline in its productivity growth in the subsequent sub periods, Gujarat had the highest TFPG during 2001–18. Chhattisgarh and Madhya Pradesh are the two other states which also experienced a secular decline in their TFPG, albeit from relatively lower values of TFPG during 2001–04.

An analysis of the adjusted TFPG estimates across the different time periods (Annexures 4.1–4.4) reveals the following.

- Taking 2001–04 as the reference, the TFPG improved for 13 out of the 19 states during the relatively high growth period 2005–09. Three out of the six states which experienced a decline
- During 2010–14 when growth had decelerated, TFPG also declined for 13 states as compared to 2005–09.
- There was slight pickup in growth in the most recent period 2015–18. During this period, TFPG improved for 11 states as compared to that in 2010–14.
- Compared to 2001–04, TFPG declined successively in the next three sub periods for three states viz, Chhattisgarh, Gujarat, and Madhya Pradesh.
- Haryana and Uttar Pradesh were the only two states which have experienced a successive improvement in their TFPG in the subsequent three sub periods as compared to 2001–04.

Annexure 4.1 Sources of Growth during 2001–04

(%)

State	*Adjusted*				*Unadjusted*			
	Output	*Productivity*	*Labour*	*Capital*	*Output*	*Productivity*	*Labour*	*Capital*
Andhra Pradesh	5.43	2.4	1.25	1.78	5.43	2.34	1.22	1.87
Bihar	0.65	1.12	0.64	–1.11	0.65	1.69	0.55	–1.59
Chhattisgarh	9.89	4.49	3.05	2.36	9.89	4.53	3.31	2.05
Gujarat	10.44	8.56	2	-0.12	10.44	8.4	2.15	-0.1
Haryana	8.07	2.64	3.91	1.51	8.07	2.51	4.23	1.33
Himachal Pradesh	6.12	1.55	1.89	2.68	6.12	1.77	2.09	2.26
Jammu and Kashmir	4.09	1.37	1.14	1.57	4.09	1.2	1.06	1.83
Jharkhand	5.79	2.02	4.77	–1	5.79	1.12	5.47	-0.81
Karnataka	3.6	-0.56	3.05	1.11	3.6	-0.59	2.66	1.53
Kerala	6.24	5.76	0.8	-0.32	6.24	5.91	0.72	-0.4
Madhya Pradesh	4.87	3.73	1.52	-0.37	4.87	3.67	1.57	-0.36
Maharashtra	6.29	3.89	2.72	-0.33	6.29	4.15	2.52	-0.38
Orissa	6.93	1.66	2.12	3.15	6.93	1.84	2.26	2.83
Punjab	3.62	1.22	1.82	0.57	3.62	1.19	1.88	0.54
Rajasthan	9.88	8.19	1.84	-0.15	9.88	8.12	1.9	-0.14
Tamil Nadu	2.06	-0.98	2.02	1.02	2.06	-1.01	1.87	1.2
Uttar Pradesh	3.72	0.93	2.47	0.32	3.72	0.9	2.5	0.32
Uttaranchal	7.69	7.79	5.58	-5.67	7.69	6.78	5.97	-5.05
West Bengal	5.77	2.82	2.29	0.66	5.77	2.82	2.28	0.67
India					5.31	2.69	2.12	0.50

Source: Estimates by the Author.
Note: Andhra Pradesh represents both Andhra Pradesh and Telangana.

Annexure 4.2 Sources of Growth during 2005–09

(%)

State	*Adjusted*				*Unadjusted*			
	Output	*Productivity*	*Labour*	*Capital*	*Output*	*Productivity*	*Labour*	*Capital*
Andhra Pradesh	9.56	4.97	0.32	4.28	9.56	4.81	0.31	4.44
Bihar	9.35	9.16	0.78	–0.59	9.35	9.48	0.67	–0.8
Chhattisgarh	8.86	1.59	0.74	6.54	8.86	2.49	0.83	5.55
Gujarat	10	6.97	0.35	2.67	10	7.25	0.38	2.37
Haryana	9.09	2.72	1.09	5.28	9.09	2.98	1.13	4.98
Himachal Pradesh	8.21	1.18	0.37	6.66	8.21	1.96	0.41	5.84
Jammu and Kashmir	5.97	–0.19	1.91	4.25	5.97	–0.68	1.77	4.88
Jharkhand	6.63	3.54	0.2	2.89	6.63	3.92	0.22	2.49
Karnataka	10.01	6.53	0.39	3.09	10.01	5.47	0.34	4.21
Kerala	8.46	7.16	–0.16	1.45	8.46	6.74	–0.14	1.86
Madhya Pradesh	6.96	3.4	0.5	3.05	6.96	3.59	0.52	2.85
Maharashtra	9.88	7.26	0.8	1.82	9.88	7.04	0.74	2.1
Orissa	10.08	1.81	0.38	7.89	10.08	2.73	0.41	6.94
Punjab	7.19	3.39	0.07	3.73	7.19	3.57	0.07	3.54
Rajasthan	6.15	2.12	0.61	3.41	6.15	2.29	0.64	3.22
Tamil Nadu	10.44	7.13	0.16	3.15	10.44	6.58	0.14	3.72
Uttar Pradesh	6.86	1.52	0.42	4.92	6.86	1.6	0.42	4.83
Uttaranchal	14.34	14.35	0.62	–0.63	14.34	14.2	0.68	–0.54
West Bengal	6.73	3.73	1.06	1.94	6.73	3.77	1.08	1.88
India					6.90	3.10	0.53	3.27

Source: Estimates by the Author.
Note: Andhra Pradesh represents both Andhra Pradesh and Telangana.

Annexure 4.3 Sources of Growth during 2010–14

(%)

State	*Adjusted*				*Unadjusted*			
	Output	*Productivity*	*Labour*	*Capital*	*Output*	*Productivity*	*Labour*	*Capital*
Andhra Pradesh	6.26	1.36	−0.22	5.12	6.26	1.09	−0.21	5.38
Bihar	7.92	4.79	−0.29	3.41	7.92	3.8	−0.26	4.37
Chhattisgarh	6.95	0.92	1.4	4.62	6.95	1.54	1.58	3.82
Gujarat	9.27	4.66	0.1	4.51	9.27	5.33	0.11	3.84
Haryana	8.66	7.38	−0.74	2.02	8.66	7.39	−0.74	2.02
Himachal Pradesh	7.53	4.19	0.77	2.58	7.53	4.44	0.84	2.25
Jammu and Kashmir	5.28	2.32	0.73	2.23	5.28	1.93	0.67	2.68
Jharkhand	8.05	2.61	0.45	4.98	8.05	3.13	0.49	4.43
Karnataka	6.16	5.13	−0.64	1.66	6.16	4.53	−0.56	2.19
Kerala	6.46	4.97	−0.35	1.84	6.46	4.3	−0.31	2.47
Madhya Pradesh	7.94	0.47	0.54	6.93	7.94	1.21	0.58	6.15
Maharashtra	7.61	5.21	0.04	2.37	7.61	4.9	0.03	2.68
Orissa	6.23	−0.74	0.02	6.96	6.23	0.1	0.02	6.11
Punjab	6.26	4.74	0.43	1.08	6.26	4.77	0.44	1.04
Rajasthan	8.19	3.99	0.28	3.92	8.19	4.34	0.29	3.56
Tamil Nadu	8.86	5.32	0.35	3.19	8.86	4.95	0.33	3.58
Uttar Pradesh	6.1	2.03	0.47	3.61	6.1	2.02	0.47	3.61
Uttaranchal	10.65	10.49	−0.7	0.86	10.65	10.74	−0.79	0.7
West Bengal	5.14	1.7	1.09	2.36	5.14	1.47	1.02	2.65
India					6.18	2.96	0.22	3.01

Source: Estimates by the Author.
Note: Andhra Pradesh represents both Andhra Pradesh and Telangana.

Annexure 4.4 Sources of Growth during 2015–18

(%)

State	*Adjusted*				*Unadjusted*			
	Output	*Productivity*	*Labour*	*Capital*	*Output*	*Productivity*	*Labour*	*Capital*
Andhra Pradesh	9.66	6.66	−0.44	3.43	9.66	6.29	−0.42	3.78
Bihar	6.29	0.04	−0.16	6.42	6.29	-1.64	−0.14	8.07
Chhattisgarh	4.87	-2.79	1.04	6.62	4.87	-1.58	1.21	5.24
Gujarat	10.29	3.91	−0.49	6.87	10.29	5.32	−0.56	5.54
Haryana	8.84	8.55	−0.16	0.45	8.84	8.52	−0.15	0.47
Himachal Pradesh	7.20	8.65	−0.43	-1.01	7.2	8.55	−0.47	−0.88
Jammu and Kashmir	6.05	3.96	1.43	0.66	6.05	3.94	1.32	0.78
Jharkhand	5.57	1.36	−0.84	5.04	5.57	1.66	−0.86	4.77
Karnataka	9.8	9.17	−0.24	0.87	9.8	8.8	−0.21	1.21
Kerala	6.41	6.42	-1.56	1.54	6.41	5.70	-1.37	2.08
Madhya Pradesh	8.06	0.13	1.5	6.43	8.06	0.97	1.66	5.43
Maharashtra	7.17	4.83	−0.09	2.43	7.17	4.47	−0.08	2.78
Orissa	8.09	6.19	-1.28	3.17	8.09	6.62	-1.36	2.84
Punjab	5.82	8.11	−0.8	-1.49	5.82	8.11	−0.80	-1.49
Rajasthan	6.48	2.41	−0.46	4.53	6.48	2.86	−0.49	4.11
Tamil Nadu	7.23	6.86	−0.05	0.41	7.23	6.83	−0.04	0.44
Uttar Pradesh	7.21	4.75	−0.46	2.91	7.21	4.72	−0.46	2.94
Uttaranchal	7.79	8.54	−0.61	−0.14	7.79	8.59	−0.69	−0.12
West Bengal	5.63	2.79	0.32	2.52	5.63	2.58	0.30	2.74
India					6.84	4.77	−0.12	2.19

Source: Estimates by the Author.
Note: Andhra Pradesh represents both Andhra Pradesh and Telangana.

TFPG and sustainability of growth process

One way to assess the sustainability of the growth process in a state is to compare the growth of its capital input with that of TFPG. TFPG falling short of growth of capital suggests that the production process is more resource intensive. In such a situation, sustainability of the growth process becomes an area of concern. We find that seven out of the 19 states failed to meet the sustainability criterion during the period 2001–18. These seven states viz, Andhra Pradesh, Chhattisgarh, Jammu and Kashmir, Jharkhand, Madhya Pradesh, Odisha, and Uttar Pradesh experienced a TFP growth less than that of the growth in the capital input used by them.

During the 2015–18 period when TFP growth was highest compared to other sub periods, we find seven states viz, Bihar, Chhattisgarh, Gujarat, Jharkhand, Madhya Pradesh, Rajasthan, and West Bengal had growth in capital input much higher than their productivity growth. When we compare across the sub periods, we find only in four states viz, Kerala, Maharashtra, Punjab, and Uttaranchal, the TFP growth was higher than that of capital in all the sub periods. In the rest 15 states, capital input grew higher than TFPG in one or more sub periods.

V Productivity growth as an argument for creation of new states

Three new states viz, Jharkhand, Chhattisgarh, and Uttaranchal were created from Bihar, Madhya Pradesh, and Uttar Pradesh, respectively, in the year 2001 as a part of administrative reorganisation.

Economic backwardness despite abundance of natural resources was one of the chief arguments for creating two out of the three newly created states. It was argued that creation of the new states would lead to better governance, effective resource utilisation and would help to meet the developmental needs of the marginalised segments in those states.[1] It was thought that because of their large size, Bihar and Madhya Pradesh could not respond effectively to the development aspiration of the tribals who were concentrated in certain pockets of these states. Specifically, southern Bihar and eastern part of Madhya Pradesh had higher concentration of tribal population and were relatively more underdeveloped despite better natural resource endowment. It was argued that these sub-regions could not develop as they did not receive the required attention of policymakers of the concerned states. It was believed that by creating new states, administrative efficacy will improve, resource utilisation will get focused attention, and growth prospects would improve.

Did the administrative reorganisation lead to higher productivity growth for the parent as well as the newly created states? The TFPG estimates can be used to assess how productivity growth evolved in the parent state vis-à-vis the new states.

It is observed that the newly created states had slightly better growth of SDP than their parent states during 2001–18. However, the slightly higher SDP growth was driven by more intensive use of both labour and capital inputs than improvement in productivity. This can be seen from the fact that capital input grew by 4.3% in Chhattisgarh compared to 3.8% in Madhya Pradesh during 2001–18 (Table 4.1). Similarly, capital in Jharkhand grew by 2.9% compared to 2.8% for Bihar. We find that during the entire period of study, the parent state of Bihar and Madhya Pradesh had a higher TFPG compared to the newly carved out states Jharkhand and Chhattisgarh, respectively. We could not find evidence to support the argument that resource utilisation will improve as a smaller administrative unit would get focussed attention for development. These findings suggest that solution to the development challenges, perhaps, needs to be seen beyond administrative reorganisation.

VI Conclusion

Few studies have attempted to estimate productivity growth in Indian states. We estimated productivity growth in 19 major Indian states from 2001 to 2015 using the growth accounting framework. A mix of NSSO Survey and Census data was utilised to derive state-wise estimates of labour and capital stock in three broad sectors to compute the TFPG. To compute aggregate capital stock and labour used in the production process for each of the 19 states, we added capital stock and workers employed in agriculture, industry, and services. Factor shares in the output were obtained from NAS data.

TFPG estimates indicated that, between 2001 and 2018, the new states of Jharkhand and Chhattisgarh did not have a higher TFPG than their parent states of Bihar and Madhya Pradesh, respectively. As a result, the argument that smaller administrative regions lead to higher productivity growth does not appear to have held true for Jharkhand and Chhattisgarh in their first 15 years of existence.

Our findings suggest that productivity growth has improved significantly in the 2015–18 period. As discussed in Chapter 1, the initiatives taken by the Government to reduce transaction costs and expand financial access in the initial years of its office would have contributed to the higher productivity. Further, certain reforms including the bankruptcy Code, the GST, and the Labour Codes, which when stabilise can contribute to higher productivity growth in the medium-term and help India achieve a 10% per annum growth in the next two decades.

Note

1 Creation of Uttarakhand was guided by considerations other than economic backwardness. Retaining cultural identity in the Kumaon and Garhwal Hilly regions of Uttar Pradesh rather than overcoming economic backwardness was the basis for creation of Uttarakhand. This is because the Hilly regions of Kumaon and Garhwal districts which became part of Uttarakhand had better economic and social development compared to the rest of the districts in Uttar Pradesh. Uttaranchal the newly carved out state had a higher TFPG than Uttar Pradesh in the entire period of study as well as in both the sub periods.

References

Agarwalla, Astha. (2011). Estimating the Contribution of Infrastructure in Regional Productivity Growth in India, *Working Paper No. WP2011-05-01*, Indian Institute of Management Ahmedabad, India.

Bosworth, B., Collins, S. and Virmani, A. (2007). Sources of Growth in Indian Economy, *Working Paper No. 12901*, NBER, Cambridge, MA.

Das, D.K., Erumban, A.A., Agarwal, S. and Wadhwa, D. (2010). Total Factor Productivity Growth in the Reform Period: A Disaggregated Sectoral Analysis, *Paper Presented in the 1st World KLEMS Conference at Harvard University*, Cambridge, Massachusetts.

Goldar, B.N. (2014). Estimates of Productivity Growth for the Indian Economy, India KLEMS project by ICRIER in collaboration with the Reserve Bank of India.

Guerriero, M. (2012). The Labour Share of Income Around the World Evidence from a Panel Data Set, *Development Economics and Public Policy Working Paper Series of Global Development Institute*, Manchester, UK.

Gupta, A. (2008). Indian Economy-TFP or Factor Accumulation: A Comprehensive Growth Accounting Exercise, *Working Paper Series*, University of British Columbia, Vancouver, Canada.

Hall, R.E. and Jones, C.I. (1999). Why do Some Countries Produce So Much More Output Per Worker Than others? *Quarterly Journal of Economics*, Vol. 114, No. 1, pp. 83–116.

Hulten, Charles R. (2000). Total Factor Productivity: A Short Biography, *NBER Working Papers 7471*, National Bureau of Economic Research, Inc. Cambridge, MA.

Isaksson, A. (2007). Determinants of Total Factor Productivity: A Literature Review, *Research and Statistics Branch, UNIDO*, Vienna, available at: http://www.rrojasdatabank.info/87573_determinants_of_total_factor_productivity.pdf (accessed 7 July 2018).

Johnson, D.G. (1954). The Functional Distribution of Income in the United States, 1850–1952, *Review of Economics and Statistics*, Vol. 36, No. 2, pp. 175–182.

Kim, Jungsuk and Park, Jungsoo. (2018). The Role of Total Factor Productivity Growth in Middle-Income Countries, *Emerging Markets Finance and Trade*, Vol. 54, No. 6, pp. 1264–1284.

Kim, Young Eun and Loayza, Norman V. (2017). Productivity and its Determinants: Innovation, Education, Efficiency, Infrastructure, and Institutions, *DECRG Kuala Lumpur Seminar Series*, World Bank, Malaysia.

Kumar, Surender and Managi, Shunsuke. (2012). Productivity and Convergence in India: State Level Analysis, *Journal of Asian Economics*, Vol. 23, No. 5, pp. 548–559.

Lakhchaura, P. (2004). Capital Formation at State Level, *New Delhi: Ministry of Statistics and Programme Implementation*, Government of India, mimeo.

Manchester.Guscina, A. (2006). Effects of Globalization on Labor's Share in National Income, *Working Paper No. 06/294*, IMF, Washington.

NSSO (2019). Annual Report, Periodic Labour Force Survey, 2017–18 (July 2017–June 2018), National Statistical Office, Ministry of Statistics and Programme Implementation Government of India (May 2019).

NSSO (2001). Employment and Unemployment Situation in India, 1999–2000, NSS Report No. 458, NSS 55th Round (July 1999–June 2000), NSSO, Ministry of Statistics and Programme Implementation, Government of India, May 2001.

NSSO (2003). Unorganised Services Sector in India, 2001–02 Salient Features, NSSO Report No. 482, NSS 57th Round (July 2001–June 2002), NSSO, Ministry of Statistics and Programme Implementation, Government of India, August 2003.

NSSO (2005). Situation Assessment Survey of Farmers, Indebtedness of Farmer Households, NSS 59th Round (January–December 2003), NSSO, Ministry of Statistics and Programme Implementation, Government of India, May 2005.

NSSO (2006). Employment and Unemployment Situation in India, 2004–05, NSS Report No. 515, NSS 61th Round (July 2004–June 2005), NSSO, Ministry of Statistics and Programme Implementation, Government of India, September 2006.

NSSO (2009). Service Sector in India, 2006–07, Economic Characteristics of Enterprises, NSS Report No. 529, NSS 63rd Round, NSSO, Ministry of Statistics and Programme Implementation, Government of India, September 2009.

NSSO (2011). Employment and Unemployment Situation in India, 2004–05, NSS Report No. 537, NSS 66th Round (July 2009–June 2010), NSSO, Ministry of Statistics and Programme Implementation, Government of India, November 2011.

NSSO (2013). Economic Characteristics of Unincorporated Non Agricultural Enterprises (Excluding Construction) in India, NSS 67TH Round (July 2010–June 2011), NSSO, Ministry of Statistics and Programme Implementation, Government of India, February 2013.

NSSO (2014). Employment and Unemployment Situation in India, 2004–05, NSS Report No. 554, NSS 68th Round (July 2011–June 2012), NSSO, Ministry of Statistics and Programme Implementation, Government of India, January 2014.

NSSO (2016). Income, Expenditure, Productive Assets and Indebtedness of Agricultural Households in India, Report No. 576, NSS 70th Round (January–December 2013), NSSO, Ministry of Statistics and Programme Implementation, Government of India, April 2016

Pallikara, R. (2004). National Report- India. In *Measuring Total Factor Productivity: Survey Report*, Asian Productivity Organization, Tokyo, pp. 52–97. https://www.apo-tokyo.org/wp-content/uploads/2014/07/ind-04-tfpg.pdf.

Rosés, Joan R. and Prados de la Escosura, Leandro. (2003). Wages and Labor Income in History: A Survey, *IFCS - Working Papers in Economic History*, Universidad Carlos III de Madrid, Instituto Figuerola.

Saha, S. (2014). Total Factor Productivity in India- A Conventional Approach, *The NEHU Journal*, Vol. XII, No.1. pp. 95–106.

Sivasubramonian, S. (2004). *The Sources of Economic Growth in India, 1950–51 to 1999–2000*. Oxford University Press, New Delhi.

Trivedi Pushpa. (2004). An Inter-State Perspective on Manufacturing Productivity in India: 1980–81 to 2000–01, *Indian Economic Review*, New Series, Vol. 39, No. 1, pp. 203–237.

Virmani, A. (2004). Sources of India's Economic Growth: Trends in Total Factor Productivity, *Working Paper No. 131*, ICRIER, New Delhi.

5 Determinants of productivity

I Introduction

In the development literature, the relevance of infrastructure in driving economic growth is well recognised. Several studies, beginning with Aschauer (1989), have confirmed relatively high elasticity of output to infrastructure (Munnell, 1990; Nadiri and Mamuneas, 1994). Aschauer (1989) found a very high elasticity of gross domestic output to total public capital (0.34) in the United States. Subsequent time series studies on the United States using different samples or refined approaches confirmed the high elasticity of output to infrastructure (Munnell, 1990; Nadiri and Mamuneas, 1994). However, spatial analysis undertaken in several studies for US regions have reported a relatively lower impact on output (Hulten and Schwab, 1991; Romp and de Haan, 2007).

Beyond the United States, evidence from cross-country studies on the impact of infrastructure on broad macroeconomic aggregates like output, growth, and productivity, using a variety of data, empirical methodologies, and infrastructure measures, also indicates that infrastructure makes a positive contribution (Estache, 2006; Romp and de Haan, 2007; Straub, 2008). Despite the general conclusion that infrastructure has a beneficial impact on growth, the degree of its impact varies depending on the country's level of development, the time period over which the impact is measured, and the type of infrastructure (Estache and Garsous, 2012).

In addition to its impact on output, several attempts have been made to discern the impact of infrastructure on productivity growth (Isaksson, 2007; Loko and Diouf, 2009; Kim and Loyola, 2017; Kim and Park, 2017, 2018; van Ark, 2017). Isaksson (2007) provides a survey of cross-country studies conducted between 1990 and 2005 to determine the infrastructure categories that drive total factor productivity growth (TFPG) in emerging countries. This survey found that (a) health should

DOI: 10.4324/9781003278351-5

take precedence over education, (b) the quality of education is just as important as the level of education, (c) public investment in infrastructure does not significantly crowd out private investment, and (d) management of public capital should be given higher priority. Kim and Loyola (2017) found physical infrastructure, education, and market efficiency to be the primary predictors of productivity in their study spanning 65 nations from 1985 to 2011. Market efficiency refers to the ability of the financial system to direct resources to the most worthy sectors and initiatives, resulting in increased productivity. As a measure of market efficiency, Kim and Loyola (2017) used the International Monetary Fund's Financial Development Index. Based on the experience of 62 countries from 1970 to 2005, further, Kim and Park (2017) found that infrastructure, whether economic, social, or financial growth, plays a crucial role, in influencing productivity.

More importantly, Hulten and Isaksson (2007) suggest that different types of infrastructure are important at different phases of development in influencing growth and productivity from their analysis of income and productivity differences among 112 countries from 1970 to 2000.

Since the mid-1990s, India has prioritised improving economic infrastructure, such as irrigation, electricity, and road connectivity, as well as social infrastructure viz, education and health as crucial components of its regionally inclusive development strategy (GoI, 2012; Misra, 2013). Increasing access to finance has also been a major policy focus since 2005 (RBI, 2015). In this backdrop, this chapter analyses the impact of economic and social infrastructure and financial development on productivity in the Indian states. We take into account spatial interdependence among states, which can have a significant impact on the financial and infrastructural development on productivity as discussed in Misra (2019). Use of spatial econometric methods helps to infer about the spillover effects while examining the impact of infrastructure on output and productivity. Our analysis spans 19 states for the period 2001–16.

The remainder of the chapter is organised in the following manner. The method of computing TFPG was the focus of Chapter 4. To ascertain the impact of infrastructure on productivity, we need to obtain TFP levels from the TFPG estimates. The methodology for obtaining TFP levels is described in Section II. This section also describes the econometric methodology for estimating the influence of infrastructure and financial development on productivity. Section III discusses some stylised facts related to the infrastructure indicators during the study period. The empirical findings are highlighted in Section IV. Section V presents concluding observations.

Methodology

Computation of TFP level

The TFP level has been computed by applying the annual growth rate of TFP to a base year TFP index for each state by using the translog index method discussed in Hulten, Bennathan, and Srinivasan (2003). Deriving the TFP index using the trans log index method involved three steps. First, the TFP index in each state in some base year is computed as the output of the state relative to the combined output of all states less the inputs in the state relative to the combined inputs of all the states, multiplied by the respective factor shares. Second, the initial year of the study period 2001 is used as the base year for the TFP index. Third, equating the average level of TFP across all the states in the base year to 100, the index values computed in the first step for a state have been calibrated to represent the base year TFP index value.

Estimation methodology

The shift parameter A_{it} in the standard Cobb Douglas Production function, $Y_{it} = A_{it}\ K\alpha^{k}{}_{it}\ L\alpha_{it}$, represents the TFP which enables the economy to produce more than the growth in inputs. Guided by the literature, we have assumed an exponential relationship between different components of infrastructure, financial depth, and productivity which gives us the following specification:

$$A_{it} = Iit^{\beta 1}Cit^{\beta 2}Rit^{\beta 3}Eit^{\beta 4}Hit^{\beta 5}Dit^{\beta 6} \tag{1}$$

The estimable form of Eq. (1) is obtained through a logarithmic transformation and which is represented as Eq. (2).

$$LAit \equiv \beta_0 + \beta_1 LIit + \beta_2 LCit + \beta_3 LRit + \beta_4 LEit + \beta_5 LHit + \beta_6 LDit + \varepsilon_{it} \tag{2}$$

where β's are the parameter to be estimated and $\varepsilon_{i,t}$ is the error term.

In Eq. (2), we have considered a broader connotation of infrastructure by including both the economic and social dimensions. In the economic dimension, we consider three indicators viz, irrigated area as proportion of total cropped area (I), per capita installed capacity of electricity (C), and road density (R). In the social dimension, we have considered two important aspects viz, education (E) and health (H). Education infrastructure is represented through the pupil-teacher ratio (PTR) ratio at the primary level and health through the availability of various categories of government health centres per lakh population. Financial depth (D) is measured through credit outstanding as a proportion of the nominal SDP.

Eq. (2) can be estimated using fixed effects (FE) model to consider the unobservable state-specific factors that can have an influence on TFP. However, it is quite possible that TFP has a momentum of its own and which can be represented by considering its lagged value in the estimation. Non-incorporation of the lagged value of TFP in the econometric estimation would blur the impact of other determinants of productivity. Use of the lagged dependent variable also helps to control the endogeneity bias while assessing the impact of various determinates of TFP. As such, we have also estimated an extended model Eq. (3) that uses lagged value of TFP in addition to the specified variables in Eq. (2).

$$LAi,t \equiv \beta_0 LAi,t-1 + \beta_1 LIit + \beta_2 LCit + \beta_3 LRit + \beta_4 LEit + \beta_5 LHit + \eta\varepsilon_{it} \quad (3)$$

Eq. (3) is a dynamic panel data model. When a lagged dependent variable is used as an explanatory variable, OLS estimates become biased as the error term and the lagged dependent variable are correlated. As such, there is a need to use an alternate approach for estimating dynamic panel data models. The typical method used for obtaining consistent estimates in such situations is to employ an instrumental variable technique, in which different lags of the dependent variable are used as instruments. Amongst the several instrumental variable methods, we have chosen the Arellano and Bover (1995) approach since it produces the most efficient estimates. Overall instrument validity is tested utilising a Sargan test of over identifying restrictions while using lagged dependent variables as instruments.

Although the use of the generalised method of moments (GMM) overcomes the problem of endogeneity, it ignores the spillover effects. To overcome this limitation, we have used spatial econometric models to account for spillover effects while estimating the impact of infrastructure and financial depth on TFP, in addition to the Fixed Effects and GMM estimates. To account for spillover effects, we employed a contiguity matrix based on Queen's first-order neighbourhood criterion. Amongst the competing spatial interaction models, the spatial Durbin model (SDM) is found to be more versatile because it takes into account the spatial lag of both the dependent and independent variables and allows for more flexibility in determining the direct and indirect effects of the explanatory variables on the dependent variable. Thus, the empirical estimates have been obtained using the SDM model. Eq (4) describes the SDM Model.

$$A_{it} = \rho WA_{it} + \beta X_{it} + \eta WX_{it} + \eta\varepsilon_{it} \quad (4)$$

ρ measures the strength of the spatial lag dependence of the dependent variable WA_{it}. The term η measures the strength of the spatial lag dependence of the independent variables. TFP is dependent variable 'A_{it}', X is the vector of explanatory variables and consists of six elements representing infrastructure and financial depth in the states. Following, Loko and Diouf (2009), we have also included the size of the industry sector measured through share of industrial output in SDP as another explanatory variable in our estimates. The spatial Durbin model specified in Eq. (4) has been estimated with state-specific fixed effects and by applying the bias correction procedure suggested by Lee and Yu (2010). We have also included a time dummy for the year 2009 in all our estimations to assess the impact of the GFC on TFP.

III Stylised facts

Before we discuss the empirical estimates, it will be instructive to take stock of the progress made in the infrastructure indicators during our study period. The mean value of the infrastructure indicators and financial depth during the study period is presented in Table 5.1. We find that during the study period, there has been improvement in Per capita installed capacity of electricity, road density, pupil teacher ratio, and financial depth. Irrigated area normalised by population, however, has fluctuated around 8% during the study period. More importantly, the number of health centres has declined during the study period.

Road density, financial depth, and pupil teacher ratio have improved in all the states between 2002 and 2016. Further, per capital installed capacity of electricity has also improved for all states except Bihar as can be seen from Table 5.2. However, irrigated area and health centres normalised by population declined for as many as 11 and 14 states, respectively, between 2001 and 2016.

IV Results

We draw our inferences from the estimation of the SDM model. Nonetheless, we have also reported the estimation results from the fixed effects and GMM equivalent of Eq. (4) as a point of reference. We have presented estimates of Eq. (4) for two distinct specifications: The first specification takes into account only economic and social infrastructure. In the second specification, financial infrastructure proxied through financial depth is also taken into account in addition to economic and social infrastructure. Thus, the financial depth variable has been excluded in the first specification (FE-1, GMM-1, and SDM-1) and it is included in the FE-2, GMM-2, and SDM-2 specifications.

Table 5.1 Progress in Economic, Social, and Financial Infrastructure during 2001–20

Year	*Irrigation*	*Road*	*Electricity*	*SHIND*	*Financial Depth*	*PTR*	*Health*
2001	8.14	2.62	10.28	32.27	18.11	43.37	18.50
2002	8.23	2.64	10.91	31.17	20.38	43.53	18.72
2003	7.57	2.67	11.13	33.11	21.68	39.32	18.48
2004	7.90	2.67	12.82	32.78	22.81	43.11	18.23
2005	8.08	2.71	12.81	34.25	26.38	44.84	18.01
2006	8.23	2.73	12.89	34.25	30.03	43.41	17.92
2007	8.32	2.87	13.21	35.34	33.01	41.84	17.67
2008	8.29	2.89	14.61	35.91	34.48	42.95	17.59
2009	8.22	3.31	15.07	35.61	34.92	40.32	17.32
2010	7.74	3.37	16.01	35.58	36.63	36.58	17.32
2011	7.91	3.45	17.14	35.27	36.64	36.89	17.22
2012	8.03	3.53	19.52	34.83	37.81	35.89	16.77
2013	7.94	3.75	21.18	34.16	38.47	31.59	17.17
2014	8.04	3.84	23.18	34.12	38.74	28.41	16.88
2015	8.03	3.86	25.74	33.50	39.34	23.65	17.03
2016	7.94	3.96	27.66	34.44	38.64	22.79	17.14
Total	8.04	3.18	16.51	34.16	31.75	37.40	17.62

Notes: Irrigation refers to irrigated area normalised by population.
Road refers to road density.
Electricity represents per capita installed capacity of electricity.
PTR refers to pupil-teacher ratio.
Health refers to number of PHCs, CHCs, and Sub centres per lakh population.
SHIND refers to share of industry in state output.
Financial depth is measured by credit outstanding as a proportion nominal SDP.

In the FE, GMM, and SDM estimates, we find that industry share has a favourable impact on TFP. This suggests that when the rate of industrialisation in Indian states accelerates, TFP improves. In both the GMM-2 and SDM-2 calculations, financial depth is statistically insignificant. The sign of the GFC dummy is negative in all the specification, but it is not statistically significant.

Except for road, education and industry share, the spatial lag coefficient of all the other explanatory factors in the SDM-2 estimates (Table 5.3) are statistically significant. This implies that spatial interaction and spillovers work through both the value of TFP and some of the explanatory variables in neighbouring states. It may be noted that the SDM estimates do not represent the marginal effects, and hence, they cannot be used to draw inferences about the impact of infrastructure indicators and financial development on productivity. As such, we have used the method suggested by Le Sage and Pace (2009) to calculate the direct, indirect, and total effect of various categories of infrastructure on the TFP.

Table 5.2 Progress in Infrastructure Indicators and Financial Depth in Indian States during 2001–16

State	*Irrigation*	*Road*	*Electricity*	*Share of Industry*	*Financial Depth*	*PTR*	*Health*
2001							
Andhra Pradesh	7.80	2.53	9.50	27.90	20.70	45.00	2.77
Bihar	5.60	0.95	3.60	11.70	9.00	67.00	2.69
Chhattisgarh	5.00	1.64	8.90	43.50	9.30	44.00	3.07
Gujarat	6.70	2.74	14.40	43.40	21.70	49.00	2.83
Haryana	25.00	1.35	14.70	31.50	13.80	42.00	2.58
Himachal Pradesh	3.00	4.86	8.90	42.00	8.70	23.00	3.69
Jammu and Kashmir	4.50	2.32	11.10	32.20	15.80	42.00	3.04
Jharkhand	0.80	0.38	6.60	54.30	10.30	65.00	2.94
Karnataka	6.20	2.90	9.60	28.00	21.70	41.00	2.95
Kerala	1.40	4.74	9.20	24.90	20.90	28.00	2.96
Madhya Pradesh	7.20	2.71	6.90	29.70	15.90	45.00	2.84
Maharashtra	4.00	2.72	14.70	35.70	50.20	36.00	2.51
Orissa	5.80	5.78	8.30	38.90	12.40	38.00	3.12
Punjab	31.50	2.53	21.20	19.80	23.40	42.00	2.65
Rajasthan	11.00	2.54	7.50	29.50	13.60	45.00	3.06
Tamil Nadu	5.60	2.62	12.80	36.90	31.90	33.00	2.80
Uttar Pradesh	10.70	1.50	4.60	24.50	12.00	49.00	2.62
Uttaranchal	6.40	3.78	15.20	32.10	11.20	35.00	3.06
West Bengal	6.40	1.13	7.70	26.60	21.50	55.00	2.48
Average	8.14	2.62	10.28	32.27	18.11	43.37	2.88
2016							
Andhra Pradesh	6.40	3.40	29.40	26.60	50.30	24.50	2.81
Bihar	4.70	1.85	2.70	20.30	21.90	48.50	2.35
Chhattisgarh	6.40	3.49	56.50	47.20	29.50	20.90	3.10
Gujarat	9.40	2.79	46.10	49.80	38.00	22.20	2.79
Haryana	22.00	1.79	32.50	32.20	35.60	26.60	2.46
Himachal Pradesh	2.90	7.80	61.90	44.60	19.10	12.40	3.62
Jammu and Kashmir	3.90	3.70	23.20	28.20	30.20	11.00	3.27
Jharkhand	0.70	1.88	7.40	41.30	22.80	30.20	2.53
Karnataka	5.80	5.38	26.50	27.60	46.70	16.30	2.92
Kerala	1.40	5.88	12.20	27.70	40.40	16.80	2.80
Madhya Pradesh	12.80	3.70	22.50	29.30	32.00	22.80	2.61
Maharashtra	4.00	5.19	34.20	35.50	114.10	24.00	2.38
Orissa	3.30	6.69	21.90	42.80	26.00	19.50	2.97
Punjab	26.40	3.68	42.30	25.20	51.90	23.10	2.48
Rajasthan	14.40	3.47	24.30	33.30	27.50	19.70	3.15
Tamil Nadu	4.80	3.51	33.20	36.20	58.00	18.00	2.64
Uttar Pradesh	9.70	1.97	8.70	28.20	29.10	39.20	2.45
Uttaranchal	5.00	5.69	29.60	53.30	19.00	16.70	3.00
West Bengal	6.80	3.32	10.50	25.00	42.10	20.70	2.50
Average	7.94	3.96	27.66	34.44	38.64	22.79	2.78

Notes: Irrigation refers to irrigated area normalised by population.
Road refers to road density.
Electricity represents per capita installed capacity of electricity.
PTR refers to pupil-teacher ratio.
Health refers to number of PHCs, CHCs, and Sub centres per lakh population.
SHIND refers to share of industry in state output.
Financial depth is measured by credit outstanding as a proportion nominal SDP.

Table 5.3 Impact of Infrastructure and Financial Depth on Productivity

	Col.1	*Col.2*	*Col.3*	*Col.4*	*Col.5*	*Col.5*
	FE-1	*FE-2*	*GMM-1*	*GMM-2*	*SDM-1*	*SDM-2*
Main						
Lag of TFP			0.896***	0.885***		
			(24.722)	(23.114)		
Irrigation	0.106*	0.0968	0.0360**	0.0334**	0.0603	0.0737
	(1.781)	(1.645)	(2.263)	(2.087)	(1.186)	(1.454)
Electricity	0.204***	0.151***	0.0117	0.0082	-0.0604*	-0.0521*
	(7.628)	(4.791)	(0.667)	(0.442)	(-1.898)	(-1.647)
Road	0.285***	0.238***	0.0093	0.0054	0.0930**	0.0942**
	(6.798)	(5.425)	(0.363)	(0.206)	(2.131)	(2.185)
Education	-0.0715**	-0.0809**	-0.0366*	-0.0375*	-0.0586*	-0.0648**
	(-2.103)	(-2.406)	(-1.659)	(-1.683)	(-1.828)	(-2.043)
Health	-0.765***	-0.599***	-0.146**	-0.123*	-0.278**	-0.292**
	(-6.009)	(-4.385)	(-2.366)	(-1.812)	(-2.407)	(-2.432)
Industry share	0.0284***	0.0261***	0.0027**	0.0027**	0.0225***	0.0220***
	(10.857)	(9.711)	(1.984)	(2.012)	(9.085)	(8.803)
GFC dummy	-0.0345	-0.0417	-0.0057	-0.0067	-0.0312	-0.0313
	(-1.115)	(-1.364)	(-0.371)	(-0.435)	(-1.193)	(-1.246)
Financial depth		0.140***		0.0200		-0.151**
		(3.075)		(0.757)		(-2.575)
Constant	5.300***	4.684***	0.886***	0.824***		
	(12.567)	(10.151)	(3.038)	(2.746)		
W. Irrigation					0.205**	0.174*
					(2.074)	(1.754)
Electricity					0.259***	0.247***
					(5.531)	(4.973)
W. Road					0.0391	0.0356
					(0.536)	(0.495)
W. Education					-0.0024	0.0001
					(-0.041)	(0.002)
W. Health					-0.5260**	-0.4890*
					(-2.270)	(-1.838)
W. Industry Share					0.0023	0.0031
					(0.524)	(0.650)
W. Financial Depth						0.1330*
						(1.705)
Spatial rho					0.2890***	0.3180***
					(4.059)	(4.355)
p-value of Sargan Test			0.182	0.121		
Hausman Statistics	40.630***	30.880***			0.0106***	0.0103***
					(11.827)	(11.791)
N	304	304	285	285	285	285

Source: Estimates by Author.
Notes: Null Hypothesis of Sargan test is that overidentifying restrictions are valid.
Hausman Statistics indicates that FE method is more appropriate.
t statistics in parentheses.
* $p < 0.1$, ** $p < 0.05$, *** $p < 0.01$.

Some interesting results are found when we consider the direct and indirect effect of the infrastructure indicators separately in the augmented model (Cols. 4–6 of Table 5.4). Irrigation and electricity have a greater indirect impact on TFP than their direct impact. This suggests that improvements in irrigation and electricity infrastructure in neighbouring states have a greater beneficial influence on TFP than improvements in the concerned state. According to the SDM-2 specification, a 1% increase in irrigation infrastructure in all neighbouring states results in a 0.27% increase in a state's TFP growth. Improvements in irrigation facilities in neighbouring states may have a favourable influence on TFP through the demand, inter linkage, or terms of trade and competitiveness channels.

When agricultural income rises as a result of improved irrigation facilities, the demand channel kicks in. For the states under consideration, we find a correlation of 0.6 between irrigation facilities and cropping intensity. In addition, increase in cropping intensity has the potential to boost farmers' earnings (Chand, 2017). As a result, improved irrigation facilities may lead to increased cropping intensity and increased agricultural income. Higher

Table 5.4 Direct and Indirect Impact of Infrastructure and Financial Depth on Productivity from SDM Models

	SDM-1			*SDM-2*		
	Col.1	*Col.2*	*Col.3*	*Col.4*	*Col.5*	*Col.6*
	Direct	*Indirect*	*Total*	*Direct*	*Indirect*	*Total*
Irrigation	0.0797	0.292**	0.372***	0.0896*	0.275**	0.365**
	(1.542)	(2.397)	(2.800)	(1.801)	(2.059)	(2.440)
Electricity	-0.0425	0.323***	0.281***	-0.0284	0.313***	0.285***
	(–1.438)	(6.199)	(5.126)	(–0.949)	(4.844)	(3.915)
Road	0.102**	0.0886	0.191*	0.101**	0.0967	0.198*
	(2.472)	(0.968)	(1.917)	(2.383)	(0.927)	(1.734)
Education	-0.0601*	-0.0270	-0.0871	-0.0659**	-0.0321	-0.0980
	(–1.942)	(–0.364)	(–1.109)	(–2.090)	(–0.403)	(–1.125)
Health	-0.320***	-0.765**	-1.085***	-0.340***	-0.765*	-1.106**
	(–2.804)	(–2.383)	(–2.894)	(–2.685)	(–1.924)	(–2.336)
Industry share	0.0234***	0.0116*	0.0350***	0.0229***	0.0139*	0.0369***
	(9.136)	(1.924)	(4.851)	(8.205)	(1.820)	(4.071)
Financial depth				-0.141**	0.121	-0.0205
				(-2.430)	(1.283)	(-0.215)

Source: Estimates by the Author.

Notes:

t statistics in parentheses.

* $p < 0.1$, ** $p < 0.05$, *** $p < 0.01$.

agricultural income increases demand for goods and services, which may lead to better capacity utilisation and productivity growth in neighbouring states. Agriculture and industry are intertwined through the inter linkage channel. Higher agricultural productivity, assisted by increased irrigation systems, benefits industries that rely on agriculture for raw materials. Higher agricultural production also has a sobering effect on agricultural commodity prices, facilitating favourable terms of trade for industry. Further, lower agricultural inflation also serves to keep demand for nominal wage growth in check, allowing industry to maintain its competitiveness.

As far as road density is concerned, only the direct effect on productivity is positive. The direct effect arises from the fact that increased road density improves connectivity, allows for faster movement of goods and people, and lowers wastage of perishables during transportation. Improved road density reduces transaction costs (Binswanger et al., 1993), and as a result, it boosts productivity. The indirect effect of increased road density in neighbouring states on productivity is also positive but not statistically significant.

The direct effect of installed capacity of electricity capacity is found to be negative but statistically insignificant. The negative sign may seem counterintuitive at first, yet it makes sense in the Indian context. This is because installed capacity of electricity is only a necessary condition for improving productivity. Electricity's productivity-enhancing effect is contingent on its unhindered availability in a cost-effective manner to consumers and businesses. India's power sector is saddled with problems in all the three aspects viz, generation, transmission, and distribution in the electricity supply chain. Lack of timely coal linkage to power plants, technology obsolescence in the transmission network, and inability of distribution companies' to collect revenue has forced big industries to rely on captive power plants and small businesses to rely on power generators. Factory production is disrupted by voltage fluctuations and power outages, which has a negative impact on productivity. In short, problems in the electricity supply chain has an adverse impact on productivity by raising the cost of doing business. The indirect effect of the installed capacity of electricity, however, is positive and statistically significant on productivity. This could be because increase in installed capacity of electricity in all the states is suggestive of traction in economic activity and, thus, a positive effect on productivity. Overall, we find that the installed capacity of electricity has a positive impact on productivity when both direct and indirect effects are considered.

Within social infrastructure, when we take into account the role played by health infrastructure, the results are quite disappointing. The direct as well as indirect impact of health infrastructure is negative and statistically significant. The results again appear counter intuitive. However, the results can be appreciated given the evolution of health infrastructure during the study period. We find that during the study period, the availability of health infrastructure has deteriorated. Moreover, there is a shortfall of 46,140 SCs (24%), 9,231 PHCs (29%), and 3,002 CHCs (38%) across the country as per the Rural Health Statistics 2020 (RHS, 2020). The RHS, 2020 has also brought out the shortage of doctors in the PHCs and CHCs. For instance, 37.6% of the sanctioned posts of Health Assistant (Male + Female) and 24.1% of the sanctioned posts of Doctors are vacant in 2020 in the PHCs.

As far as impact of education is concerned, we find the direct effect of PTR is statistically significant and positive. It may be recalled that we have used PTR which is a negative indicator to represent academic infrastructure. Thus, a negative coefficient is indicative of a positive impact on productivity. A reduction in PTR can be due to increase in number of teachers or decline in number of students. As enrolment ratios have improved in India in the last two decades, the decline in PTR is mostly reflective of increase in the number of teachers. As teachers play the most important role in the education system, addressing the shortage of teachers is crucial, and hence, the direct effect of improved educational infrastructure reflected through the PTR is positive and statistically significant. The indirect effect of improved pupil teacher ratio in neighbouring states is also positive but statistically insignificant. Overall, we find the education infrastructure though positive is not statistically significant in impacting productivity in the states. The results are partly guided by the fact PTR is quite high for many states during the study period. Further, smaller classroom size can make an impact on productivity if it leads to improved learning outcomes. However, as has been pointed out in the literature, classroom size may not lead to improved learning outcomes in the face of teacher absenteeism, relevant curriculum, and teacher effort (Muralidharan, 2013).

We also find that, despite policy emphasis, increased financial depth has no impact on the productivity of the state. This inference is based on the finding that overall effect of financial depth turns out to be statistically insignificant. It may be noted that the direct effect of financial depth is negative and statistically significant. However, the indirect effect is positive but statistically insignificant. During the study period, we find a perceptible improvement in the credit extended by banks. The results, however, suggests that financial institutions have not been able to put their resources to their best possible use. There are several reasons why credit penetration did not augment productivity. It has been documented in the literature that the high NPAs of Indian banks in the post-GFC period are mostly accounted by the public sector banks and in the infrastructure sector. As a bank group, public sector banks (PSBs) account for the largest share in the credit portfolio of the banking system. The reason for high NPAs of PSBs during the study period is well documented in Misra and Cocorrese (2022). Lack of expertise in the PSBs to assess infrastructure projects was also partly responsible for the high NPAs. With the encouragement from the government, PSBs extended loans to infrastructure projects to support the economy after the GFC. However, many infrastructure projects which were financed after GFC lost financial viability owing to time and cost overruns and subsequently became NPA. This explains why the financial development has not been effective in improving productivity.

V Conclusion

This chapter investigated the impact of infrastructure and financial depth on state-level productivity. The impacts were estimated using the SDM model, which took into account spatial interaction across Indian states. We found prevalence of positive spillover effects in productivity across Indian states. According to our findings, irrigation facilities had the greatest influence on productivity, followed by installed capacity of power and road density. We also observed that expanding credit penetration and improvement in PTR have not been sufficient and also there is a lack of focus on improving leaning outcomes. The deterioration in health infrastructure is reflected through its negative impact on productivity. The findings of this chapter indicate the need for serious policy interventions in improving the social infrastructure to improve productivity of Indian states.

References

Aschauer, D. (1989). Is Public Expenditure Productive?, *Journal of Monetary Economics*, Vol. 23, No. 2, pp. 177–200.

Binswanger, H.P., Khandker, S.R. and Rosenzweig, Mark R. (1993). How Infrastructure and Financial Institutions Affect Agricultural Output and Investment in India, *Journal of Development Economics*, Vol. 41, No. 2, pp. 337–366.

Chand, R. (2017). Doubling Farmers' Income- Rational Strategy Prospects and Action Plan, *NITI Policy Paper No. 1, National Institution for Transforming India*, Government of India, New Delhi.

Estache, A. and Fay, M. (2007). Current Debates on Infrastructure Policy, *Paper prepared for Growth Commission,* Workshop on Global Trends and Challenges held on Sep 28–29, 2007 at Yale University.

Estache, A. and Garsous, G. (2012). The Impact of Infrastructure on Growth in Developing Countries, *IFC Economics Notes*, Note 1.

Hulten, C. R. and Schwab, R. M. (1991). Public Capital Formation and the Growth of the Regional Manufacturing Industries, *National Tax Journal*, Vol. 44, No. 4, pp. 121–134.

Hulten, C. and Isaksson, A. (2007). Why Development Levels Differ: The Sources of Differential Economic Growth in a Panel of High and Low Income Countries, *NBER Working Paper* No. 13469, NBER, Cambridge, MA.

Isaksson, A. (2007). Determinants of Total Factor Productivity: A Literature Review, *Research and Statistics* Branch, UNIDO, Vienna, available at: http://www.rrojasdatabank.info/87573_determinants_of_total_factor_productivity.pdf.

Kim, J. and Park, J. (2017a). *The Role of Total Factor Productivity Growth in Middle-Income Countries ADB Economics Working Paper Series*, Asian Development Bank, Philippines.

Kim, J. and Park, J. (2017b). *The Role of Total Factor Productivity Growth in Middle-Income Countries ADB Economics Working Paper Series.* Asian Development Bank, Philippines.

Kim, J. and Park, J. (2018). The Role of Total Factor Productivity Growth in Middle-Income Countries, *Emerging Markets Finance and Trade*, Vol. 54, No. 6, pp. 1264–1284.

Kim, Y.E. and Loayza, N.V. (2017). Productivity and its Determinants: Innovation, Education, Efficiency, Infrastructure, and Institutions, *DECRG Kuala Lumpur Seminar Series*, World Bank, Washington.

Lee, L., and Yu, J. (2010). Some Recent Developments in Spatial Panel Data Models, *Regional Science and Urban Economics*, Vol.40, No. 5, pp. 255–271.

LeSage, J.P. (2014). What Regional Scientists Need to Know about Spatial Econometrics, *The Review of Regional Studies,* Vol. 44, No. 1, pp. 13–32.

Lesage, J.P. and Pace, R.K. (2009). *Introduction to Spatial Econometrics.* Taylor & Francis/CRC Press, New York.

Loko, B. and Diouf, M.A. (2009). Revisiting the Determinants of Productivity Growth: What's New?, *Working Paper No. WP/09/225*, IMF, Washington.

Misra, B.S. (2013). *Revisiting Regional Growth Dynamics in India in the Post-Economic Reforms Period.* Palgrave Macmillan, London.

Munnell, A.H. (1990). Why Has Productivity Declined? Productivity and Public Investment, *New England Economic Review*, Federal Reserve Bank of Boston, January/February, pp. 3–22.

Nadiri, M.I. and Mamuneas, T.P. (1994). The Effects of Public Infrastructure and R&D Capital on the Cost Structure and Performance of U.S. Manufacturing Industries, *Review of Economics and Statistics*, Vol. 76, No. 1, pp. 22–37.

Romp, W. and De Haan, J. (2007). Public Capital and Economic Growth: A Critical Survey, *Perspektiven der Wirtschaftspolitik*, Vol. 8, No. 1, pp. 6–52.

Straub, S. (2008). Infrastructure and Growth in Developing Countries: Recent Advances and Research Challenges, *World Bank Policy Research Working Paper 4460*, World Bank, Washington DC.

van Ark, B. (2014), Total Factor Productivity: Lessons from the Past and Directions for the Future, *Working paper No. 271*, October 2014, National Bank of Belgium, Belgium.

6 Infrastructure and regional inequality

I Introduction

In the empirical literature, there is broad agreement that infrastructure improves a country's growth prospects (Aschauer, 1989; Munnell, 1990; Hulten and Schwab, 1991; Nadiri and Mamuneas, 1994; Romp and de Haan, 2007; Calderon and Serven, 2014). Infrastructure can also have an impact on spatial inequality if it leads to relatively higher growth in the relatively underdeveloped regions of a country (Calderon and Serven, 2004, 2014; Estache and Fay, 2010; ADB, 2012). In Bangladesh, China, Peru, Vietnam, and South Africa, studies have revealed that different kinds of economic infrastructure, such as roads, electricity, and irrigation, have a positive impact on rural development (Zhu and Luo, 2006; Mu and Vande Walle, 2007; Escobal and Ponce, 2014; Dinkelman, 2011). Physical infrastructure, in general, and transportation and communications, in particular, facilitate access to information, enhance labour mobility, stimulate nonfarm activity, and thus, reduce poverty in the poorer regions of a country. There is also a large body of literature that takes into account both physical and human infrastructure and analyses how they help to reduce regional disparity (Dan and Tatsuaki, 2003; Fan et al., 2004; Belton et al., 2007). These studies conclude that, while both physical and social infrastructure are beneficial, education has a larger impact in reducing inter-regional disparities. However, Estache and Fay (2007) argue that infrastructure investment especially in transport is a necessary but not sufficient condition for regional growth, based on the experiences of France, Italy, and Brazil. Based on the experience from China, Fan et al. (2011) argue that returns to infrastructure investment in lagging regions are, in general, high but deciphering which category of infrastructure has the highest returns in specific regions needs detailed investigation. Furthermore, the empirical evidence on the relationship between infrastructure investment and inequality are less conclusive (UNCTAD, 2013). In light

DOI: 10.4324/9781003278351-6

of the foregoing discussion, this chapter investigates how various types of infrastructure affect intra-state inequality in India. Understanding the relationship between infrastructure and inequality assumes significance in light of the importance accorded to balanced regional development as a key objective of India's policy (Misra, 2007).

India's post-independence development goals were expressed through five-year plans, which began in 1951. Concerns about balanced regional development to some extent were addressed in the second five-year plan (1956–61). The second five-year plan had a focus on state-led heavy industrialisation and it envisaged establishing mega infrastructure projects in the relatively poorer states to create forward and backward linkages for development. Fiscal incentives were also given to the private sector to set up industry in the backward states. Commitment to balanced regional development in the third five-year plan can be ascertained from explicit pronouncements such as 'balanced development of different parts of the country, extension of the benefits of economic progress to the less developed regions, and 'widespread diffusion of industry are among the major aims of planned development'. The fourth five-year plan also acknowledged the importance of locating large central projects in backward States. Attempts were made for balanced regional development in the subsequent plans through launching welfare schemes, special area programmes, and favourable disposition of central assistance to less developed states.

Even when market forces were given a bigger role in resource allocation as India pursued economic reforms in the year 1991, development of the lagging states continued to receive policy attention. In the post reform period, reducing inter-state disparity gained added significance in the 10th five-year plan (2002–07), with the launch of the Rashtriya Sam Vikas Yojana (RSVY), a new initiative by the central government to reduce regional disparity (Misra, 2013). The RSVY was launched as an independent programme in 2003–04 and was later subsumed into the Backward Regions Grant Fund (BRGF) programme in 2006–07. As alluded in Chapter 1, the scope of RSVY which was limited to 147 districts in 27 states was expanded under the BRGF to include 250 districts. The BRGF could be utilised for a variety of purposes, including education, health, clean water, and electrification. Given the continuous policy emphasis on promoting balanced regional development, with infrastructure as a key area of intervention, it would be important from a policy perspective to examine how infrastructure impacts output and inequality in the states.

The rest of the chapter is organised as follows. Section II covers the findings from India-specific studies on the infrastructure–inequality relationship. The methodology used to study the infrastructure–inequality relationship is discussed in Section III. Section IV prevents some stylised facts related to intra-state inequality and progress in economic and social infrastructure during the study period. Section V deliberates on the empirical findings with an exploratory analysis of the provision of basic infrastructure in the backward districts to appreciate the findings. Section VI provides the concluding observations.

II Literature on the infrastructure–inequality relationship for India

There are very few India-based research studies on the relationship between infrastructure and regional inequality. Two relevant studies in this context are by Bajar and Rajeev (2015) and Majumder (2012). Both of these studies investigate the impact of infrastructure on consumption inequality using data from the quinquennial consumer spending surveys undertaken by the National Sample Survey Organization (NSSO). Bajar and Rajeev (2015) have investigated inequality in consumption spending in 17 major states classified as high and low income for the years 1983, 1988, 1994, 2005, and 2010. This study, which solely looked at components of physical infrastructure, found that provision of road and electricity accentuate inter-personal consumption inequality in low-income states. This seemingly paradoxical result, according to Bajar and Rajeev (2015), is due to the improved access of the rich to opulent products made feasible by improvements in the road and electricity networks. Majumder (2012) used consumption-based inequality to create a composite index by combining physical, financial, and social infrastructure between 1991 and 2005. According to this study, economic infrastructure increases disparity in consumption, whereas social infrastructure tends to reduce inequality. A limitation of both these studies is that they have not addressed the methodological nuances associated with the estimation of infrastructure and inequality relationships. The analysis by Bajar and Rajeev (2015) has the additional limitation of excluding social infrastructure.

India-specific studies have analysed state-level consumption inequality rather than income inequality. Instead, we have used sub-state or district level income to compute intra-state inequality. We analyse how provision of infrastructure affects income disparities between districts. Moreover, unlike the existing literature, which focuses on either the 'quantity' and/or 'quality' of infrastructure, we take a different approach. We take into account 'availability' and 'usage' of economic infrastructure and 'availability' and 'adequacy' of social infrastructure.

III Methodology for computing infrastructure index

A standard approach in empirical studies is to use monetary measures of public investment to denote infrastructure while studying the relationship between infrastructure and inequality (Straub, 2004). However, if the private sector plays a large part in the provision of infrastructure, then using public investment to represent infrastructure might lead to systematic measurement errors. This was notably true in India after 1990 when the private sector accounted for a large share of total infrastructure expenditure (Misra, 2013). Another drawback of using public capital stock as a proxy for infrastructure is that it may not accurately reflect the effective capital stock. This is because, due to inefficiency, corruption, and inaccurate accounting techniques, the costs incurred over time may overstate the values associated with public infrastructure stock. The flaw in employing public capital may be seen in the fact that roughly 48% of studies that utilise aggregate public capital to denote infrastructure do not find that it has a positive impact on output (Straub, 2004).

Infrastructure has often been proxied through a single indicator in the empirical literature. Incorrect conclusions may be drawn by omitting crucial indicators and having too many indicators can result in erroneous estimations (Calderon and Serven, 2014). Infrastructure indices can help solve these issues. To achieve more precise estimates of the impact of infrastructure on output and inequality, we have employed a composite index in this study. We have constructed a composite index that considers both the social and economic dimensions of infrastructure. Economic infrastructure includes essential facilities such as water, electricity, and roads. Provision of healthcare and educational facilities are used to represent social infrastructure.

The literature suggests combining quantity indicators of infrastructure to create a composite index of physical infrastructure. Similarly, indicators that represent the quality of physical infrastructure services are often used to create aggregate indexes of infrastructure quality (Louis and Servon, 2004). Instead of looking at infrastructure in terms of 'quantity' and 'quality', we look at economic infrastructure in terms of 'availability' and 'usage'. This is especially important for India, a low-middle-income country where infrastructure availability and its usage can differ owing to demand and supply forces.

Supply side constraints can lead to divergence between availability and usage of infrastructure services. For example, despite having adequate installed capacity, electricity available for consumption can be relatively low due to poor maintenance or higher transmission and distribution losses. Likewise usage of available capacity can be relatively low due to demand side factors such as inability to purchase power. In the economic dimension, the indicators employed to measure availability and usage for water are 'gross irrigated area as a per cent of gross cropped area' and 'fertiliser consumption per hectare', respectively. Indicators such as 'installed capacity' and 'per capita electricity consumption' are used as indicators to describe availability and usage for electricity. We have used 'road density' to indicate availability and 'surfaced road as a percentage of total road' to describe its effective use to facilitate trade and commerce.

When it comes to social infrastructure, building schools and hospitals is important, but it is not enough to secure better education and health outcomes. This is because schools and hospitals without the requisite manpower and resources may not have a significant impact on human capital formation. As such, for social infrastructure, we have considered 'availability' as well as 'adequacy' of education and health facilities.

Education as a component of social infrastructure is represented through the 'number of teachers per school in a state' and the 'Pupil Teacher Ratio'. These two indicators depict the availability of teachers, an essential component of academic infrastructure and adequacy of teachers to impart effective education, respectively.

The number of health centres in a state represents the 'availability' of health infrastructure. Adequacy of health infrastructure involves several dimensions, and it is difficult to obtain information on all aspects. As such, we have used infant survival rate, an output indicator to describe the 'adequacy' of health infrastructure.

For each infrastructure indicator in the economic and social dimensions, the index for a specific state in a given year is calculated using the following formula: Component Index = (actual–minimum)/(maximum–minimum).

To calculate the composite index, one needs to assign weights to the component indicators. One standard approach to assign weights in the literature is to use principal component analysis (PCA). The weights for the various components of the economic infrastructure index are calculated using PCA. Because there is no tangible output or production in the social infrastructure, equal weights were assigned to indicators underlying the health and education sub-indices. PCA-based weights were assigned to the health and education sub-indices to compute the social infrastructure index. We have again used PCA to assign weights to the economic and infrastructure indices after they have been computed to get the composite infrastructure index. The economic, social, and composite infrastructure indices created using the PCA weights are labelled ECOINFPCA, SOCINFPCA, and INFPCA.

We employed yet another way to assign weights to evaluate the robustness of our findings. The three economic infrastructure indicators are given weights in the alternative method depending on the relative importance of the sector they represent in the state domestic product (SDP), a measure of output. We assign the share of agriculture, industry, and services in SDP as weights for water, electricity, and road, respectively, as water is vital for agriculture, electricity for industry, and road network for services. Because the share of each sector in SDP might vary both among states for a year and within a single state over time, the weights for the various components of the economic infrastructure index according to this alternate method are dynamic in nature. We assigned equal weights to the health and education sub-indices to compute the social infrastructure index in the alternate method. To generate the composite infrastructure index for each year from 2000–01 to 2011–12, the economic and social infrastructure indices were additionally given weights based on PCA. The economic, social, and composite infrastructure indices as per the alternate method is labelled as ECOINFSS, SOCINFSS, and INFSS.

Measurement of inequality

The Gini index, which is calculated from the income of sub-state entities, or districts within a state, represents state-level inequality. To calculate income at the district level, we used the district domestic product with 2004–05 as the base year. We chose 12 states for the analysis based on the availability of reliable data at the district level.

These 12 states contributed for 75% of the India's GDP in 2001 and 74.2% in 2012. Moreover, these 12 states accounted for 80% of India's population, both in 2001 and 2012.

Classification of states

We conceptualise states to be classified in two broad categories viz, leading and lagging. To categorise states as leading or lagging, we have taken into account per capita income of the state and the prevalence of backwardness at the district level within states. In September 2017, the Niti Aayog identified 115 of India's most backward districts. We have used the condition that a state be classified as lagging if at least five of its districts appear on this list of 115 backward districts. Six states, namely, Bihar, Madhya Pradesh, Odisha, Rajasthan, Uttar Pradesh, and West Bengal, are found to be lagging by this criterion. In both 2001 and 2012, we found that the six lagging states had a real per capita SDP lower than the average for all 12 states when we used income classification at the state level. The remaining six states, Andhra Pradesh, Karnataka, Kerala, Maharashtra, Punjab, and Tamil Nadu, were classified as leading since the number of backward districts in these states were relatively low, and their actual per capita SDP was higher than the average for the 12 states in both 2001 and 2012.

The appropriateness of our classification of states can be ascertained from the fact that it broadly concurs with that of the Raghuram Rajan Committee (GoI, 2013). Based on composite index scores of less than 0.4, 0.4–0.6, and beyond 0.6, the Raghuram Rajan Committee (2013) classified states as relatively developed, less developed, and least developed, respectively. With the exception of West Bengal, with a score of 0.55, all other states categorised by us as lagging are also classified as least developed by the Rajan Committee.

Estimation methodology

We have used panel data econometric techniques to examine the impact of infrastructure on output and inequality. The general specifications used for studying the infrastructure–output relationship are given by Eqs. (1–2), and the infrastructure–inequality relationship is studied using Eqs. (3–4). Inequality, financial depth, and inflation are used as conditioning variables in Eqs. (1–2) to assess the influence of infrastructure on output. Eq. 2 estimates the impact of economic and social infrastructure individually, whereas Eq. (1) estimates the impact of composite infrastructure. Eqs. (3–4) use SDP, squared SDP, financial depth, and inflation as conditioning variables to quantify the influence of infrastructure on income disparity. We chose conditioning variables based on the literature and the context of our study. For example, conditioning variables like external orientation were left out because they are largely relevant at the country level.

$$SDP_{i,t} = h_1 + h_2 INFR_{i,t} + h_3 GINI_{i,t} + h_4 INFL_{i,t} + h_5 DPTH_{i,t} + e_{I,t} \quad (1)$$

$$\begin{aligned} SDP_{i,t} = {} & h_6 + h_7 ECOINFR_{i,t} + h_8 SOCINFR_{i,t} + h_9 GINI_{i,t} \\ & + h_{10} INFL_{i,t} + h_{11} DPTH_{i,t} + e_{i,t} \end{aligned} \quad (2)$$

$$\begin{aligned} GINI_{i,t} = {} & h_{12} + h_{13} INFR_{i,t} + h_{14} PSDP_{i,t} + h_{15} SDPSQ_{i,t} \\ & + h_{16} INFL_{i,t} + h_{17} DPTH_{i,t} + e_{i,t} \end{aligned} \quad (3)$$

$$\begin{aligned} GINI_{i,t} = {} & h_{18} + h_{19} ECOINFR_{i,t} + h_{20} SOCINFR_{i,t} \\ & + h_{21} SDP_{i,t} + h_{22} SDPSQ_{i,t} + h_{23} INFL_{i,t} + h_{24} DPTH_{i,t} + e_{i,t} \end{aligned} \quad (4)$$

where

INFR = Composite infrastructure index. This variable can be either *INFPCA* or *INFSS*.

INFPCA = Composite infrastructure index where the economic infrastructure index is computed by assigning weights to indicator using *PCA*.

INFSS = Composite infrastructure index where the economic infrastructure index is computed by assigning weights to indicator using sectoral shares.

ECOINFR = Economic infrastructure index. This variable can be either *ECOINFPCA* or *ECOINFSS*.

ECOINFPCA and *ECOINFSS* represent economic infrastructure index computed with PCA and sectoral share-based weights, respectively.

SOCINFR = Social infrastructure index. This variable can be either *SOCINFPCA* or *SOCINFSS*. *SCOINFPCA* represents social infrastructure index computed using *PCA*-based weights to the indicators.

To compute *SOCINFSS* as well as *SOCINFFSS* equal weights are assigned to indicators underlying health and education indices.

PSDP = Per capita real-state domestic product at 2011–12 base

SDPSQ = Square of real per capita SDP

INFL = Inflation

DPTH = Financial depth measured as credit outstanding as a percentage of nominal state domestic product

GINI = Income inequality in a state measured through Gini Coefficient computed from district domestic product at 2004–05 base

$\varepsilon_{i,t}$ = Error term

η's are the parameter to be estimated. We use the log of each variable in the estimation.

In the estimation, we have used the log of each variable. We have used econometric methods that are appropriate for the small size of the dataset, which contains only 144 observations. The data points are further reduced when we classify states as leading and lagging states, resulting in a total of 72 data points for each category of states. Whether panel data models should be estimated using fixed effects or random effects models is widely debated in the literature. Field (2001) has observed that, while fixed-effects (FE) models are used extensively, they are only useful for drawing conditional inferences. When making unconditional inferences, random effects (RE) models are more appropriate. A Hausman test is commonly used to determine whether a random effects model is appropriate vis-à-vis the fixed effects model. According to Monte Carlo simulations by Clark and Lazer (2015), random effects estimation should be preferred in very small datasets, even when the condition of zero correlation between the fixed effects and the independent variables is violated. Thus, the random effect estimation is better suited for the dataset available for this study. As such, we have used RE model for estimation. Further, we have used the first lag of infrastructure variables to overcome the problems of endogeneity in estimation, following Seneviratne and Sun (2013).

The use of random effects model requires specifying the variance component method that needs to be used in the estimation. In this regard, several GLS estimators have been developed such as those by Wansbeck and Kapteyn (WK), Wallace and Hussain (WH), and Swamy and Arrora (SA). Based on the Monte-Carlo Simulation of the random effect model, Mohammadi(2012) suggest that SA is inadequate for small samples. When the number of cross sections equals the number of parameters, the SA model favours the fixed effects model incorrectly, according to Mohammadi (2012). When the number of cross sections is less than the number of parameters, SA becomes mathematically infeasible, while WH and WK are feasible. As a result, we have not used the SA estimator. When estimating the random effects model, Baltagi (2011) suggests using more than one of the GLS estimators to draw robust inferences. As such, we have used the WK and WH estimators in our estimation of random effects model. We have also used the Maximum Likelihood (ML) approach of estimating the random effect model in addition to the GLS estimators because it is more efficient. Thus, to determine their impact on output and inequality, we have used RE model with three alternate variance component methods (RE-WH, RE-WK, and RE-ML). Further, the three estimation methods are applied to infrastructure indices derived using PCA-and SS-based weights.

In sum, we conduct six sets of regressions (RE-WH-SS, RE-WK-SS, RE-ML-SS, RE-WH-PCA, RE-WK-PCA, and RE-ML-PCA) to draw inferences. Given the six different specifications for estimations, we use a majority criteria decision rule to infer the impact of infrastructure on output and intra-state inequality. The congruence of results from at least three specifications has been used to reflect weak impact of regressors on output and inequality. Congruence of results from four or more specifications is used to classify the impact as strong.

We conduct empirical estimation for three groups of states: a single group of 12 states (Group A), and distinct groups of leading (Group B) and lagging (Group C). The term 'infrastructure' has been used throughout the study to refer to composite infrastructure. We explore some of the stylised facts about the evolution of inequality and availability of infrastructure in the 12 states for the beginning and end of our study period before discussing the results from empirical estimations.

IV Stylised facts

Inequality had risen in each of the 12 states between 2001 and 2012. Both in the first and in the last year of the study period, Odisha and Punjab had the highest and lowest inter-district income inequality (Table 6.1). Despite the fact that inequality increased in both the leading and lagging states in 2012 compared to 2001, the former had a consistently lower Gini coefficient than the latter.

Table 6.1 Evolution of Intra-State Inequality in Indian States

State	*2001*	*2002*	*2003*	*2004*	*2005*	*2006*	*2007*	*2008*	*2009*	*2010*	*2011*	*2012*
High-Income States												
Andhra Pradesh	0.12	0.13	0.14	0.14	0.14	0.13	0.15	0.14	0.14	0.15	0.16	0.17
Karnataka	0.16	0.18	0.19	0.19	0.20	0.20	0.20	0.20	0.21	0.23	0.22	0.23
Kerala	0.09	0.09	0.09	0.08	0.08	0.09	0.09	0.10	0.11	0.11	0.11	0.11
Maharashtra	0.20	0.20	0.20	0.21	0.22	0.22	0.22	0.22	0.24	0.25	0.21	0.21
Punjab	0.08	0.08	0.08	0.08	0.08	0.07	0.08	0.09	0.08	0.10	0.09	0.09
Tamil Nadu	0.16	0.17	0.17	0.18	0.19	0.18	0.18	0.19	0.20	0.21	0.21	0.21
Average	0.13	0.14	0.15	0.15	0.15	0.15	0.15	0.16	0.16	0.17	0.17	0.17
Low-Income States												
Bihar	0.16	0.17	0.17	0.18	0.19	0.18	0.18	0.19	0.20	0.21	0.21	0.21
Madhya Pradesh	0.18	0.17	0.18	0.17	0.18	0.18	0.19	0.19	0.19	0.19	0.20	0.19
Orissa	0.21	0.20	0.23	0.23	0.24	0.24	0.25	0.26	0.27	0.26	0.26	0.24
Rajasthan	0.13	0.13	0.13	0.12	0.13	0.14	0.14	0.14	0.15	0.15	0.14	0.14
Uttar Pradesh	0.20	0.19	0.21	0.20	0.22	0.21	0.23	0.24	0.23	0.23	0.22	0.23
West Bengal	0.12	0.12	0.13	0.14	0.16	0.16	0.17	0.17	0.18	0.18	0.19	0.19
Average	0.17	0.16	0.18	0.17	0.18	0.18	0.19	0.20	0.20	0.20	0.20	0.20
Average for 12 States	0.15	0.15	0.16	0.16	0.17	0.17	0.17	0.18	0.18	0.19	0.18	0.18

Source: The Author

Note: The state level inequality is computed from district level income for each state.

Regardless of the technique used to assign weights, Bihar had the lowest composite infrastructure index at the start and end of the study period. However, when viewed in terms of its variants, Madhya Pradesh and Bihar had the lowest levels of economic infrastructure in 2001 as per the SS- and PCA-based weights, respectively. However, in the year 2012, Bihar had the lowest economic infrastructure index values under both methods of assigning weights. Irrespective of the methods used to assign weights, Punjab had the highest economic infrastructure index value in 2001 and 2012. In terms of social infrastructure, Bihar had the lowest and Kerala had the highest index value in both 2001 and 2012. Except for Bihar and Punjab, the economic infrastructure index value increased for all other states in 2012 compared to 2001. In the group of lagging states, except West Bengal, the social infrastructure index value declined for all other states between 2001 and 2012. However, the social infrastructure index value improved for all states except Kerala in the group of leading states. It needs to be mentioned that the decline for Kerala was marginal and albeit from very high levels.

Between 2001 and 2012, the economic and social infrastructure for both the lagging and leading states improved irrespective of the SS and PCA method of assigning weights. However, the improvement was more pronounced in the provision of economic infrastructure for the leading states. As a result, we find that the composite infrastructure of the lagging states has made little progress, whereas the composite infrastructure of the leading states has improved significantly. We also found that between 2001 and 2012, the gap between the leading and lagging states grew in terms of both economic and social infrastructure. Thus, the groups of leading states had higher growth, lower inequality, and better infrastructure than the group of lagging states during the study period.

For the 12 states as a group, financial depth measured as credit outstanding as a percentage of nominal SDP increased from 21 in 2001 to 45 in 2012 (Table 6.2). However, there was a substantial difference in the financial depth between the lagging and leading regions. In both 2001 and 2012, credit as a percentage of nominal SDP for the leading states was twice that for the lagging states.

V Estimation results

Impact of Infrastructure on Output: We first present the results for all states taken as one group. When we consider all the 12 states as one group (Group A), estimation of Eq. (1) unequivocally brings out the positive impact of composite infrastructure in influencing state income (Cols. 1, 3, and 5 of Tables 6.3 and 6.4). As far as the leading (Cols. 1, 3, and 5 of

Table 6.2 Evolution of Infrastructure in High- and Low-Income States during 2001 and 2012

2001								
State	*ECOINFSS*	*SOCINFSS*	*INFSS*	*ECOINFPCA*	*SOCINFPCA*	*INFPCA*	*FINLDPTH*	*INFL*
Leading States								
Andhra Pradesh	0.53	0.33	0.43	0.50	0.33	0.42	20.66	3.90
Karnataka	0.49	0.44	0.46	0.47	0.44	0.45	21.69	5.50
Kerala	0.36	0.92	0.64	0.36	0.92	0.64	20.87	1.50
Maharashtra	0.54	0.44	0.49	0.54	0.44	0.49	50.18	4.00
Punjab	0.88	0.40	0.64	0.87	0.40	0.64	23.39	7.00
Tamil Nadu	0.62	0.55	0.59	0.62	0.55	0.59	31.91	3.30
Average	**0.57**	**0.52**	**0.54**	**0.56**	**0.52**	**0.54**	**28.12**	**4.20**
Lagging States								
Bihar	0.31	0.16	0.23	0.19	0.16	0.17	8.96	–1.70
Madhya Pradesh	0.26	0.31	0.29	0.28	0.31	0.30	15.94	6.20
Orissa	0.32	0.47	0.39	0.34	0.47	0.41	12.39	2.60
Rajasthan	0.32	0.44	0.38	0.34	0.44	0.39	13.58	1.70
Uttar Pradesh	0.44	0.25	0.34	0.35	0.25	0.30	11.99	1.40
West Bengal	0.37	0.25	0.31	0.32	0.25	0.29	21.48	2.20
Average	**0.34**	**0.31**	**0.33**	**0.30**	**0.31**	**0.31**	**14.06**	**2.07**
Average for 12 States	**0.45**	**0.41**	**0.43**	**0.43**	**0.41**	**0.42**	**21.09**	**3.13**

(*Continued*)

2012

State	*ECOINFSS*	*SOCINFSS*	*INFSS*	*ECOINFPCA*	*SOCINFPCA*	*INFPCA*	*FINLDPTH*	*INFL*
Leading States								
Andhra Pradesh	0.60	0.54	0.57	0.59	0.54	0.56	52.00	6.60
Karnataka	0.66	0.62	0.64	0.68	0.62	0.65	48.32	6.90
Kerala	0.56	0.90	0.73	0.54	0.90	0.72	42.08	12.00
Maharashtra	0.65	0.44	0.55	0.71	0.44	0.58	109.71	6.70
Punjab	0.87	0.46	0.66	0.86	0.46	0.66	52.47	6.40
Tamil Nadu	0.71	0.63	0.67	0.72	0.63	0.67	62.04	6.20
Average	**0.67**	**0.60**	**0.63**	**0.68**	**0.60**	**0.64**	**61.10**	**7.47**
Lagging States								
Bihar	0.26	0.15	0.21	0.11	0.15	0.13	16.75	8.40
Madhya Pradesh	0.35	0.28	0.31	0.40	0.28	0.34	29.95	6.70
Orissa	0.46	0.43	0.45	0.51	0.43	0.47	25.46	7.40
Rajasthan	0.46	0.42	0.44	0.57	0.42	0.50	31.48	13.00
Uttar Pradesh	0.45	0.19	0.32	0.34	0.19	0.26	26.20	8.20
West Bengal	0.38	0.49	0.44	0.32	0.49	0.41	45.88	9.40
Average	**0.39**	**0.33**	**0.36**	**0.38**	**0.33**	**0.35**	**29.29**	**8.85**
Average for 12 States	**0.53**	**0.46**	**0.50**	**0.53**	**0.46**	**0.50**	**45.19**	**8.16**

Note: INFPCA=Composite infrastructure index where the economic infrastructure index is computed by assigning weights to indicator using PCA.
INFSS= Composite infrastructure index where the economic infrastructure index is computed by assigning weights to indicator using sectoral shares.
ECOINFSS=economic infrastructure index computed using sectoral share-based weights.
SOCINFSS=social infrastructure index computed using equal weights to health and education indices.
ECOINFPCA=economic infrastructure index computed with PCA-based weights.
SOCINFPCA=social infrastructure index computed using PCA-based weights to health and education indices.
FINLDPTH=Financial depth is measured as outstanding bank credit as a percentage of nominal SDP
Inflation is measured as annual percentage change in SDP deflator.

Tables 6.5 and 6.6) and lagging (Cols. 1, 3, and 5 of Tables 6.7 and 6.8) states are concerned, we find that in three out of six specifications, composite infrastructure impacts output positively. Thus, at a disaggregated level, we find infrastructure weakly impacts output.

When we consider economic and social infrastructure separately for all states (Cols. 2, 4, and 6 of Tables 6.3 and 6.4) treated as one group, we find the former positively impacts output in all the six specifications. As far as social infrastructure is concerned, though directionally it impacts output

Table 6.3 Impact of Infrastructure on Output-All States (Sectoral Share-Based Weights)

	Col.1	*Col.2*	*Col.3*	*Col.4*	*Col.5*	*Col.6*
	RE-ML-SS	*RE-ML-SS*	*RE-WH-SS*	*RE-WH-SS*	*RE-WK-SS*	*RE-WK-SS*
Constant	8.884* (22.477)	9.425* (22.744)	8.947* (24.913)	9.126* (30.013)	9.194* (21.116)	9.699* (22.063)
Lpgini	0.138 (1.172)	0.296 (2.347)	-0.033 (-0.370)	-0.101 (-1.485)	0.322** (2.333)	0.419* (3.064)
Lfinldpth	0.719* (12.577)	0.662* (11.432)	0.654* (11.540)	0.579* (11.442)	0.694* (11.602)	0.637* (10.722)
Linfss(-1)	0.388* (3.431)	–	0.618* (6.057)	–	0.252*** (2.057)	–
Linflation	0.000 (0.046)	-0.003 (-0.176)	0.024 (1.114)	0.045** (2.141)	-0.001 (-0.103)	-0.004 (-0.247)
Lecoinfpca(-1)	–	0.386* (4.117)	–	0.348* (4.616)	–	0.375* (3.964)
Lsocinfpca(-1)	–	0.073 (1.376)	–	0.345* (7.491)	–	0.040 (0.747)
Hausman Test (Signif)	17.642 (0.001)	15.753 (0.007)	15.753 (0.007)	15.753 (0.007)	7.990 (0.091)	8.797 (0.117)

Source: The Author

Notes:

Lpgini = Log of Gini Coefficient;

Linfss= Log of Composite Infrastructure Index computed using SS-based weights;

Lecoinfss = Log of Economic Infrastructure Index computed using SS-based weights;

Lsocinfss = Log of Social Infrastructure Index computed using SS-based weights

Lfinldpth = Log of Financial Depth;

Linflation = Log of Inflation;

Parenthesis to coefficient estimates indicates t-statistics;

Parenthesis to Hausman Statistics refers to the significance level.

*, **, and *** refer to 1%, 5%, and 10% level of significance, respectively.

Table 6.4 Impact of Infrastructure on Output-All States (PCA-Based Weights)

	Col.1	*Col.2*	*Col.3*	*Col.4*	*Col.5*	*Col.6*
	RE-ML-PCA	*RE-ML-PCA*	*RE-WH-PCA*	*RE-WH-PCA*	*RE-WK-PCA*	*RE-WK-PCA*
Constant	8.875* (23.214)	9.127* (21.892)	9.039* (31.528)	8.901* (31.074)	9.212* (21.505)	9.480* (20.982)
Lpgini	0.131 (1.138)	0.257 (1.997)	-0.076 (-1.074)	-0.123 (-1.785)	0.319** (2.338)	0.417* (2.932)
Lfinldpth	0.710* (12.512)	0.688* (11.546)	0.590* (11.958)	0.600* (11.841)	0.687* (11.516)	0.656* (10.640)
Linfpca(-1)	0.351* (3.864)		0.575* (8.476)	–	0.246* (2.482)	–
Linflation	0.004 (0.257)	0.002 (0.125)	0.046* (2.243)	0.048* (2.283)	0.000 (0.011)	0.000 (0.032)
Lecoinfpca(-1)	–	0.209* (3.022)	–	0.265* (4.488)	–	0.191* (2.741)
Lsocinfpca(-1)	–	0.074 (1.362)	–	0.280* (5.793)	–	0.033 (0.593)
Hausman Test (Signif)	18.124 (0.001)	16.828 (0.004)	16.828 (0.004)	16.828 (0.004)	8.069 (0.089)	8.604 (0.125)

Source: The Author
Notes:
Lpgini = Log of Gini Coefficient;
Linfpca= Log of Composite Infrastructure Index computed using PCA-based weights;
Lecoinfpca = Log of Economic Infrastructure Index computed using PCA-based weights;
Lsocinfpca = Log of Social Infrastructure Index computed using PCA-based weights;
Lfinldpth = Log of Financial Depth;
Linflation = Log of Inflation;
Parenthesis to coefficient estimates indicates t-statistics;
Parenthesis to Hausman Statistics refers to the significance level.

positively but the effect is not statistically significant. We find that social infrastructure positively impacts output only in the WH-SS and WH-PCA specifications. In the rest four specifications, impact of social infrastructure on output is positive but not statistically significant.

Estimate of Eq. (2) suggests that the economic infrastructure positively impacts output for both the leading (Cols. 2, 4, and 6 of Tables 6.5 and 6.6) and the lagging (Cols. 2, 4, and 6 of Tables 6.7 and 6.8) states. However, economic infrastructure impact output positively as per all the six estimates for the leading states. In the lagging states, economic

Table 6.5 Impact of Infrastructure on Output-Leading States (Sectoral Share-Based Weights)

	Col.1	*Col.2*	*Col.3*	*Col.4*	*Col.5*	*Col.6*
	RE-ML-SS	*RE-ML-SS*	*RE-WH-SS*	*RE-WH-SS*	*RE-WK-SS*	*RE-WK-SS*
Constant	9.320*	9.335*	9.389*	9.655*	9.377*	9.350*
	(16.766)	(18.929)	(15.866)	(19.738)	(16.464)	(18.578)
Lpgini	0.339**	0.336**	0.048	−0.043	0.405*	0.355*
	(2.201)	(2.386)	(0.356)	(−0.443)	(2.542)	(2.491)
Lfinldpth	0.714*	0.723*	0.608*	0.501*	0.722*	0.726*
	(9.086)	(10.625)	(6.765)	(6.407)	(9.202)	(10.680)
Linfss(-1)	0.384	–	0.902*	–	0.295	–
	(1.579)		(3.517)		(1.195)	
Linflation	0.016	−0.004	0.051	0.080*	0.013	−0.005
	(0.636)	(−0.188)	(1.516)	(2.390)	(0.501)	(−0.255)
Lecoinfss(-1)	–	0.584*	–	0.555*	–	0.579*
		(4.058)		(3.558)		(4.012)
Lsocinfss(-1)	–	−0.124	–	0.466*	–	−0.140
		(−1.102)		(4.329)		(−1.243)
Hausman Test	7.300	6.506	6.506	6.506	4.291	4.713
(Signif)	(0.120)	(0.260)	(0.260)	(0.260)	(0.367)	(0.451)

Source: The Author
Notes:
Lpgini = Log of Gini Coefficient;
Linfss= Log of Composite Infrastructure Index computed using SS-based weights;
Lecoinfss = Log of Economic Infrastructure Index computed using SS-based weights;
Lsocinfss = Log of Social Infrastructure Index computed using SS-based weights
Lfinldpth = Log of Financial Depth;
Linflation = Log of Inflation;
Parenthesis to coefficient estimates indicates t-statistics;
Parenthesis to Hausman Statistics refers to the significance level.
*, **, and *** refer to 1%, 5%, and 10% level of significance, respectively.

infrastructure impacts state output but weakly. When we look at social infrastructure, we do not find a clear pattern for the high-income states. However, for the low-income states, social infrastructure has a positive and weakly impact on output.

Conditioning variables in Infrastructure and output relationship: Inflation does not have a statistically significant impact on state income in any of the three state groupings irrespective of whether infrastructure is taken as a composite index (Eq. 1) or in terms of its economic and social

Table 6.6 Impact of Infrastructure on Output-Leading States (PCA-Based Weights)

	Col.1	*Col.2*	*Col.3*	*Col.4*	*Col.5*	*Col.6*
	RE-ML-PCA	*RE-ML-PCA*	*RE-WH-PCA*	*RE-WH-PCA*	*RE-WK-PCA*	*RE-WK-PCA*
Constant	9.339*	9.392*	9.756*	9.661*	9.403*	9.405*
	(17.026)	(19.591)	(20.845)	(19.426)	(16.736)	(19.217)
Lpgini	0.337**	0.333*	0.001	−0.058	0.398*	0.348*
	(2.194)	(2.443)	(0.012)	(−0.608)	(2.508)	(2.525)
Lfinldpth	0.705*	0.696*	0.475*	0.475*	0.711*	0.698*
	(8.874)	(10.421)	(6.286)	(5.802)	(8.974)	(10.467)
Linfpca(-1)	0.366***	–	0.943*	–	0.302	–
	(1.729)		(4.784)		(1.413)	
Linflation	0.020	0.002	0.094*	0.091*	0.016	0.000
	(0.750)	(0.093)	(2.874)	(2.731)	(0.608)	(0.035)
Lecoinfpca(-1)	–	0.614*	–	0.509*	–	0.612*
		(4.682)		(3.410)		(4.665)
Lsocinfpca(-1)	–	−0.199***	–	0.432*	–	−0.212**
		(−1.870)		(4.149)		(−1.986)
Hausman Test	7.133	6.402	6.402	6.402	4.329	4.764
(Signif)	(0.129)	(0.269)	(0.269)	(0.269)	(0.363)	(0.445)

Source: The Author
Notes:
Lpgini = Log of Gini Coefficient;
Linfpca= Log of Composite Infrastructure Index computed using PCA-based weights;
Lecoinfpca = Log of Economic Infrastructure Index computed using PCA-based weights;
Lsocinfpca = Log of Social Infrastructure Index computed using PCA-based weights
Lfinldpth = Log of Financial Depth;
Linflation = Log of Inflation;
Parenthesis to coefficient estimates indicates t-statistics;
Parenthesis to Hausman Statistics refers to the significance level.

variants (Eq. 2). As far as financial depth is concerned, it has a statistically significant positive impact on state output in all the six estimates for both Eqs. (1–2) for all the three groups of states.

The impact of inequality on income for Group-A states is nuanced. This is because when we consider Eq. (1), in only two (RE-WH-SS and RE-WK-PCA) out of six specifications, inequality has a statistically significant positive impact. In four specifications, inequality does not have a

Table 6.7 Impact of Infrastructure on Output-Lagging States (Sectoral Share-Based Weights)

	Col.1	*Col.2*	*Col.3*	*Col.4*	*Col.5*	*Col.6*
	RE-ML-SS	*RE-ML-SS*	*RE-WH-SS*	*RE-WH-SS*	*RE-WK-SS*	*RE-WK-SS*
Constant	9.124*	9.733*	8.830*	8.985*	9.514*	10.492*
	(15.329)	(13.820)	(18.286)	(26.263)	(14.193)	(12.927)
Lpgini	0.261	0.447***	0.032	-0.004	0.447***	0.731*
	(1.225)	(1.845)	(0.201)	(-0.042)	(1.834)	(2.622)
Lfinldpth	0.636*	0.563*	0.710*	0.696*	0.572*	0.4628
	(7.083)	(5.716)	(8.397)	(9.672)	(5.889)	(4.240)
Linfss(-1)	0.233	–	0.516*	–	0.127	–
	(1.562)		(3.608)		(0.825)	
Linflation	-0.005	-0.005	-0.011	-0.006	-0.001	-0.003
	(-0.193)	(-0.210)	(-0.378)	(-0.236)	(-0.067)	(-0.142)
Lecoinfss(-1)	–	0.240***	–	0.332*	–	0.270**
		(1.865)		(2.918)		(2.091)
Lsocinfss(-1)	–	0.057	–	0.332*	–	0.002
		(0.851)		(6.097)		(0.035)
Hausman Test	8.580	9.325	9.325	9.325	4.155	4.252
(Signif)	(0.072)	(0.096)	(0.096)	(0.096)	(0.385)	(0.513)

Source: The Author
Notes:
Lpgini = Log of Gini Coefficient;
Linfss= Log of Composite Infrastructure Index computed using SS-based weights;
Lecoinfss = Log of Economic Infrastructure Index computed using SS-based weights;
Lsocinfss = Log of Social Infrastructure Index computed using SS-based weights;
Lfinldpth = Log of Financial Depth;
Linflation = Log of Inflation;
Parenthesis to coefficient estimates indicates t-statistics;
Parenthesis to Hausman Statistics refers to the significance level.
*, **, and *** refer to 1%, 5%, and 10% level of significance, respectively.

statistically significant impact on income. However, when Eq. (2) is used, in three (RE-ML-SS, RE-ML-PCA, and RE-WK-PCA) out of six specifications, inequality has a positive impact on output. A similar nuanced pattern is also observed for the low-income states. However, inequality turns out to have a statistically significant positive impact on output in the high-income states for Eqs. (1–2) in four out of the six estimates.

Impact of infrastructure on inequality

We first consider Group A states to ascertain the impact of infrastructure on inequality. Applying majority criterion to the empirical estimates of

Table 6.8 Impact of Infrastructure on Output-Lagging States (PCA-Based Weights)

	Col.1	*Col.2*	*Col.3*	*Col.4*	*Col.5*	*Col.6*
	RE-ML-PCA	*RE-ML-PCA*	*RE-WH-PCA*	*RE-WH-PCA*	*RE-WK-PCA*	*RE-WK-PCA*
Constant	8.952* (22.632)	8.934* (16.845)	9.022* (28.804)	8.936* (28.307)	9.554* (14.455)	9.961* (12.455)
Lpgini	0.071 (0.535)	0.158 (0.864)	0.033 (0.320)	0.036 (0.348)	0.434*** (1.821)	0.610** (2.161)
Lfinldpth	0.671* (9.027)	0.671* (7.915)	0.651* (9.425)	0.671* (9.589)	0.571* (5.943)	0.516* (4.694)
Linfpca(-1)	0.440* (5.344)	–	0.513* (7.671)	–	0.169 (1.422)	–
Linflation	-0.001 (-0.062)	-0.004 (-0.160)	0.006 (0.228)	0.005 (0.179)	-0.001 (-0.047)	0.000 (0.000)
Lecoinfpca(-1)		0.156*** (1.984)		0.239* (3.798)		0.103 (1.186)
Lsocinfpca(-1)		0.139** (2.216)		0.242* (4.252)		0.013 (0.189)
Hausman Test (Significance)	14.780 (0.005)	13.787 (0.017)	13.787 (0.017)	13.787 (0.017)	3.973 (0.409)	4.098 (0.535)

Source: The Author
Notes:
Lpgini = Log of Gini Coefficient;
Linfpca= Log of Composite Infrastructure Index computed using PCA-based weights;
Lecoinfpca = Log of Economic Infrastructure Index computed using PCA-based weights;
Lsocinfpca = Log of Social Infrastructure Index computed using PCA-based weights;
Lfinldpth = Log of Financial Depth;
Linflation = Log of Inflation;
Parenthesis to coefficient estimates indicates t-statistics;
Parenthesis to Hausman Statistics refers to the significance level.
*, **, and *** refer to 1%, 5%, and 10% level of significance, respectively.

Eq. (3) (Cols. 1, 3, and 5 of Tables 6.9 and 6.10), we can infer that the composite infrastructure does not lower inequality in a statistically significant manner. However, when seen separately (Eq. 4), only the economic infrastructure is found to have a statistically significant ameliorating impact on inequality as per five out of the six estimates (Cols. 2, 4, and 6 of

Table 6.9 Impact of Infrastructure on Inequality-All States (Sectoral Share-Based Weights)

	Col.1	*Col.2*	*Col.3*	*Col.4*	*Col.5*	*Col.6*
	RE-ML-SS	*RE-ML-SS*	*RE-WH-SS*	*RE-WH-SS*	*RE-WK-SS*	*RE-WK-SS*
Constant	-7.580*	-5.4538*	-4.968	-4.390	-7.580*	-2.588
	(-2.502)	(-1.833)	(-1.055)	(-0.843)	(-2.502)	(-0.505)
Lrpsdp	0.840	0.405	0.356	0.209	0.840	-0.120
	(1.513)	(0.739)	(0.412)	(0.218)	(1.513)	(-0.128)
Sdpsq	-0.031	-0.010	-0.011	-0.002	-0.031	0.011
	(-1.246)	(-0.410)	(-0.285)	(-0.045)	(-1.246)	(0.274)
Lfinldpth	0.125*	0.123*	0.157**	0.134***	0.125*	0.155**
	(2.627)	(2.697)	(2.143)	(1.680)	(2.627)	(1.985)
Linfss(-1)	0.068		-0.080		0.068	
	(0.938)		(-0.748)		(0.938)	
Linflation	0.007	0.008	0.013	0.010	0.007	0.014
	(0.678)	(0.833)	(0.801)	(0.604)	(0.678)	(0.828)
Lecoinfss(-1)		-0.125**		-0.154		-0.203**
		(-2.131)		(-1.521)		(-2.089)
Lsocinfss(-1)		0.069**		0.053		0.026
		(2.217)		(0.987)		(0.504)
Hausman Test	7.473	8.417	8.417	8.417	7.473	7.393
(Signif)	(0.187)	(0.209)	(0.209)	(0.209)	(0.187)	(0.286)

Source: The Author

Notes:

Linfss= Log of Composite Infrastructure Index computed using SS-based weights;
Lecoinfss = Log of Economic Infrastructure Index computed using SS-based weights;
Lsocinfss = Log of Social Infrastructure Index computed using SS-based weights;
Lrpsdp = Log of real per capita SDP;
Sdpsq = Square of real per capita SDP;
Lfinldpth = Log of Financial Depth;
Linflation = Log of Inflation;
Parenthesis to coefficient estimates indicates t-statistics;
Parenthesis to Hausman Statistics refers to the significance level.
*, **, and *** refer to 1%, 5%, and 10% level of significance, respectively.

Tables 6.9 and 6.10). In contrast, following the majority criterion, we find that social infrastructure accentuated inequality in a statistically significant but weak manner. This is because in three (RE-ML-SS, RE-ML-PCA, and RE-WK-PCA) out of the six specifications, the coefficient of social infrastructure variable is positive and statistically significant.

Seen through the lens of the leading and lagging states, we find composite infrastructure does not have statistically significant impact on income inequality (Cols. 1, 3, and 5 of Tables 6.11 – 6.14). Again, neither economic nor social infrastructure had a statistically significant impact on inequality for the leading states (Cols. 2, 4, and 6 of Tables 6.11 and 6.12).

Table 6.10 Impact of Infrastructure on Inequality-All States (Sectoral Share-Based Weights)

	Col.1	*Col.2*	*Col.3*	*Col.4*	*Col.5*	*Col.6*
	RE-ML-PCA	*RE-ML-PCA*	*RE-WH-PCA*	*RE-WH-PCA*	*RE-WK-PCA*	*RE-WK-PCA*
Constant	-7.404*	-4.224	-4.591	-0.440	-7.500*	-4.329
	(-2.429)	(-1.365)	(-0.890)	(-0.075)	(-2.462)	(-1.399)
Lrpsdp	0.800	0.186	0.283	-0.504	0.818	0.205
	(1.431)	(0.326)	(0.299)	(-0.465)	(1.464)	(0.359)
Sdpsq	-0.029	-0.000	-0.007	0.028	-0.030	-0.001
	(-1.165)	(-0.029)	(-0.184)	(0.571)	(-1.195)	(-0.061)
Lfinldpth	0.127*	0.134*	0.161**	0.177**	0.126*	0.133*
	(2.670)	(2.928)	(2.006)	(2.019)	(2.650)	(2.907)
Linfpca(-1)	0.029		-0.093		0.033	
	(0.481)		(-0.971)		(0.547)	
Linflation(-1)	0.007	0.006	0.013	0.011	0.007	0.006
	(0.740)	(0.644)	(0.723)	(0.598)	(0.724)	(0.630)
Lecoinfpca(-1)		-0.099*		-0.170**		-0.097**
		(-2.348)		(-2.212)		(-2.300)
Lsocinfpca(-1)		0.068**		0.021		0.069**
		(2.175)		(0.362)		(2.214)
Hausman Test	8.636	8.592	8.592	8.592	7.489	7.496
(Signif)	(0.124)	(0.197)	(0.197)	(0.197)	(0.186)	(0.277)

Source: The Author

Notes:

Linfpca= Log of Composite Infrastructure Index computed using PCA-based weights;
Lecoinfpca = Log of Economic Infrastructure Index computed using PCA-based weights;
Lsocinfpca = Log of Social Infrastructure Index computed using PCA-based weights;
Lrpsdp = Log of real per capita SDP;
Sdpsq = Square of real per capita SDP;
Lfinldpth = Log of Financial Depth;
Linflation = Log of Inflation;
Parenthesis to coefficient estimates indicates t-statistics;
Parenthesis to Hausman Statistics refers to the significance level.
*, **, and *** refer to 1%, 5%, and 10% level of significance, respectively.

However, for the lagging states (Cols. 2, 4, and 6 of Tables 6.13 and 6.14), the ameliorating impact of infrastructure on inequality is accounted for by economic infrastructure.

The impact, however, is weak as per the majority criterion. This is because only three (RE-ML-SS, RE-ML-PCA, and RE-WK-PCA) out of six estimates had a statistically significant negative coefficient for economic infrastructure when Eq.(2) is used. As far as impact of social infrastructure on inequality is concerned, we find it tends to accentuate inequality but again weakly as estimations from only three specifications viz, RE-ML-SS,

Table 6.11 Impact of Infrastructure on Inequality-Leading States (Sectoral Share-Based Weights)

	Col.1	*Col.2*	*Col.3*	*Col.4*	*Col.5*	*Col.6*
	RE-ML-SS	*RE-ML-SS*	*RE-WH-SS*	*RE-WH-SS*	*RE-WK-SS*	*RE-WK-SS*
Constant	29.130	31.720	41.278	109.901*	29.130	45.999
	(1.457)	(1.581)	(1.313)	(4.587)	(1.457)	(1.448)
Lrpsdp	-5.749	-6.225***	-7.934	-20.263*	-5.749	-8.770
	(-1.620)	(-1.746)	(-1.423)	(-4.744)	(-1.620)	(-1.554)
Sdpsq	0.262***	0.284***	0.356	0.892*	0.262***	0.393
	(1.688)	(1.816)	(1.454)	(4.689)	(1.688)	(1.583)
Lfinldpth	0.128	0.122	0.265***	0.689*	0.128	0.261***
	(1.221)	(1.145)	(1.750)	(16.480)	(1.221)	(1.702)
Linfss(-1)	0.214		0.042		0.214	
	(1.177)		(0.148)		(1.177)	
Linflation	-0.009	-0.008	-0.017	0.035	-0.009	-0.016
	(-0.497)	(-0.457)	(-0.581)	(1.338)	(-0.497)	(-0.542)
Lecoinfss(-1)		0.038		-0.686*		0.001
		(0.296)		(-8.270)		(0.007)
Lsocinfss(-1)		0.126		-0.164*		0.082
		(1.326)		(-2.412)		(0.559)
Hausman Test	4.873	6.192	6.192	6.192	4.873	4.882
(Signif)	(0.431)	(0.401)	(0.401)	(0.401)	(0.431)	(0.558)

Source: The Author

Notes:

Linfss= Log of Composite Infrastructure Index computed using SS-based weights;

Lecoinfss = Log of Economic Infrastructure Index computed using SS-based weights;

Lsocinfss = Log of Social Infrastructure Index computed using SS-based weights;

Lrpsdp = Log of real per capita SDP;

Sdpsq = Square of real per capita SDP;

Lfinldpth = Log of Financial Depth;

Linflation = Log of Inflation;

Parenthesis to coefficient estimates indicates t-statistics;

Parenthesis to Hausman Statistics refers to the significance level.

*, **, and *** refer to 1%, 5%, and 10% level of significance, respectively.

RE-ML-PCA, and RE-WK-PCA, suggest that social infrastructure accentuated inequality.

The empirical estimates suggest that the adverse impact of social infrastructure in the lagging states is neutralising the sobering impact of economic infrastructure on income inequality to render the impact of composite infrastructure ineffective in reducing inequality. As both variants of infrastructure were not statistically significant for the leading

Table 6.12 Impact of Infrastructure on Inequality-Leading States (PCA-Based Weights)

	Col.1	*Col.2*	*Col.3*	*Col.4*	*Col.5*	*Col.6*
	RE-ML-PCA	*RE-ML-PCA*	*RE-WH-PCA*	*RE-WH-PCA*	*RE-WK-PCA*	*RE-WK-PCA*
Constant	27.382	31.648	40.416	45.819	26.524	30.778
	(1.391)	(1.572)	(1.308)	(1.455)	(1.346)	(1.529)
Lrpsdp	-5.448	-6.232***	-7.783	-8.752	-5.295	-6.078***
	(-1.558)	(-1.740)	(-1.418)	(-1.562)	(-1.513)	(-1.696)
Sdpsq	0.249	0.285***	0.349	0.393	0.242	0.279***
	(1.626)	(1.811)	(1.449)	(1.591)	(1.582)	(1.769)
Lfinldpth	0.133	0.115	0.262***	0.254***	0.124	0.106
	(1.266)	(1.085)	(1.716)	(1.682)	(1.179)	(0.992)
Linfpca(-1)	0.143		0.030		0.149	
	(0.917)		(0.122)		(0.960)	
Linflation	−0.008	−0.008	−0.016	−0.016	−0.008	−0.007
	(−0.458)	(−0.432)	(−0.561)	(−0.545)	(−0.429)	(−0.403)
Lecoinfpca(-1)		−0.015		−0.032		−0.015
		(−0.121)		(−0.170)		(−0.121)
Lsocinfpca(-1)		0.125		0.083		0.128
		(1.306)		(0.582)		(1.336)
Hausman Test	6.179	6.180	6.180	6.180	4.881	4.878
(Signif)	(0.289)	(0.289)	(0.289)	(0.289)	(0.430)	(0.430)

Source: The Author
Notes:
Linfpca= Log of Composite Infrastructure Index computed using PCA-based weights;
Lecoinfpca = Log of Economic Infrastructure Index computed using PCA-based weights;
Lsocinfpca = Log of Social Infrastructure Index computed using PCA-based weights;
Lrpsdp = Log of real per capita SDP;
Sdpsq = Square of real per capita SDP;
Lfinldpth = Log of Financial Depth;
Linflation = Log of Inflation;
Parenthesis to coefficient estimates indicates t-statistics;
Parenthesis to Hausman Statistics refers to the significance level.
*, **, and *** refer to 1%, 5%, and 10% level of significance, respectively.

states, the results for all the states under study seem to be driven by the results for lagging states.

Conditioning variables in infrastructure and inequality relationship

When composite infrastructure is used in Eq. (3), we find that output does not impact inequality in a statistically significant manner for all the three groups of states. Similar results are also obtained when Eq. (4) is used for

Table 6.13 Impact of Infrastructure on Inequality-Lagging States (Sectoral Share-Based Weights)

	Col.1	*Col.2*	*Col.3*	*Col.4*	*Col.5*	*Col.6*
	RE-ML-SS	*RE-ML-SS*	*RE-WH-SS*	*RE-WH-SS*	*RE-WK-SS*	*RE-WK-SS*
Constant	-11.192*	-1.402	-8.776	-33.074*	-11.192*	-2.790
	(-2.343)	(-0.318)	(-0.810)	(-3.925)	(-2.343)	(-0.240)
Lrpsdp	1.611***	-0.345	1.183	6.166*	-0.346***	-0.008
	(1.750)	(-0.403)	(0.566)	(3.811)	(1.750)	(-0.003)
Sdpsq	-0.071	0.023	-0.053	-0.298*	-0.071	0.004
	(-1.613)	(0.574)	(-0.531)	(-3.830)	(-1.613)	(0.039)
Lfinldpth	0.187*	0.202*	0.174	-0.156**	0.187*	0.182
	(3.706)	(4.768)	(1.515)	(-1.957)	(3.706)	(1.602)
Linfss(-1)	0.095		0.000		0.095	
	(1.346)		(0.005)		(1.346)	
Linflation	0.011	0.008	0.025	0.116*	0.011	0.024
	(0.963)	(0.874)	(0.960)	(5.189)	(0.963)	(0.935)
Lecoinfss(-1)		-0.186*		0.195**		-0.145
		(-3.446)		(2.384)		(-1.044)
Lsocinfss(-1)		0.088*		-0.065		0.039
		(3.479)		(-1.179)		(0.588)
Hausman Test	5.057	6.042	6.042	6.042	5.057	5.042
(Signif)	(0.408)	(0.302)	(0.302)	(0.302)	(0.408)	(0.410)

Source: The Author

Notes:

Linfss= Log of Composite Infrastructure Index computed using SS-based weights;
Lecoinfss = Log of Economic Infrastructure Index computed using SS-based weights;
Lsocinfss = Log of Social Infrastructure Index computed using SS-based weights;
Lrpsdp = Log of real per capita SDP;
Sdpsq = Square of real per capita SDP;
Lfinldpth = Log of Financial Depth;
Linflation = Log of Inflation;
Parenthesis to coefficient estimates indicates t-statistics;
Parenthesis to Hausman Statistics refers to the significance level.
*, **, and *** refer to 1%, 5%, and 10% level of significance, respectively.

the lagging states and 'all states' as a group. However, we find evidence for a Kuznet curve relationship between output and inequality for the leading states when Eq. (4) is used. The coefficients of output and squared output are positive and negative, respectively, in the ML-SS, WH-SS, ML-PCA, and WK-PCA specifications. This suggests an increase in inequality followed by a decline as output increases rapidly for the leading states. We also find that financial depth accentuates inter-district inequality, primarily in the lagging states. This could be due to the preference by the commercial banks to concentrate their lending activities in the relatively well-off districts of the lagging states.

Table 6.14 Impact of Infrastructure on Inequality-Lagging States (PCA-Based Weights)

	Col.1	*Col.2*	*Col.3*	*Col.4*	*Col.5*	*Col.6*
	RE-ML-PCA	*RE-ML-PCA*	*RE-WH-PCA*	*RE-WH-PCA*	*RE-WK-PCA*	*RE-WK-PCA*
Constant	-11.170**	1.601	-8.464	1.605	-11.254	1.569
	(-2.289)	(0.328)	(-0.796)	(0.132)	(-2.306)	(0.321)
Lrpsdp	1.598***	-0.899	1.098	-0.868	1.614***	-0.894
	(1.696)	(-0.951)	(0.535)	(-0.370)	(1.713)	(-0.944)
Sdpsq	-0.070	0.049	-0.048	0.046	-0.071	0.049
	(-1.561)	(1.083)	(-0.491)	(0.408)	(-1.577)	(1.077)
Lfinldpth	0.187*	0.212*	0.170	0.187	0.187*	0.212*
	(3.673)	(4.954)	(1.509)	(1.649)	(3.678)	(4.959)
Linfpca(-1)	0.050		-0.042		0.053	
	(0.868)		(-0.373)		(0.909)	
Linflation	0.012	0.005	0.024	0.017	0.012	0.005
	(1.078)	(0.563)	(0.940)	(0.683)	(1.058)	(0.548)
Lecoinfpca(-1)		-0.1318		-0.145		-0.131*
		(-3.399)		(-1.635)		(-3.379)
Lsocinfpca(-1)		0.086*		0.047		0.087*
		(3.345)		(0.723)		(3.364)
Hausman Test	6.105	6.041	6.041	6.041	5.035	5.002
(Signif)	(0.296)	(0.418)	(0.418)	(0.418)	(0.411)	(0.543)

Notes:
Linfpca= Log of Composite Infrastructure Index computed using PCA-based weights;
Lecoinfpca = Log of Economic Infrastructure Index computed using PCA-based weights;
Lsocinfpca = Log of Social Infrastructure Index computed using PCA-based weights;
Lrpsdp = Log of real per capita SDP;
Sdpsq = Square of real per capita SDP;
Lfinldpth = Log of Financial Depth;
Linflation = Log of Inflation;
Parenthesis to coefficient estimates indicates t-statistics;
Parenthesis to Hausman Statistics refers to the significance level.
*, **, and *** refer to 1%, 5%, and 10% level of significance, respectively.

Given the policy focus on the upliftment of lagging states, our finding that social infrastructure accentuates inequality in these states appears to be counter intuitive. However, our findings can be appreciated if the relatively backward districts within the lagging states do not get a preferential treatment in the provision of health and education facilities despite the policy intent. To evaluate such a possibility, we undertake an exploratory analysis of the evolution of some key social (education and health) infrastructure in the backward districts in different states.

We make use of the list of backward districts identified by the NITI Aayog (GoI, 2017) for this purpose. To assess if backward districts in the states under study have got preferential treatment in the creation of health facilities, we look at the progress made in the availability of government health centres in the backward districts during the study period. We look at different types of healthcare centres such as primary health centres, community health care centres, and sub centres in a state between 2004 and 2011. In case of education, we take into account two indicators viz, the proportion of 'primary schools with single teacher' and the percentage of 'primary schools with single classroom' out of the total number of such schools in a state. We look at how the percentage of such schools in backward districts has changed between 2002 and 2011. If policies are implemented in accordance with the objective of reducing regional disparity, we would expect education and health infrastructure to improve at a faster pace in backward districts over time.

The NITI Aayog has designated 61 districts in the 12 states under study as backward. The lagging state accounts for 47 of the 61 districts (Table 6.3). We find that the backward districts have not received any special treatment in terms of creating education or healthcare facilities. In fact, heath infrastructure deteriorated in more than half of the backward districts in the lagging states during the study period. In contrast, health infrastructure has deteriorated in around two-fifths of the backward districts in the leading states. In terms of educational infrastructure, the percentage of 'schools with a single classroom' and 'schools with a single teacher' increased in one-fourth and more than one-third of the backward districts in the lagging states, respectively. For the leading states, these numbers were one-fifth and one-third, respectively.

Thus, notwithstanding the policy intent to uplift backward districts across the country, the facts on the ground show no discernible change in the social infrastructure in backward districts in both leading and lagging states during our study period. The discord between policy intent and actual provision of social infrastructure is most pronounced in the backward districts of the lagging states. This could explain why social infrastructure had a statistically significant negative influence on inequality in as many as three out of six specifications in the lagging states. The empirical finding that social infrastructure has negative repercussions for inequality is due to the inability of the states to implement the policy intent and should not lead to drawing wrong inferences regarding the importance of social infrastructure in Indian states in general, and lagging states in particular.

The empirical findings reflect the state governments' inability to carry out a policy of balanced development of districts rather than the ineffectiveness of social infrastructure in achieving more equitable outcomes. We only considered the quantitative aspect of social infrastructure. Studying the 'quality' of social infrastructure will perhaps make the disparities in the delivery of education and health infrastructure in lagging states more pronounced.

Table 6.15 Changing Share of Education and Health Infrastructure in the Backward Districts

State	*District Name*	*Percentage of Schools with Single Classroom at Primary level*		*Percentage of Schools with Single Teacher at Primary level*		*Share in total number of PHCs, CHCs and Sub Centres*	
		2002–03	*2010–11*	*2002–03*	*2010–11*	*2004*	*2011*
Lagging States							
Bihar	Araria	9.10	3.56	14.00	4.97	2.42	2.03
Bihar	Aurangabad (Bihar)	27.50	9.31	26.60	11.49	2.78	2.50
Bihar	Banka	16.90	9.46	35.40	14.01	1.96	2.70
Bihar	Begusarai	5.40	1.54	7.40	3.75	2.89	2.86
Bihar	Gaya	6.30	3.57	42.90	7.65	5.40	4.45
Bihar	Jamui	16.30	3.50	55.50	14.81	1.11	2.94
Bihar	Katihar	30.20	9.86	17.20	1.24	2.76	3.41
Bihar	Khagaria	9.30	3.40	5.20	3.77	0.48	1.72
Bihar	Muzaffarpur	8.70	3.70	34.10	6.66	4.66	4.98
Bihar	Nawada	31.40	4.37	23.10	7.36	2.28	3.42
Bihar	Purnia	11.20	0.23	21.80	16.18	2.29	3.29
Bihar	Sheikhpura	25.70	18.58	36.20	10.62	4.25	3.71
Bihar	Sitamarhi	6.10	3.15	9.30	12.77	1.12	0.94
Madhya Pradesh	Barwani	11.40	11.17	31.10	23.00	3.18	3.22
Madhya Pradesh	Chhatarpur	17.40	10.92	3.70	16.21	2.27	2.36
Madhya Pradesh	Damoh	8.70	3.07	7.70	18.40	1.73	1.81
Madhya Pradesh	Guna	5.10	0.00	10.60	11.92	3.15	2.07
Madhya Pradesh	Khandwa	10.20	5.89	12.70	17.94	2.39	1.37
Madhya Pradesh	Rajgarh	4.90	5.34	7.20	16.96	1.95	1.97
Madhya Pradesh	Sidhi	2.50	4.11	22.80	18.31	3.42	3.33
Madhya Pradesh	Vidisha	4.30	4.80	17.20	24.39	1.63	1.72

Orissa	Balangir	15.70	19.44	19.30	29.34	3.96	3.98
Orissa	Dhenkanal	8.50	8.13	26.10	15.60	2.96	2.94
Orissa	Gajapati	34.90	20.38	59.30	32.18	2.20	2.31
Orissa	Kalahandi	4.70	3.90	7.40	31.97	4.13	4.23
Orissa	Kandhamal	10.70	21.21	39.90	39.59	4.13	3.12
Orissa	Koraput	13.90	15.59	16.20	32.78	6.39	5.22
Orissa	Malkangiri	9.10	14.33	31.40	25.36	2.59	2.68
Orissa	Rayagada	19.50	17.83	29.10	27.64	3.82	3.96
Rajasthan	Barmer	5.20	3.32	64.00	66.36	4.17	4.64
Rajasthan	Dhaulpur	6.70	5.82	35.60	36.58	1.57	1.66
Rajasthan	Jaisalmer	5.00	7.21	75.90	76.50	1.21	1.18
Rajasthan	Karauli	3.30	5.43	31.20	31.19	2.16	2.15
Rajasthan	Sirohi	2.20	3.45	46.50	28.50	1.84	1.64
Uttar Pradesh	Bahraich	3.00	0.67	55.00	35.69	1.35	1.34
Uttar Pradesh	Balrampur	0.50	0.47	48.50	44.84	1.04	1.03
Uttar Pradesh	Chandauli	4.60	0.00	16.30	10.92	1.17	1.16
Uttar Pradesh	Chitrakoot	1.10	0.11	33.40	17.00	0.70	0.70
Uttar Pradesh	Fatehpur	0.20	0.74	10.10	7.84	1.51	1.50
Uttar Pradesh	Shrawasti	3.30	0.36	23.90	38.52	0.79	0.79
Uttar Pradesh	Siddharthnagar	0.10	0.00	21.60	21.60	1.48	1.46
Uttar Pradesh	Sonbhadra	0.30	0.30	37.50	31.18	0.82	0.82
West Bengal	Birbhum	19.10	13.20	3.80	5.11	4.83	4.83
West Bengal	Dakshin Dinajpur	47.90	30.72	2.00	10.06	2.35	2.35
West Bengal	Maldah	30.40	16.85	2.00	1.48	4.83	4.83
West Bengal	Murshidabad	11.80	15.18	2.90	0.76	7.99	7.99
West Bengal	Nadia	18.10	12.72	1.30	2.21	4.60	4.59

(*Continued*)

State	District Name	Percentage of Schools with Single Classroom at Primary level		Percentage of Schools with Single Teacher at Primary level		Share in total number of PHCs, CHCs and Sub Centres	
		2002–03	2010–11	2002–03	2010–11	2004	2011
Leading States							
Andhra Pradesh	Cuddapah	45.50	43.53	10.40	20.18	3.78	3.78
Andhra Pradesh	Visakhapatnam	24.50	43.16	40.00	36.46	4.59	4.59
Andhra Pradesh	Vizianagaram	39.80	42.99	19.70	27.12	3.75	3.73
Karnataka	Gadag	7.50	0.52	5.30	6.22	1.33	1.55
Karnataka	Gulbarga	20.10	6.46	8.90	12.92	5.27	5.08
Kerala	Wayanad	2.10	2.08	0.00	0.00	3.83	2.97
Maharashtra	Gadchiroli	41.30	20.00	43.60	22.96	4.24	3.92
Maharashtra	Jalgaon	6.90	3.84	6.80	2.30	4.87	4.88
Maharashtra	Nanded	17.70	8.69	13.80	5.87	4.46	4.13
Maharashtra	Nandurbar	23.90	13.73	0.00	0.00	3.12	3.28
Punjab	Firozpur	6.40	3.11	2.90	17.24	8.34	8.64
Punjab	Moga	7.00	4.31	7.80	6.20	3.88	4.69
Tamil Nadu	Ramanathapuram	52.20	5.91	6.10	4.83	2.92	3.04
Tamil Nadu	Virudhunagar	0.10	12.25	0.00	4.53	2.94	2.94

Annex 6.1 Data Source for Various Indicators

Indicator	*Source*
a) Per capita Installed Capacity of Electricity b) Per capita Electricity consumption	1. Annual Report of Central Electricity Authority, Ministry of Power, Government of India (various issues) 2. Energy Statistics, Central Statistical Office, Ministry of Planning and Programme Implementation, Government of India (various issues)
c) Gross Irrigated Area as Percentage of Gross Cropped Area d) Fertiliser consumption in a State	1. Pocket Book on Agricultural Statistics, Department of Agriculture and Cooperation, Ministry of Agriculture, Government of India (various issues) 2. State of Indian Agriculture, Department of Agriculture and Cooperation, Ministry of Agriculture, Government of India (various issues)
e) Road Density f) Surfaced Road as Percentage of Total Road	1. Infrastructure Statistics, Central Statistical Office, Ministry of Planning and Programme Implementation, Government of India (various issues)
g) Number of PHCs, CHCs, and Sub centres per lakh population h) Infant Mortality Rate	1. National Health Profile (various issues) 2. The survival index is a residual index derived from the IMR. Handbook of Statistics on Indian States, Reserve Bank of India
i) Average number of teachers per school at the primary level j) Pupil Teacher Ratio	1. Selected Educational Statistics, Ministry of HRD, Government of India (Various Issues) 2. Unified District Information System for Education (U-DISE), Government of India
k) State Domestic Product	1. Statistical Handbook, Directorate of Economics and Statistics of different State Governments (various issues)
l) District Income	District Statistical Handbook from Each State (various issues)

VI Conclusion

This chapter used data from 12 states in India, divided into leading and lagging states, to examine how infrastructure affects inter-district disparity from 2001 to 2012. Income data from 388 districts were used to compute state-wise Gini coefficients. Unlike previous research, which has looked at either the 'quantity' and/or the 'quality' of infrastructure, this study takes into account both the 'availability' and the 'usage' of economic infrastructure and 'availability' and 'adequacy' of social infrastructure. We studied how the economic and social variants of infrastructure affect output and inequality in the Indian states.

We found only economic infrastructure has a significant impact on inter-district income inequality in the lagging states. In the lagging states, social infrastructure was found to exacerbate income disparity, albeit weakly. The findings appear to be guided by the deterioration of social infrastructure in backward districts of both leading and lagging states, particularly in the lagging ones.

Our findings appear to be at odds with those of Bajar and Rajeev (2015). This could be due to the fact that previous studies have focused on the impact of infrastructure on personal consumption inequality rather than inter-district income inequality. The lack of social infrastructure in a state's backward districts may cause human and material resources to be channelled away from it, exacerbating inter-district income inequality. Policymakers need to place greater emphasis on the provision of social infrastructure in general, as well as giving preference to backward districts in the creation of such infrastructure, in order to promote balanced regional development.

References

ADB (2012). Infrastructure for Supporting Inclusive Growth and Poverty Reduction in Asia, *Asian Development Bank, Summary of the Papers and Presentations in Workshops on Economics of Infrastructure in a Globalized World*, funded by ADB Manila, Philippines.

Aschauer, D. (1989). Is Public Expenditure Productive?, Journal *of Monetary Economics*, Vol. 23, No. 2, pp. 177–200.

Bajar, S. and Rajeev, M. (2015). The Impact of Infrastructure Provisioning on Inequality: Evidence from India, *ISEC Working Paper 337*, Bangalore, India.

Baltagi, B. (2011). *Econometrics Analysis of Panel Data*, Fourth Edition, Wiley International, Chichester, England.

Belton Fleisher, Haizheng, Li. and Min Qiang, Z. (2007). Human Capital, Economic Growth, and Regional Inequality in China, *William Davidson Institute*

Working Papers Series, Working Paper No. 857, William Davidson Institute, University of Michigan.

Calderón, César. and Servén, L. (2004). The Effects of Infrastructure Development on Growth and Income Distribution, *World Bank Policy Research Working Paper No.3400*, World Bank, Washington, DC.

Calderon, Cesar and Serven, L. (2014). Infrastructure, Growth, and Inequality: An Overview, *World Bank Policy Research working paper No. 7034*, Washington, DC.

Clark Tom, S. and Linzer Drew, A. (2015). Should I Use Fixed or Random Effects?, *Political Science Research and Methods*, Vol. 3, No. 2, pp. 399–408.

Dan, Z. and Tatsuaki, K. (2013). The Role of Public Infrastructure in C hina's Regional Inequality and Growth: A Simultaneous Equations Approach, *The Developing Economies, Institute of Developing Economies*, Vol. 51, No. 1, pp. 79–109, March.

Dinkelman, T. (2011). The Effects of Rural Electrification on Employment: New Evidence from South Africa, *American Economic Review*, Vol. 101 No. 7, pp. 3078–3108.

Escobal, Javier. and Ponc, C. (2014), *Enhancing Income Opportunities for the Rural Poor: The Benefits of Rural Roads*, Available at: https://www.researchgate.net/publication/228969202.

Estache A. and Fay, M. (2007). Current Debates on Infrastructure Policy. Paper prepared for Growth Commission. Workshop on Global Trends and Challenges held on Sep 28-29, 2007, Yale University.

Estache, A. and Fay, M. (2010). Current Debates on Infrastructure Policy, *Commission on Growth and Development, Working Paper No. 49*, Washington, DC.

Fan, S., Kanbur, R. and Zhang, Xaobo. (2011). China's Regional Disparities: Experience and Policy, *Review of Development Finance*, Vol. 1, No. 1, pp. 47–56.

Fan, S., Zhang, L. and Zhang, X. (2004). Reforms, Investment, and Poverty in Rural China. *Economic Development and Cultural Change*, Vol. 52, No. 2, pp. 395–421.

Field, A.P. (2001). Meta-Analysis of Correlation Coefficients: A Monte Carlo Comparison of Fixed and Random Effects Methods, *Psychological Methods,* Vol. 6, No. 2, pp. 161–180

Hulten, C.R. and Schwab, R.M. (1991). Public Capital Formation and the Growth of the Regional Manufacturing Industries, *National Tax Journal*, Vol. 44, No. 4, pp. 121–134.

Majumder, R. (2012). Removing Poverty and Inequality in India: The Role of Infrastructure, *MPRA Paper No.* 4094, pp.1–25.

Misra Biswa Swarup. (2007). *Regional Growth Dynamics in India in the Post-Economic Reforms Period.* Palgrave Macmillan, London.

Misra B. S. (2013). *Revisiting Regional Growth Dynamics in India in the Post-economic Reforms Period.* Palgrave Macmillan, London.

Mohammadi Teimour. (2012). Relative Performance of Components Variance Estimators in Random Effects Models, *Iranian Journal of Economic Research*, Vol. 17, No. 5, pp. 83–98.

Munnell, A.H. (1990). Why Has Productivity Declined? Productivity and Public Investment, New *England Economic Review*, Federal Reserve Bank of Boston, January/February, pp. 3–22.

Mu Ren, Van de Walle Dominique. (2007). Rural Roads and Local Market Development in Vietnam, *World Bank Policy Research Working Paper No. 4340*, World Bank, Washington, DC.

Nadiri M.I. and Mamuneas, T.P. (1994). The Effects of Public Infrastructure and R&D Capital on the Cost Structure and Performance of U.S. Manufacturing Industries, *Review of Economics and Statistics*, Vol. 76, No. 1, pp. 22–37.

Romp, W. and De Haan, J. (2007). Public Capital and Economic Growth: A Critical Survey, *Perspektiven der Wirtschaftspolitik*, Vol. 8, No. 1, pp. 6–52.

Seneviratne, Dulani. and Sun, Yan. (2013). Infrastructure and Income Distribution in ASEAN–5: What Are the Links?, *IMF Working Paper No. 13/41.*

Straub, S. (2008). Infrastructure and Development: A Critical Appraisal of the Macro Level Literature, *Policy Research Working Paper Series 4590*, The World Bank.

UNCTAD (2013). Supporting Infrastructure Development to Promote Economic Integration: The Role of the Public and Private Sectors, *Note by UNCTAD Secretariat at the Multi Year Expert Meeting on Promoting Economic Integration and Cooperation*, Geneva, pp. 11–12, April 2013.

Zhu, N. and Luo, X. (2006). Nonfarm Activity and Rural Income Inequality: A Case Study of Two Provinces in China, *World Bank Research Working Paper No. 3811*, The World Bank, Washington DC.

7 Political accountability and development in Indian States

I Introduction

The power vested on the people to choose their representative is the most essential feature of a democracy. The elected representative is expected to act as the agent of the principal, the electorate. The possibility of re-election in this principal–agent framework can act as a disciplining mechanism and also as an incentive for elected officials to align their interests with those of the voters (Alt et al., 2011, Ferraz and Finan, 2012, Bobonis et al., 2015, Aruoba et al., 2017, Fouirnaies and Hall, 2018). However, another body of research argues that, rather than serving as a disciplining mechanism, re-election may be indicative of perpetuation of power without accountability. Historical and structural forces may explain why informal institutions dominate over formal institutions, leading to perpetuation of power de facto, without yielding the benefits of a de jure democracy (Khemani et al., 2016; Foldvari, 2017). Furthermore, because political institutions are prone to local-level elite capture in developing countries like India, Bardhan (2002) and Bardhan and Mookherjee (2006) are sceptical whether the elected officials are accountable. According to Banerjee and Iyer (2005), Pandey (2010), and Anderson et al. (2015), historical institutions and clientelism dominate in India without providing much benefit to the voter. However, none of the previous studies take the re-election dimension into consideration when determining political accountability in India. In this context, we investigate whether the possibility of re-election acts as sufficient incentive for elected leaders in India to be more accountable to the citizens.

Undertaking such an analysis is useful since India is the world's largest democracy, where elections are held on a regular basis and there are no term limits. In the absence of term limits, re-elections to India's highest legislative body are pervasive. In the first 16 Lok Sabha elections during 1952–14, for instance, 246 legislators were elected for five terms from the

DOI: 10.4324/9781003278351-7

same constituency, while 119 members were elected for six terms. Besides, the per capita income was lower than that of the state average in more than half of the constituencies in the 14 large states that exhibited re-election for four consecutive terms, or nearly 20 years, in the first 13 Lok Sabha elections between 1952 and 1999.

This raises the question whether re-election had the necessary disciplining effect as suggested in the literature. The issue is vexed because despite the best efforts of the elected representative, a constituency may remain relatively underdeveloped due to region-specific constraints or inadequate infrastructure and financial underdevelopment. Furthermore, one must account for reverse causality when evaluating the influence of re-election on development. This is because the economic voting literature suggests that if economic conditions have improved during the incumbent's tenure, the likelihood of re-election increases significantly (Pacek and Radcliff, 1995; Lewis-Beck and Stegmaier, 2000; Duch and Stevenson, 2008; Dassonneville and Lewis-Beck, 2014; Rumayya et al., 2020). For example, Brender and Drazen (2008) found that in less developed nations, a higher GDP growth rate is associated with a higher probability of re-election, based on the experience of 74 countries in 350 election episodes from 1960 to 2003. Gupta and Panagariya (2014) based on their analysis of elections to 464 parliamentary constituencies in 18 states of India in the 2009 parliamentary elections found that economic growth had a statistically significant and substantial impact on the electoral prospects of candidates of the incumbent party. As such, to overcome the possibility of reverse causality, we have created an index of re-election which is time invariant as on the year 1999. We have studied the impact of re-election on per capita state income through the re-election index during 2001–16. Our objective is to ascertain whether the disciplining effect of re-election holds for Indian states after considering the various other determinants of development[1].

The remainder of this chapter is organised in the following manner. In Section II, we discuss the findings from theoretical and empirical studies on electoral accountability using the political agency framework. This section also discusses the role played by historical institutions and clientelism in influencing political accountability. The study's research design is discussed in Section III. Section IV discusses the role elected representatives play in influencing the development of their constituencies as well as some stylised facts about the prevalence of re-election across India's states. In Section V, the empirical methods and rationale for selecting the control variables are discussed. The findings from the empirical estimations are discussed in Section VI. Section VII provides concluding observations.

II Literature review

The political agency theory provides a framework for understanding the elected representative's accountability to the voters. According to the agency theory, the elected representative, as the agent, should work in the best interests of the principal, the voter. In the agency theory, the possibility of re-election serves as a disciplining tool for politicians to align their interests with those of the voters. However, the politician can avoid accountability to the voters by taking advantage of information asymmetry.

Asworth (2012) has identified two key takeaways from the theoretical models of political agency. First, the politician's actions to impress voters can be counterproductive to voters' interests. Second, rationality of voters need not ensure that the politician serves voters' interests. The predictions of theoretical models are contingent on the voter's efforts to be aware, alert, and vigilant about the actions of the politicians.

The limitations of voter rationality in generating a reaction from politicians that best suits the voter's interests have been highlighted in literature. Daley and Snowberg (2011) provide an example of how rationality need not serve the voter's interests. They look at a politician who can devote time to shaping policy or campaigning. Given the information content in campaign activities, rational voters prefer candidates who devote time to campaigning. As a result, politicians prefer to devote more time to campaigning than to policymaking. In the process, the rationality of voters results in a sub-optimal outcome. Smart and Sturm (2013) established a compelling case for term limits. Using a political agency model, Smart and Sturm argue that term limits lower the value of retaining office and elicits truthful behaviour of incumbents. Thus, enabling voters to re-elect high-quality leaders for a second term.

In the midst of unhealthy political arrangements when leaders are chosen for extending private gains rather than providing public goods, the principal–agent relationship gets inverted (Khemani et al., 2016). When political norms permit actions such as violence, clientelist strategies, vote buying, and political patronage, citizens become accountable to political leaders for the patronage they receive. Political representatives take advantage of knowledge asymmetry to promote their own interests at the expense of the voters. Information that is necessary to ensure discipline is presented to the voters in a curated manner. Further, elected representatives present partial information that voters use to evaluate the performance of governments and elected leaders through their control of official media. In the absence of comprehensive disclosure standards, official media are used to feed voters selective information, which can lead to faulty assessments of politicians' performance.

In the United States and other nations where there is a limit on the number of times someone can be elected, such as Brazil, extensive empirical study has been done to understand how re-election possibilities influence the behaviour of people's representatives. Besley and Case (1995) in their seminal study concluded that term limits had no impact on per capita income in US states during 1950–96. Nonetheless, they argued that term limits are beneficial because they limit the buildup of political capital. The Besley and Case (1995) study was based on the behaviour of US state governors who were allowed to run for re-election for only one more term. Re-election incentives, on the other hand, were found to diminish corruption in Brazil in the study by Ferraz and Finan (2012). Re-election, according to Aruoba et al. (2019), enhances political leaders' accountability to voters and has a powerful disciplining effect. The Aruoba et al. (2019) study undertaken for the United States ascribe two-thirds of the improvement in voter welfare to the discipline effect. Given the mixed results, findings from India on how re-election prospects influence the behaviour of elected representatives will add to the literature. We next discuss how historical institutions and clientelism act as impediments to political accountability in India.

Clientelism and the importance of historical institutions

Banerjee and Iyer (2005) and Pandey (2005) highlight the importance of the colonial land administration system in different states before India's independence as an indicator of historical institutions (2010). The British administration used three different types of land tenure systems: Zamindari, Ryotwari, and Mahal Wari in different parts of India (Banerjee and Iyer, 2005). In the Ryotwari and Mahal Wari systems, land revenue was collected directly from the peasant and village community, respectively. However, the power of revenue collection was vested in the landlords, who served as intermediaries between the government and the peasants, in the Zamindari system. In the Zamindari system of revenue collection, the landlord wanted to extract the maximum from the peasants. According to Pandey (2010), because land was the foundation for all economic activity and social interactions prior to independence, the land revenue system had a significant impact on people's perceptions of power structures and political representatives' accountability in the post-independence period.

Another historical institution that influences Indian politics is the caste system (Sen, 2012). When the recommendation of the Mandal Commission was adopted in 1990 to provide quota for 400 backward castes, state action reinforced the influence of caste on Indian politics. Because caste identification is so strongly ingrained in Indian society, voters may be hesitant to hold elected politicians from their own caste, accountable.

Anderson et al. (2015) have investigated electoral practices in rural Maharashtra and found evidence of deep rooted clientelist vote-trading structures sustained through non-political means. The poor elect the landowners as political representatives through a democratic election process that is highly participatory and non-coercive. Despite having the necessary traits, the authors warn that the election process should not be construed as an ideal democracy at work because voting is governed by the need of the poor for insurance against future contingencies. The poor vote for the landlord in expectation of receiving support at the time of need. The poor are aware that once elected, the landlord will deprive them of benefits from government welfare programmes. Nevertheless, they vote for the landlord as they prefer exchanging welfare benefits for insurance. Thus, India-specific literature suggests that historical institutions may be the reason for lack of political responsibility. In this backdrop, we investigate whether re-election acts as an incentive for promoting political accountability.

III Research design

Our objective is to examine the impact of re-election on development. However, as alluded in the introduction, re-election possibilities may be contingent on development of the constituency. As a result, it is critical that our estimation process account for reverse causality. Quantifying re-election without term limits is another challenge in assessing whether re-election matters for development. We address both of these concerns by constructing a time invariant re-election index. Following Gerring et al. (2005), who employed a stock measure of democracy to reflect the accumulation of democratic capital, we have computed a re-election index which embodies persistent re-election. For this purpose, we conceptualise re-election without term limits to describe persistent re-election. We define a constituency to exhibit persistent re-election when the same individual is elected in four successive Lok Sabha elections or for about 20 years from that constituency.

The re-election index (RI) is calculated by dividing the total number of constituencies demonstrating persistent re-election in the first 13 Lok Sabha elections held during 1952–99 (R) by the total number of constituencies in the state (M). As a result, we can write $RI = R/M$.

The re-election index is computed for each state in the year 1999 to reflect the pervasiveness of persistent re-election.

We have also computed three variants of the RI to ensure that the impact of re-election on development is not influenced by constituencies that are relatively underdeveloped. As such, we use three variants of the *RI*. The variants of RI are computed as follows:

$$RIv = (R - Uv)/M \quad (v = 1, 2, \text{ and } 3),$$

where *U* is the total number of constituencies that exhibit persistent re-election coupled with relative underdevelopment (Table 7.1).

We have taken into account both the economic and social dimensions of development in categorising constituencies as relatively underdeveloped. In each of the 14 states under study, we conducted an exploratory analysis of the economic and social development of the constituencies that displayed persistent re-election. In India, development indicators for constituencies are not available. What are available are the development indicators for the districts in which a constituency is nested. As such, we have mapped constituencies to districts to see how far they have progressed. An implicit assumption in our analysis is that a constituency has the same level of development as the district to which it belongs. We use the development indicators as of 2001 to determine the relative underdevelopment of a constituency, taking into account the fact that the process of development takes time. We look at both economic and social indicators to provide a more comprehensive picture of development. The economic status of the district is reflected in its income. At the district level, we have used infant mortality rate (IMR) and female literacy rate to reflect the state of health and education, respectively, under social indicators.

To determine a constituency's relative development, we first map it to the district in which it is located. In the next step, we compare that district's per capita income, IMR, and female literacy to the average for all the district in a state on these three indicators. When the district to which a constituency belongs has a per capita income less than the state average in 2001, we categorise the constituency as relatively underdeveloped in economic terms. We classify constituencies in a district to be relatively undeveloped in the social dimension when female literacy is below the state average or IMR is above the state average in 2001. We looked at each of these factors alone and in combination to determine a district's relative underdevelopment to compute the three variants of re-election index.

RI_1 is calculated by excluding constituencies (U_1) that are economically undeveloped. Constituencies that fare poorly in terms of education or health are excluded to compute RI_2. Specifically, we consider *IMR* for health and female literacy for education to assess relative underdevelopment. By excluding constituencies (U_3) that indicate relative underdevelopment in any of the three measures, RI_3 treats development in its broadest sense. The *RI* and its variants were augmented by a factor that

Table 7.1 Persistence of Re-election in Indian States and Backwardness.

State	*Number of Constituencies*	*Constituencies that had Re-election in Four Terms*	*Constituencies that had Re-election in Four Terms and Relatively Economically Underdeveloped*	*No. of Constituencies that had Re-election Four times and having IMR Below Average for 2001*	*No. of Constituencies that had Re-election Four Times and Having Female Literacy Below Average for 2001*	*No. of Re-elected Constituencies Having IMR or Female Literacy above Average for 2001*	*No. of Re-elected Constituencies having Either Income or IMR or Female Literacy below Average for 2001*
Andhra Pradesh	42	10	5	2	4	4	7
Gujarat	26	11	4	2	5	5	5
Haryana	10	2	1	2	1	2	2
Karnataka	28	13	4	3	6	7	7
Kerala	20	6	5	3	3	5	6
Maharashtra	48	18	10	6	12	13	14
Tamil Nadu	39	9	6	3	4	5	7
Punjab	13	1	1	0	0	0	1
Leading States	**226**	**70**	**36**	**21**	**35**	**41**	**49**
Bihar	40	13	8	3	6	8	11
Madhya Pradesh	29	16	7	8	6	8	10
Odisha	21	5	5	3	4	4	5
Rajasthan	25	6	2	3	3	5	4
Uttar Pradesh	80	25	12	8	6	11	18
West Bengal	42	29	18	11	12	12	20
Lagging States	**237**	**94**	**52**	**36**	**37**	**48**	**68**
All States	**463**	**164**	**88**	**57**	**72**	**89**	**117**

Note: Figures presented are numbers.
The number of constituencies listed for Bihar, Madhya Pradesh, and Uttar Pradesh is excluding those for Jharkhand, Chhattisgarh, and Uttarakhand, respectively. This is done to maintain compatibility of the democracy index with the indicators of development for the 2001–15 period. Telangana was created out of Andhra Pradesh in the year 2014. As such, we have considered the undivided Andhra Pradesh for our calculations.

reflects a state's share in the combined Lok Sabha seats of all the 14 states under study. The RI as well as its variants RI_1, RI_2, and RI_3 are stock measures of persistent re-election in various states as on the year 1999.

The chances of reverse causality are minimised when we assess regress the re-election index estimated as on 1999 on per capita state income for the next 16 years between 2001 and 2016. Apart from estimating the impact of RI and its variants on development, we also buttress our findings by looking at the availability of essential services in constituencies with persistent re-election compared to the state average. Exploratory analysis of the basic utilities such as electricity, piped water, school classrooms, and health clinics in the districts in which the constituencies are nested will help us to appreciate the empirical findings. We present our findings for 14 large Indian states as one group as well as these states divided into groups of 'leading' and 'lagging' states. To identify states as leading or lagging, we consider per capita income at the state level and pervasive backwardness at the district level. In September 2017, the Niti Aayog had identified 115 of India's most backward districts. If at least five districts of a state appear on this list of 115 backward districts, that state has been classified as lagging. Using this criterion, we find six states, namely, Bihar, Madhya Pradesh, Odisha, Rajasthan, Uttar Pradesh, and West Bengal, are categorised as lagging. When we used income classification, we found that the six lagging states had a real per capita SDP lower than the average for all 14 states in 2001 as well as 2016. The remaining eight states, namely, Andhra Pradesh, Gujarat, Haryana, Karnataka, Kerala, Maharashtra, Punjab, and Tamil Nadu, have been classified as leading. The leading states had relatively less number of backward districts and a real per capita SDP that was higher than the average for all the 14 states during the entire period of study lending credence to our classification. The role elected representatives can play in influencing development and the re-election patterns found in the states are discussed in the next section.

IV Stylised facts on re-election

Role of elected representatives and pattern of re-election

Indian Parliament is the highest legislative body in India comprising the President of India and two legislative bodies, the Lower House (Lok Sabha) and the Upper House (Rajya Sabha). The Lok Sabha plays the most important role in the Indian political system because its members are elected directly using the first-past-the-post voting procedure. Furthermore, money bills can only be introduced in the Lok Sabha, and the government at the Centre is formed by the party or coalition that has the majority in the Lok Sabha. Each state is assigned a specific number of seats in the Lok Sabha.

A Member of Parliament (MP) elected to the Lok Sabha can influence the development of his constituency in several ways. First, the elected representative has the opportunity to flag the developmental needs of his constituency and seek government assistance to promote development. Second, by utilising funds allocated under the Members of Parliament Local Area Development Scheme (MPLADS) for development projects. In December 1993, during the tenure of the Tenth Lok Sabha, the MPLADS was introduced in 1993 which empowered MPs to spend up to Rs.5 crore (US$780,000) per year in their constituency for development activities. As a result, MPs are endowed with dedicated funds to use for the development of their constituencies. Third, if an MP is a member of the government or belongs to the ruling party or coalition that has formed the government, can use political influence for development of his own constituency. We now analyse the state-wise re-election pattern seen in the first 13 Lok Sabha elections.

Re-election Pattern

The Lok Sabha, or Lower House of Indian Parliament, has 543 seats distributed among 37 administrative regions classified as 'States' and 'Union Territories', with each seat representing a geographical constituency. We analyse extreme situations of recurrent political representation in the Lok Sabha to better understand the consequences of re-election for development outcomes. Following the general elections, the first Lok Sabha was constituted on April 17, 1952. We have analysed instances when an MP has been elected consecutively for at least four times from a constituency in the first 13 Lok Sabha elections to identify persistent re-election. We limited our study to 14 large states for whom we have complete information on election results. The output of these 14 states accounts for 90% of the total output of all the states. These 14 states accounted for 463 seats in the Lok Sabha (Table 7.1). Re-election in four successive Lok Sabha elections was observed in 34.7% of the total constituencies in these 14 states. Each of the 14 states in our analysis has at least ten seats in the Lok Sabha.

We find that leading states accounted for 42% of constituencies that were characterised by persistent re-election, while lagging states accounted for the rest 58% (Table 7.1).

It is also observed that compared to the leading states, the lagging states had a higher proportion of constituencies that were relatively underdeveloped. For example, amongst the 14 states under study, the lagging states accounted for 60%, 54%, and 58% of total constituencies that exhibited persistent re-election and were undeveloped in the economic, social, and economic or social dimensions, respectively. The next section focuses on the econometric methodology used for studying the impact of re-election on development.

V Estimation methodology

Our empirical estimation of the impact of re-election on development takes into account several control variables. The control variables include state-specific structural factors that do not change over time as well as infrastructure facilities and financial development. As our study is based on a panel of 14 states during the period 2001–15, the effect of unobserved state-specific structural characteristics is incorporated by using the fixed effects estimation method.

The model we are interested to estimate is given in Eq. (1)

$$\Upsilon_{i,t} = \alpha_i + \beta_1 X_{i,t} + \beta_2 RI_i + e_{i,t} \tag{1}$$

Where i and t denote state and year, respectively. The state specific unobserved factors are presented by αi and Xi,t includes the control variables which are the other state-specific determinants of development. *RI* represents the time-invariant re-election index and εi,t is the error term. The time invariant characteristic of the *RI* in Eq (1) helps to avoid reverse causality. However, use of the time invariant regressor prevents the use of FE method as the fixed effects are wiped out during the estimation process. The time invariant regressor *RI* can be estimated using a random effect model. The random effects model, on the other hand, makes the very restrictive assumption that there is no relationship between cross-section-specific heterogeneity and time-varying regressors. Relaxing the assumption of no correlation, Pesaran and Zhou (2016) proposed the fixed effects filter (FEF) technique, which allows for arbitrary degrees of correlation between the time-varying regressor and the individual fixed effects. Hence, we have used the FEF estimation approach proposed by Pesaran and Zhou (2016) to estimate Eq (1). The FEF estimation involves a two-step procedure. In the first step, time-varying effects are filtered out by using FE estimation with the time-varying regressors. The residuals from the first-stage regression are averaged over time and are used as the dependent variable in the second step. In the second stage, the time invariant re-election measure and intercept are used as explanatory variables to get efficient estimates. FEF estimation method, however, assumes that time invariant regressors are strictly exogenous, i.e. that there is no correlation between the time-varying and the time-invariant regressors. In practice, strict exogeneity of a time invariant regressor may not hold true. Hence, as an alternative to the FEF, the correlated random effects (CRE) model is often preferred since it assumes conditional exogeneity. The CRE model allows correlation between individual-specific effects with time-varying regressors but assumes the individual effects are uncorrelated with time-invariant regressors (Schunck, 2013). Individual-specific heterogeneity is assumed to be linearly dependent on time-varying regressors in the CRE, which we believe to be a more reasonable assumption than the FEF. As a result, we base our conclusions on the CRE estimates. We do, however, present estimates from the RE and FEF models for comparison.

Based on the literature, we have used indicators of economic and social infrastructure, as well as financial development, as control variables under Xi,t to estimate Eq. (1). The importance of infrastructure in shaping state-level growth has been highlighted by Bajar and Rajeev (2015), Majumder (2012), and Misra (2015, 2019). Financial development enables savings to be channelised into productive investment. Given its importance in reducing transaction and information costs, financial development is, sometimes, used as a control variable (Misra, 2013; Purfield, 2016).

Economic infrastructure indicators that we have considered are the basic facilities such as water, electricity, and road. Health and education facilities are taken to represent social infrastructure. We have used two indicators each for water, electricity, and road, to indicate their 'availability' and 'usage', respectively, under economic infrastructure. The need for considering 'availability' and 'usage' in the Indian context has been discussed in (Misra, 2019). Following Misra (2019), we have used 'irrigated area as a percentage of cropped area' and 'fertilizer consumption' for water, 'installed capacity of electricity' and 'per capita power consumption for electricity', and 'road density' and 'surfaced road as a percentage of total road' to indicate availability and usage, respectively.

IMR and literacy rate are used to represent health and education facilities under social infrastructure. We use the infant survival rate per 1,000 births because IMR is a negative indicator. The survival index is computed from the IMR as a residual measure. The literacy rate in the states is taken from the Census and is available for only two years 2001 and 2011 during the study period. Hence, the annual literacy rate in each state is interpolated using exponential growth from 2001 to 2011, the most recent year for which data is available. The literacy rate for 2012–16 is obtained by extrapolating the annual exponential growth rate during 2001–11.

For each infrastructure indicator in the economic and social dimension, the index for a particular state in a given year is computed using the following formula:

Component Index = (actual–minimum)/(maximum–minimum)

To calculate the aggregate social infrastructure index for a state, we added the component indices for health and education assigning them equal weight. The two component indices, one for 'usage' and the other for 'availability', were combined by assigning equal weights to create separate infrastructure indices for water, power, and road. We derived the economic infrastructure index by assigning weights to the indices for water, electricity, and road using principal component analysis to construct the economic infrastructure index. The overall infrastructure index for a state was computed by combining the economic and social infrastructure indices using weights derived from PCA. We have used indices instead of indicators to save degrees of degrees of freedom in the estimation. Credit outstanding as a percentage of nominal SDP has been used to gauge financial development. Annexure 7.1 lists the sources of data for the various indicators considered in the study.

VI Empirical findings

We looked at the effect of persistent re-election on per capita income for all states as one group as well as for the groups of leading and lagging states separately. We find that the control variables used in the estimation, namely, economic infrastructure, social infrastructure, and financial depth, have a favourable impact on per capita income. Our findings on the positive effects of infrastructure and financial development on state income are consistent with the previous research (Misra, 2019). Financial development has the greatest impact on income among the control variables, followed by economic infrastructure and social infrastructure. For example, at 1% level of significance, CRE estimates for all the 14 states show that financial depth, economic infrastructure, and social infrastructure had coefficient values of 0.871, 0.361, and 0.184, respectively (Table 7.2, Col. 3). These findings are valid for both leading and lagging states as well as for all the three estimation methods (Tables 7.2–7.4).

When we evaluate all 14 states as a group, as well as the group of leading states, we find that the re-election index (*RI*) has no statistically significant impact on per capita income (Table 7.2, Col. 3 and Table 7.4, Col. 3). Persistent re-election, on the other hand, has a statistically significant negative influence on per capita income, with a coefficient value of -0.337 from the CRE estimates for the lagging states at a 1% level of significance (Table 7.3, Col. 3). In terms of variants of *RI*, we find that RI_1 and RI_2 are not statistically significant for the leading states (Table 7.3, Cols. 6 and 9) as well as for the entire group of 14 states (Table 7.2, Cols. 6 and 9). In the lagging

Annexure 7.1 Data source for various indicators

Indicator	*Source*
State domestic product	Statistical handbook, directorate of economics, and statistics of different state governments (various issues)
District income	District statistical handbook from each state (various issues)
District-wise households having electricity as main source of lighting. In addition to electricity, the other sources of lighting for households considered are 'Kerosene', 'Solar energy', 'Oil other than Kerosene', any other. There is also a category of Households having no lighting.	Census 2001
District-wise households having access to Tap water. The access to tap water includes from 'Within', 'near', and 'away' from the premises of the household.	Census 2001
State-wise credit outstanding	Basic statistical returns, Reserve Bank of India
Female literacy rate	Census 2001, Census 2011
District-wise number of primary health centres (PHCs), Community health centres (CHCs), and Sub centres per lakh population	National health profile (various issues)
District-wise school with single classroom at the primary level	School Report Card (various issues), District Information System for Education (DISE), Government of India
State-wise Gross irrigated area as percentage of gross cropped area	Pocket Book on Agricultural Statistics, Department of Agriculture and Cooperation, Ministry of Agriculture, Government of India (various issues)
State-wise fertiliser consumption in a State	State of Indian Agriculture, Department of Agriculture and Cooperation, Ministry of Agriculture, Government of India (various issues)
State-wise road density and state-wise surfaced road as percentage of total road	Infrastructure Statistics, Central Statistical Office, Ministry of Planning and Programme Implementation, Government of India (various issues)
State-wise per capita installed capacity of electricity	Annual Report of Central Electricity Authority, Ministry of Power, Government of India (various issues)
State-wise per capita electricity consumption	Energy Statistics, Central Statistical Office, Ministry of Planning and Programme Implementation, Government of India (various issues)

Table 7.2 Impact of Persistent Re-election on Per Capita Income-All States

	(1)	*(2)*	*(3)*	*(4)*	*(5)*	*(6)*	*(7)*	*(8)*	*(9)*	*(10)*	*(11)*	*(12)*
	RE	*FEF*	*CRE*	*RE*	*FEF*	*CRE*	*RE*	*FEF*	*CRE*	*RE*	*FEF*	*CRE*
Financial Depth	0.844***	0.871***	0.871***	0.845***	0.899***	0.899***	0.814***	0.876***	0.876***	0.774***	0.894***	0.894***
	(24.862)	(17.938)	(25.718)	(22.162)	(17.618)	(23.655)	(22.025)	(15.705)	(23.635)	(17.795)	(14.751)	(20.316)
Economic Infrastructure	0.366***	0.361***	0.361***	0.339***	0.252**	0.252***	0.384***	0.364***	0.364***	0.391***	0.229*	0.229**
	(5.323)	(3.456)	(5.095)	(4.077)	(2.184)	(2.739)	(5.789)	(3.400)	(4.987)	(4.653)	(1.739)	(2.247)
Social Infrastructure	0.177***	0.184**	0.184***	0.153***	0.168**	0.168***	0.174***	0.165**	0.165***	0.170***	0.146**	0.146***
	(4.546)	(2.568)	(4.415)	(3.742)	(2.558)	(3.731)	(4.501)	(2.499)	(3.778)	(4.102)	(2.398)	(2.999)
RI	−0.125**	-0.125	0.00705									
	(−2.281)	(−1.309)	(0.094)									
State Average of Financial Depth			−0.702***			−0.711***			−0.665***			−0.683***
			(−3.896)			(−4.767)			(−5.629)			(−6.527)
State Average of Economic Infrastructure			0.454*			0.587***			0.274*			0.483***
			(1.849)			(3.083)			(1.857)			(3.033)
State Average of Social Infrastructure			0.200*			0.178			0.299***			0.259***
			(1.649)			(1.607)			(3.171)			(2.934)
RI1				−0.201***	−0.211***	−0.0792						
				(−3.789)	(−2.903)	(−1.349)						
RI2							−0.0702**	−0.0754*	0.0288			
							(−1.990)	(−1.834)	(0.732)			
RI3										0.0498	0.0473	0.0651
										(0.830)	(0.521)	(1.201)
Constant	7.974***		11.36***	7.512***		10.92***	8.210***		11.23***	8.887***		11.42***
	(27.133)		(11.431)	(22.796)		(13.781)	(31.541)		(18.513)	(25.367)		(22.956)
N	252	252	252	216	216	216	234	234	234	180	180	180

Notes: t statistics in parentheses; *p < 0.10; **p < 0.05; and ***p < 0.01; the dependent variable is Y_{it}.

Table 7.3 Impact of persistent re-election on per capita income-leading states.

	(1)	*(2)*	*(3)*	*(4)*	*(5)*	*(6)*	*(7)*	*(8)*	*(9)*	*(10)*	*(11)*	*(12)*
	RE	*FEF*	*CRE*	*RE*	*FEF*	*CRE*	*RE*	*FEF*	*CRE*	*RE*	*FEF*	*CRE*
Financial Depth	0.840***	0.901***	0.901***	0.836***	0.937***	0.937***	0.811***	0.935***	0.935***	0.465***	0.965***	0.965***
	(16.151)	(12.832)	(18.262)	(14.841)	(11.808)	(16.632)	(13.760)	(10.369)	(15.500)	(9.481)	(9.131)	(12.110)
Economic Infrastructure	0.595***	0.579**	0.579***	0.786***	0.505**	0.505***	0.653***	0.570**	0.570***	1.042***	0.602	0.602*
	(3.324)	(2.483)	(3.284)	(4.229)	(2.100)	(2.611)	(3.760)	(2.137)	(2.908)	(6.068)	(1.448)	(1.899)
Social Infrastructure	0.286***	0.304**	0.304***	0.247**	0.332*	0.332***	0.332***	0.210	0.210*	0.331***	0.180	0.180
	(3.075)	(2.041)	(3.298)	(2.410)	(1.885)	(3.059)	(3.011)	(1.296)	(1.921)	(2.896)	(0.784)	(1.149)
RI	-0.126*	-0.140	-0.0212									
	(-1.918)	(-0.903)	(-0.276)									
State Average of Financial Depth			-0.849***			-0.821***			-0.818***			-0.748***
			(-5.207)			(-4.809)			(-5.801)			(-8.173)
State Average of Economic Infrastructure			-0.657			-0.228			-0.417			-0.103
			(-1.384)			(-0.399)			(-1.006)			(-0.292)
State Average of Social Infrastructure			-0.361			-0.333			0.00866			0.0702
			(-1.527)			(-1.306)			(0.027)			(0.376)
RI1				-0.232***	-0.253**	-0.0668						
				(-3.447)	(-2.080)	(-0.945)						
RI2							-0.0503	-0.0748	-0.0117			
							(-0.755)	(-0.569)	(-0.173)			
RI3										0.233***	0.377**	0.157***
										(4.056)	(2.528)	(3.652)
Constant	8.153***		10.98***	7.679***		10.74***	8.526***		11.02***	11.38***		11.64***
	(18.554)		(11.920)	(16.291)		(12.510)	(17.400)		(14.722)	(34.785)		(46.375)
N	144	144	144	126	126	126	126	126	126	90	90	90

Notes: t statistics in parentheses; *$p < 0.10$; **$p < 0.05$; and ***$p < 0.01$; the dependent variable is Y_{it}

Table 7.4 Impact of persistent re-election on per capita income-lagging states.

	(1)	(2)	(3)	(4)	(5)	(6)	(7)	(8)	(9)	(10)	(11)	(12)
	RE	*FEF*	*CRE*	*RE*	*FEF*	*CRE*	*RE*	*FEF*	*CRE*	*RE*	*FEF*	*CRE*
Financial Depth	0.808***	0.761***	0.761***	0.789***	0.770***	0.770***	0.811***	0.761***	0.761***	0.799***	0.770***	0.770***
	(16.806)	(11.248)	(15.477)	(14.714)	(15.065)	(14.823)	(17.518)	(11.248)	(15.476)	(14.463)	(15.065)	(14.823)
Economic Infrastructure	0.439***	0.341**	0.341***	0.503***	0.163	0.163*	0.430***	0.341**	0.341***	0.487***	0.163	0.163*
	(7.666)	(2.203)	(4.672)	(6.687)	(0.920)	(1.710)	(7.667)	(2.203)	(4.672)	(6.493)	(0.920)	(1.710)
Social Infrastructure	0.192***	0.135*	0.135***	0.209***	0.111*	0.111**	0.186***	0.135*	0.135***	0.229***	0.111*	0.111**
	(7.437)	(1.661)	(3.056)	(7.578)	(1.702)	(2.439)	(7.363)	(1.661)	(3.056)	(8.600)	(1.702)	(2.439)
RI	−0.108***	−0.132***	−0.337***									
	(−4.315)	(−2.684)	(−4.759)									
State Average of Financial Depth			0.930***			0.417**			0.569***			0.479**
			(3.732)			(2.049)			(3.161)			(2.218)
State Average of Economic Infrastructure			0.0397			0.619***			0.102			0.560***
			(0.346)			(4.802)			(0.936)			(4.345)
State Average of Social Infrastructure			−0.273***			−0.0360			−0.140*			0.00429
			(−2.579)			(−0.412)			(−1.692)			(0.053)
RI1				−0.128***	−0.104	−0.274***						
				(−3.438)	(−0.717)	(−4.253)						
RI2							−0.0682***	−0.0813***	−0.139***			
							(−4.880)	(−3.011)	(−4.759)			
RI3										−0.0894***	−0.0440	−0.203***
										(−3.304)	(−0.394)	(−4.253)
Constant	8.265***		4.191***	8.260***		6.532***	8.308***		6.125***	8.346***		6.496***
	(31.785)		(3.522)	(27.226)		(6.748)	(35.599)		(7.678)	(28.570)	–	(6.659)
N	108	108	108	90	90	90	108	108	108	90	90	90

Notes: t statistics in parentheses; $^{*}p < 0.10$; $^{**}p < 0.05$; and $^{***}p < 0.01$; the dependent variable is Y_{it}.

states, we find that *RI* and its three variants have a negative impact on per capita income (Table 7.4, Cols. 3, 6, 9, and 12). The asymmetric impact of re-election on development is highlighted when we evaluate re-election after excluding states that were underdeveloped in the broadest sense (RI_3). With a coefficient value of 0.157 at a 1% level of significance for the leading states, the estimates indicate that RI_3 had a positive impact on development (Table 7.3, Col. 12). For the lagging states, however, the coefficient value of RI_3 is −0.203 at a 1% level of significance (Table 7.4, Col. 12). We find that the impact of RI_3 on development for all states (Table 7.2, Col. 12) with a coefficient value of 0.065 is statistically insignificant even at the 10% level of significance. This could be because the positive impact for leading states is offset by the negative impact for lagging states.

The empirical findings show that re-election has an asymmetric impact on development for the leading and lagging states. When we analyse the importance of historical institutions, we find they act as a drag for the development of the lagging states. It is worth noting that the six states that we have classified as lagging were also characterised by an extractive land administration system in the pre-independence period (Banerjee and Iyer, 2005). Thus, historical institutions seem to have facilitated perpetuation of power without accountability in the lagging states.

As a result, our findings do not support the contention that re-election has a disciplining impact, as has been suggested in the literature. The favourable impact of re-election for the leading states is also limited, as it is obtained only after excluding constituencies that were underdeveloped in the broadest sense.

We analysed how re-election affects development by aggregating constituency-wise re-election patterns to construct a re-election index for each state. We reviewed the prevalence of persistent re-election along with underdevelopment in Table 7.1. We looked at per capita district income, IMR, and female literacy as indicators of development in a district where persistent re-election was observed. However, it may be argued that even if a member of parliament is re-elected for multiple terms, he or she can have little direct influence on an aggregate measure like per capita income, which is influenced by a variety of factors such as the district's resource endowments, specific government policies, structural characteristics, and entrepreneurial culture. Similarly, IMR and female literacy may be influenced by societal awareness, cultural norms, and the effectiveness of government institutions (Misra, 2019). As a result, evaluating an MP's contribution to influencing these broad indicators of societal growth may not be appropriate.

However, it is reasonable to expect that a MP, who has served a constituency for four consecutive terms, can influence availability of basic amenities with some efforts. As such, we study whether provision of basic amenities have improved to appreciate the findings from empirical estimations. For this purpose, we assess relative availability of electricity, piped water, classroom facilities in primary schools, and health centres in the districts where the constituencies exhibiting persistent re-election are located.

Specifically, we compare the percentage of houses with electricity and running water in districts exhibiting re-election to the state average. To assess the availability of school infrastructure, we compare the percentage of primary schools with a single classroom in the districts characterised by persistent re-election with the state average. The number of primary health centres (PHCs), community health centres (CHCs), and sub centres per lakh people in districts showing persistent re-election is compared to the state average to assess availability of health infrastructure. To reflect the cumulative effect of persistent re-election, we examine the availability of electricity and tap water as on the year 2001, school infrastructure as on 2003, and health facilities as on the year 2004 (Table 7.5).

We find that households with electricity connection were below the state average in 43% of the districts showing persistent re-election in the leading states. As far as availability of tap water was concerned, it was below the state average for 59% of the districts with persistent re-election in the leading states. However, 62% of the districts exhibiting persistent re-election in the lagging states had availability of electricity and tap water below the state average. Moreover, among districts displaying persistent re-election, education and health infrastructure were below the state average for 58% and 62% of the districts, respectively, in the lagging states. In contrast, only 39% and 57% of the districts showing persistent re-election had relatively worse education and health infrastructure, respectively, compared the state average in the leading states.

The negative impact of re-election for lagging states can be appreciated from the fact that availability of basic infrastructure on all four indicators was below state average for around 60% of the districts. As far as districts in the leading states are concerned, they fared much better in terms availability of electricity and school infrastructure and had relatively lower provision of water and heath infrastructure compared to the state average. Thus, the overall impact of re-election turns out to be statistically insignificant for the leading states.

VII Concluding observations

The objective of this chapter was to examine how persistent re-election affects per capita income based on the experience of 14 Indian states that account for 90% of Indian GDP. We approached this question by using

Table 7.5 Availability of Basic Infrastructure in Backward Districts.

State	*District*	*Households with Electricity (%)*	*Households with Tap Water (%)*	*Schools with Single Classroom at Primary level (%)*	*Health centres per lakh population*
		2001	*2001*	*2003*	*2004*
Andhra Pradesh	East Godavari	62.17	39.80	30.60	17.93
Andhra Pradesh	Khammam	61.82	31.59	36.20	24.78
Andhra Pradesh	Hyderabad	96.97	91.58	8.60	1.36
Andhra Pradesh	Krishna	74.11	50.78	38.60	16.00
Andhra Pradesh	Medak	63.26	57.87	21.50	20.30
Andhra Pradesh	Cuddapah	76.28	53.13	45.50	19.97
Andhra Pradesh	Guntur	66.75	34.42	27.80	16.78
Andhra Pradesh	Kurnool	67.98	56.80	14.00	15.09
Andhra Pradesh	**State Average**	**66.79**	**47.75**	**30.67**	**18.53**
Bihar	Bhojpur	9.98	3.18	12.30	15.53
Bihar	Pashchim Champaran	6.25	2.26	19.90	13.73
Bihar	Patna	42.79	26.63	22.80	6.18
Bihar	Jamui	7.03	1.71	16.30	8.75
Bihar	Rohtas	16.54	5.38	22.50	11.60
Bihar	Aurangabad	7.81	2.21	27.50	15.25
Bihar	Banka*	4.74	1.15	16.90	13.39
Bihar	Gopalganj	5.99	1.61	13.60	14.25
Bihar	Vaishali	9.04	2.15	27.20	13.44
Bihar	Jehanabad	4.62	2.34	11.30	6.99
Bihar	Purba Champaran	6.30	2.17	30.30	13.78
Bihar	Nalanda	10.44	6.68	29.60	14.46
Bihar	**State Average**	**9.58**	**3.19**	**6.40**	**13.79**
Gujarat	Ahmadabad	91.37	82.55	3.40	5.29
Gujarat	Bharuch	77.68	70.24	14.30	14.34
Gujarat	Surat	84.75	65.13	7.70	14.65

(*Continued*)

State	*District*	*Households with Electricity (%)*	*Households with Tap Water (%)*	*Schools with Single Classroom at Primary level (%)*	*Health centres per lakh population*
		2001	*2001*	*2003*	*2004*
Gujarat	Junagadh	94.36	56.22	12.70	18.04
Gujarat	Amreli	89.64	46.60	16.90	20.85
Gujarat	Dohad	39.22	10.98	20.80	22.82
Gujarat	Jamnagar	87.20	55.74	34.30	15.78
Gujarat	Kachchh	80.36	77.58	21.40	17.43
Gujarat	**State Average**	**76.84**	**56.27**	**14.70**	**18.91**
Haryana	Kaithal	33.55	33.59	5.60	12.68
Haryana	Karnal	34.25	47.85	5.10	17.21
Haryana	**State Average**	**33.65**	**48.64**	**8.00**	**14.18**
Karnataka	Bangalore	94.53	77.75	18.70	18.84
Karnataka	Belgaum	77.56	49.49	21.30	17.11
Karnataka	Dharwad	82.54	73.43	13.30	12.25
Karnataka	Bangalore Rural	85.95	69.89	33.40	5.05
Karnataka	Udupi	69.73	12.62	6.50	28.37
Karnataka	Dakshina Kannada	71.45	31.02	7.60	27.10
Karnataka	Bagalkot	69.50	54.02	18.70	12.61
Karnataka	Chamarajanagar	64.48	46.74	33.10	26.28
Karnataka	Kolar	85.72	70.97	28.30	32.66
Karnataka	Tumkur	79.92	55.25	35.10	20.09
Karnataka	**State Average**	**75.68**	**55.41**	**25.17**	**21.99**
Kerala	Alappuzha	74.60	26.86	3.20	20.87
Kerala	Idukki	56.78	24.11	0.40	25.74
Kerala	Malappuram	63.84	7.56	0.00	16.28
Kerala	Kollam	73.00	13.62	5.90	20.13

Kerala	Kozhikode	64.15	11.67	0.70	15.95
Kerala	**State Average**	**67.51**	**18.85**	**1.77**	**20.44**
Maharashtra	Pune	87.85	75.20		7.70
Maharashtra	Chandrapur	62.04	36.26	5.80	19.31
Maharashtra	Thane	89.67	76.46	–	–
Maharashtra	Kolhapur	89.38	76.85	21.60	12.58
Maharashtra	Mumbai	97.84	96.60	–	–
Maharashtra	Mumbai (Suburban)	97.91	98.23	–	–
Maharashtra	Nandurbar	47.24	52.44	23.90	22.50
Maharashtra	Ahmadnagar	63.99	47.90	10.30	14.03
Maharashtra	Buldana	62.24	51.02	0.00	13.88
Maharashtra	Solapur	60.78	54.71	14.50	10.19
Maharashtra	Ratnagiri	90.17	41.04	29.80	26.93
Maharashtra	Satara	82.55	69.15	18.10	13.61
Maharashtra	Wardha	80.21	50.66	26.80	17.06
Maharashtra	Yavatmal	54.79	40.74	16.10	17.57
Maharashtra	Latur	73.24	54.02	4.10	13.22
Maharashtra	**State Average**	**72.30**	**54.49**	**16.94**	**16.07**
Madhya Pradesh	Bhopal	96.34	68.33	10.50	3.77
Madhya Pradesh	Chhindwara	84.62	38.19	4.30	20.59
Madhya Pradesh	Guna	69.17	17.04	5.10	23.19
Madhya Pradesh	Hoshangabad	81.46	31.39	11.10	14.53
Madhya Pradesh	Indore	95.16	54.43	11.90	5.22
Madhya Pradesh	Jabalpur	82.37	44.75	8.50	9.55
Madhya Pradesh	Mandsaur	86.78	31.02	7.20	16.20
Madhya Pradesh	Ratlam	81.38	34.75	12.80	15.20
Madhya Pradesh	Ujjain	90.15	36.34	15.50	10.79
Madhya Pradesh	Chhatarpur	46.58	8.45	17.40	15.04

(*Continued*)

State	*District*	*Households with Electricity (%)*	*Households with Tap Water (%)*	*Schools with Single Classroom at Primary level (%)*	*Health centres per lakh population*
		2001	*2001*	*2003*	*2004*
Madhya Pradesh	West Nimar	84.36	48.35	11.30	21.90
Madhya Pradesh	Mandla	49.42	14.39	6.20	26.62
Madhya Pradesh	Rajgarh	85.24	15.29	4.90	15.05
Madhya Pradesh	Seoni	66.74	19.82	14.30	15.21
Madhya Pradesh	Vidisha	68.45	16.77	4.30	13.09
Madhya Pradesh	**State Average**	**69.20**	**23.76**	**10.28**	**18.27**
Odisha	Ganjam	33.70	11.11	0.00	16.27
Odisha	Jajapur	30.04	4.15	0.00	17.89
Odisha	Kalahandi	13.22	2.76	4.70	18.96
Odisha	Koraput	18.26	8.02	0.00	33.32
Odisha	Nabarangapur	7.89	2.65	0.00	24.90
Odisha	**State Average**	**24.51**	**7.94**	**4.36**	**20.62**
Punjab	Gurdaspur	89.47	23.47	4.70	15.32
Punjab	**State Average**	**91.73**	**32.68**	**2.80**	**15.08**
Rajasthan	Bikaner	51.00	51.25	2.70	16.69
Rajasthan	Ganganagar	63.28	59.80	5.60	21.72
Rajasthan	Jaipur	75.34	50.72	2.70	10.89
Rajasthan	Udaipur	45.95	22.27	7.60	20.31
Rajasthan	Dausa	44.50	16.76	4.00	19.20
Rajasthan	Jhalawar	55.83	16.12	3.00	22.00
Rajasthan	**State Average**	**51.95**	**32.62**	**4.45**	**20.81**
Tamil Nadu	Kanniyakumari	77.25	44.21	1.00	17.17
Tamil Nadu	Namakkal	79.68	60.74	8.60	18.42

Tamil Nadu	Tiruchirappalli	77.22	74.49	3.00	14.66
Tamil Nadu	Dindigul	69.09	68.94	15.50	18.78
Tamil Nadu	Salem	79.44	60.19	14.20	15.59
Tamil Nadu	Sivaganga	71.79	52.95	10.20	25.74
Tamil Nadu	Tirunelveli	83.56	67.22	17.60	15.76
Tamil Nadu	Thanjavur	71.87	64.49	7.20	16.60
Tamil Nadu	The Nilgiris	72.99	71.12	2.60	29.45
Tamil Nadu	**State Average**	**76.21**	**62.07**	**17.66**	**17.81**
Uttar Pradesh	Aligarh	34.50	28.47	2.60	12.38
Uttar Pradesh	Bareilly	36.69	40.49	3.30	12.56
Uttar Pradesh	Bijnor	41.55	29.69	4.00	12.71
Uttar Pradesh	Kanpur Nagar	63.81	33.38	3.60	10.24
Uttar Pradesh	Bulandshahr	28.66	26.49	3.30	15.43
Uttar Pradesh	Ghaziabad	70.63	42.94	1.60	9.39
Uttar Pradesh	Hathras	30.45	19.54	6.90	14.49
Uttar Pradesh	Jhansi	43.26	25.37	8.70	20.57
Uttar Pradesh	Lucknow	63.57	50.52	3.50	9.72
Uttar Pradesh	Pilibhit	25.83	31.91	1.70	13.28
Uttar Pradesh	Faizabad	32.19	17.34	1.60	13.66
Uttar Pradesh	Ballia	24.40	12.82	2.30	15.80
Uttar Pradesh	Kaushambi	16.56	8.24	0.30	15.17
Uttar Pradesh	Deoria	27.96	14.38	4.30	15.80
Uttar Pradesh	Etah	18.03	25.10	2.80	17.65
Uttar Pradesh	Fatehpur	15.80	9.19	0.20	15.45
Uttar Pradesh	Ghazipur	20.82	10.69	2.10	14.77
Uttar Pradesh	Mau	39.83	9.67	1.50	14.23
Uttar Pradesh	Kushinagar	21.15	17.65	0.60	13.25
Uttar Pradesh	Pratapgarh	25.77	14.71	1.10	15.47

(Continued)

State	*District*	*Households with Electricity (%)*	*Households with Tap Water (%)*	*Schools with Single Classroom at Primary level (%)*	*Health centres per lakh population*
		2001	*2001*	*2003*	*2004*
Uttar Pradesh	Rae Bareli	20.34	13.73	2.20	14.99
Uttar Pradesh	Barabanki	19.97	15.02	3.70	14.63
Uttar Pradesh	**State Average**	**30.03**	**22.23**	**2.57**	**14.63**
West Bengal	Hugli	57.69	30.38	14.60	14.23
West Bengal	Birbhum	27.48	10.47	19.10	17.79
West Bengal	Medinipur	21.02	11.87	3.50	16.98
West Bengal	Haora	56.07	33.16	27.80	11.36
West Bengal	Jalpaiguri	32.29	19.47	27.70	16.66
West Bengal	Dakshin Dinajpur	19.41	2.91	47.90	17.59
West Bengal	Bankura	27.73	8.91	38.30	19.83
West Bengal	North 24 Parganas	55.35	37.83	25.00	11.25
West Bengal	South 24 Parganas	27.95	10.19	35.60	12.53
West Bengal	Murshidabad	18.26	4.74	11.80	14.95
West Bengal	Barddhaman	43.90	30.72	8.80	12.66
West Bengal	Nadia	29.71	7.84	18.10	11.22
West Bengal	Maldah	18.54	8.31	30.40	16.11
West Bengal	Puruliya	19.33	7.31	29.20	21.07
West Bengal	**State Average**	**35.10**	**18.97**	**24.84**	**14.72**

a re-election index to quantify persistent re-election in each state as on 1999. The re-election index was calculated by taking the ratio of the number of constituencies exhibiting persistent re-election to the total the total number of constituencies of the state in the Lok Sabha. Constituencies where the same person was elected for four terms in a row in the first 13 Lok Sabha elections between 1952 and 1999 were identified as exhibiting persistent re-election. We used the correlated random effects model to calculate the influence of the time invariant re-election index on per capita income during the period 2000–16. The incorporation of a stock measure of persistent re-election in the estimation helped to overcome endogeneity of re-election. To reflect the state of economic and social infrastructure, as well as financial progress, we included several control variables.

When all 14 states were considered as a group, we found no statistically significant influence of persistent re-election on per capita income. Re-election, on the other hand, had a negative influence on per capita income in the lagging states. To ensure that our empirical results were not influenced by constituencies exhibiting both re-election and underdevelopment, we computed three variants of the re-election index that exclude such constituencies.

We mapped a constituency's level of development to the district in which it is located. When constituencies that are either economically or socially underdeveloped are excluded, we find that re-election has a favourable impact in the leading states, a negative impact for the lagging states, and is statistically insignificant for all of the states as a group. The negative impact of re-election on development for the lagging states can be explained by the historical institution of land administration system in colonial India and the caste system. Our findings do not support the notion that re-election has a positive impact on the development of Indian states measured through per capita income. Re-election has a negative influence on lagging states, as evidenced by the relatively low basic infrastructure facilities in electricity, water, education, and health in districts associated with persistent re-election when compared to the state average. As a result, re-election does not result in increased accountability from elected representatives in the lagging states, even in terms of making efforts to improve basic infrastructure. Re-election turns out be statistically insignificant for development in the leading states because provision of power and school infrastructure above the state average in majority of districts in these states appears to be offset by water and health infrastructure below the state average. When the leading and lagging states are considered together, the effect of re-election on development is negative but statistically insignificant. In the absence of political accountability, our findings suggest the need to revisit the provision of re-election without term limits especially in the lagging states of India.

Note

1 In the Indian context, the non-economic aspects like quality of candidates which influence election has been discussed in Dutta and Gupta (2014).

References

Alt, J., Ethan, B.M. and Shanna, R. (2011). Disentangling Accountability And Competence in Elections: Evidence from U.S. Term Limits, *Journal of Politics*, Vol. 73, No. 1, pp.171–186.

Alvarez, M., Cheibub, J.A., Limongi, F. and Przeworski, A. (1996). Classifying Political Regimes, *Studies in Comparative International Development*, Vol. 31, No. 2, pp. 3–36.

Anderson, S., Patrick, F. and Kotwal, A. (2015). Clientelism in Indian Villages, *American Economic Review*, Vol.105, No. 6, pp. 1780–1816.

Ashworth, S. (2012). Electoral Accountability: Recent Theoretical and Empirical Work, *Annual Review of Political Science*, Vol. 15, pp. 183–201.

Aruoba, S.B., Drazen, A. and Vlaicu, R. (2019). A Structural Model of Electoral Accountability, *International Economic Review*, Vol. 60, No. 2, pp. 517–545.

Austen-Smith, D. and Banks, J. (1989). Electoral Accountability and Incumbency, In P. Ordeshook (Ed.), *Models of Strategic Choice in Politics*. University of Michigan Press, Ann Arbor

Banerjee, A. and Iyer, L. (2005). History, Institutions, and Economic Performance: The Legacy of Colonial Land Tenure Systems in India, *American Economic Review*, Vol. 95, No. 4, pp. 1190–1213.

Banks, J.S. and Sundaram, R.K. (1993). Moral Hazard and Adverse Selection in a Model of Repeated Elections, In W. Barnett (Ed.), *Political Economy: Institutions, Information Competition, and Representation*. Cambridge University Press, Cambridge, pp. 295–312.

Bardhan, P. (2002). Decentralization of Governance and Development, *Journal of Economic Perspectives*, Vol.16, No. 4, pp. 185–205.

Bardhan, P. (2005). *Scarcity, Conflicts, and Cooperation: Essays in Political and Institutional Economics of Development*. MIT Press, Massachusetts, United States.

Bardhan, P. and Mookherjee, D. (2006). Decentralization and Accountability in Infrastructure Delivery in Developing Countries, *The Economic Journal*, Vol. 116, No. 508, pp. 101–127.

Barro, R. (1973). The Control of Politicians: An Economic Model, *Public Choice*, Vol. 14, No. 1, pp. 19–42.

Besley, T. and Anne, C. (1995). Does Electoral Accountability Affect Economic Policy Choices? Evidence from Gubernatorial Term Limits, *Quarterly Journal of Economics*, Vol. 110, No. 3, pp. 769–798.

Bobonis, G.J., Luis, R.F. and Rainer, S. (2016). Monitoring Corruptible Politicians, *American Economic Review*, Vol. 106, No. 8, pp. 2371–2405.

Brendan, D. and Erik, S. (2011). Even if it Is Not Bribery: The Case for Campaign Finance Reform, *Journal of Law, Economics, and Organization*, Oxford University Press, Vol. 27, No. 2, pp. 324–349.

Brender, Adi and Drazen, Allan. (2008). How Do Budget Deficits and Economic Growth Affect Reelection Prospects? Evidence from a Large Panel of Countries, *The American Economic Review*, Vol. 98, No. 5, pp. 2203–2220.

Bruce, B.M., Smith, A., Siverson, R.M. and Morrow, J.D. (2003). *The Logic of Political Survival Cambridge*. MA, MIT Press, Massachusetts, United States.

Burgat, C. (2018). Five Reasons to Oppose Congressional Term Limits, *Washington Post*, Thursday, January 18, 2018, available at: www.brookings.edu/blog/fixgov/2018/01/18/five-reasons-to-oppose-congressional-term-limits/ [accessed 4 May 2020].

Dassonneville, R. and Lewis-Beck, M.S. (2014). The Economic Voter and Economic Crisis, *Acta Politica*, Vol. 49, No. 4, pp. 369–371.

Duch, R.M. and Stevenson, R.T. (2008). *The Economic Vote: How Political and Economic Institut*ions *Condition Election Results*. Cambridge University Press, New York.

Dutta, Bhaskar and Gupta, Poonam. (2014). How Do Indian Voters Respond to Candidates with Criminal Charges: Evidence from the 2009 Lok Sabha Elections, *Economic and Political Weekly*, Vol. 49, No. 4, pp. 43–51.

Elhauge, E. (1997). Are Term Limits Undemocratic?, *The University of Chicago Law Review*, Vol. 64, No. 1, pp. 83–201.

Ferejohn, J. (1986). Incumbent Performance and Electoral Control, *Public Choice*, Vol. 50, pp. 5–25.

Ferraz, C. and Finan, F. (2011). Electoral Accountability and Corruption: Evidence from the Audits of Local Governments, *American Economic Review*, Vol. 101, No. 4, pp. 1274–1311.

Foldvari, P. (2017). De Facto Versus de Jure Political Institutions in the Long-Run: A Multivariate Analysis, 1820–2000, *Social Indicators Research*, Vol. 130, No. 2, pp. 759–777.

Furnaces, A. and Hall, A.B. (2018). How Do Electoral Incentives Affect Legislator Behavior?, *Unpublished Working Paper*, available at: www.andrewbenjaminhall.com/Fouirnaies_Hall_Electoral_Incentives.pdf [accessed 9 December 2019].

Gerring, J., Philip, B., William, B. and Carola, M. (2005). Democracy and Economic Growth: A Historical Perspective, *World Politics*, Vol. 57, No. 3, pp. 323–364.

Government of India (2013). Report of the Committee for Evolving A Composite Development Index of States, *Ministry of Finance*, New Delhi, available at: https://finmin.nic.in/sites/default/files/Report_CompDevState.pdf [accessed 8 June 2019].

Government of India (2014). Backwardness Index for Sub Districts, *Planning Commission*, New Delhi, available at: www.indiaenvironmentportal.org.in/content/397012/backwardness-index-for-sub-districts-prepared-by-planning-commission-for-use-in-identifying-blocks-for-ippe [accessed 27 June 2019].

Government of India (2017). Transforming 115 Backward Districts Across the Country, *Niti Aayog*, New Delhi, available at: https://pmawards.gov.in/public/List-of-Backward-Districts.pdf [accessed 17 June 2019].

Gupta, P. and Panagariya, A. (2014). Growth and Election Outcomes in a Developing Country, *Economics and Politics*, Vol. 26, No. 2, pp. 332–354.

Khemani,S.,DalBó,E.,Ferraz,C.,Finan,F.S.,Stephenson,J.Corinne,L.Odugbemi, A.M., Thapa, D. and Abrahams, S.D. (2016). Making Politics Work for Development : Harnessing Transparency and Citizen Engagement, *Policy Research Reports,* Washington, DC, World Bank Group, available at: http://documents.worldbank.org/curated/en/268021467831470443/Making-politics-work-for-development-harnessing-transparency-and-citizen-engagement [accessed 24 March 2020].

Lewis-Beck, M.S. and Stegmaier, M. (2000). Economic Determinants of Electoral Outcomes, *Annual Review of Political Science,* Vol. 3, No.1, pp. 183–219.

Misra, B.S. (2013). *Revisiting Regional Growth Dynamics in India in the Post-economic Reforms Period.* Palgrave Macmillan, London.

Misra, B.S. (2015). Which Infrastructure Matters More for Growth-Economic or Social?Evidence from Indian States During 2001–2010, *Review of Urban & Regional Development Studies,* Applied Regional Science Conference (ARSC) and Wiley Publishing Asia Pty Ltd, Vol. 27, No. 3, pp.177–196.

Misra, B.S. (2019). Impact of Economic and Social Infrastructure on Income Inequality-Evidence form Indian States, *Australasian Journal of Regional Studies,* Vol. 25, No.1, pp. 81–114.

Pacek, A.C. and Radcliff, B. (1995). Economic Voting and the Welfare State: A Cross-National Analysis, *The Journal of Politics,* Vol. 57, No. 1, pp. 44–61 .

Pandey, P. (2010). Service Delivery and Corruption in Public Services: How Does History Matter?, *American Economic Journal: Applied Economics,* Vol. 2, No. 3, pp. 190–204.

Pesaran, H.M. and Zhou, Q. (2018). Estimation of Time-Invariant Effects in Static Panel Data Models, *Econometric Reviews,* Vol. 37, No. 10, pp. 1137–1171.

Purfield, C. (2006). Mind the Gap - Is Economic Growth in India Leaving Some States Behind?, *IMF Working Paper No. 103,* pp. 1–28.

Rumayya, Anu Rammohan, Rudi Purwono, Iman Harymawan. (2020). The Local Economy and Re-Election of Incumbent District Leaders in Indonesia, *Heliyon,* Vol. 6, No. 5, pp. 1–9.

Schunck, R. (2013). Within and Between Estimates in Random-Effects Models: Advantages and Drawbacks of Correlated Random Effects and Hybrid Models, *The Stata Journal,* Vol. 13, No. 1, pp. 65–76.

Sen, R. (2012). The Persistence of Caste in Indian Politics, *Pacific Affairs,* Vol. 85, No. 2, pp. 363–369.

Index

For Product Safety Concerns and Information please contact our EU
representative GPSR@taylorandfrancis.com
Taylor & Francis Verlag GmbH, Kaufingerstraße 24, 80331 München, Germany

www.ingramcontent.com/pod-product-compliance
Ingram Content Group UK Ltd.
Pitfield, Milton Keynes, MK11 3LW, UK
UKHW020130200926
475702UK00005B/681
* 9 7 8 1 0 3 2 2 4 3 8 8 7 *